BAAC

BBC

DOCTOR WHO

FOUR DOCTORS

D1203400

"Sparkily captivating dialogue smartly turns the promise of a team-up into a dramatic pleasure. A beguiling story, well worth your time."
TOO BUSY THINKING ABOUT COMICS

"If you don't know squat about *Doctor Who*, everything you need to know is held in the pages of this singular, sensational book."
THE BUY PILE

"Brilliant writing from Paul Cornell, excellent artwork from Neil Edwards and an amazing color palette from Ivan Nunes make this a perfect comic!"
FLICKERING MYTH

"A fun ride that packs a punch!"
FANSIDED

"Brilliant internal dialogue and subtle interactions!"
DAVID TENNANT NEWS

"Something special!"
NEED TO CONSUME

"I never expected anything as awesome as this! A must-have."
SNAP POW

"An airtight, continuity-packed time-traveling crossover epic delivered at breakneck pace!"
INFINITE COMIX

"This was great! A+"
SCIFI PULSE

"Delivers the most interesting insight so far into what makes the Doctor tick."
BIG COMIC PAGE

"Fun, thrilling and surprising in equal measures, sure to be just what any fan wants from a Doctor Who event."
NERDS UNCHAINED

"Not only a good media tie-in comic, it's a good comic, period!"
COMIC BOOK RESOURCES

"Worth the cover price for the staggering artwork and the intriguing storyline!"
STARBURST

TITAN COMICS

EDITOR
Andrew James

ASSISTANT EDITOR
Kirsten Murray

COLLECTION DESIGNER
Rob Farmer

SENIOR EDITOR
Steve White

TITAN COMICS EDITORIAL
Lizzie Kaye, Tom Williams

PRODUCTION SUPERVISORS
Jackie Flook, Maria Pearson

PRODUCTION MANAGER
Obi Onuora

STUDIO MANAGER
Selina Juneja

SENIOR SALES MANAGER
Steve Tothill

SENIOR MARKETING & PRESS OFFICER
Owen Johnson

COMICS BRAND MANAGER
Lucy Ripper

DIRECT SALES & MARKETING MANAGER
Ricky Claydon

COMMERCIAL MANAGER
Michelle Fairlamb

PUBLISHING MANAGER
Darryl Tothill

PUBLISHING DIRECTOR
Chris Teather

OPERATIONS DIRECTOR
Leigh Baulch

EXECUTIVE DIRECTOR
Vivian Cheung

PUBLISHER
Nick Landau

Special thanks to Steven Moffat, Brian Minchin,
Matt Nicholls, James Dudley, Edward Russell,
Derek Ritchie, Scott Handcock, Kirsty Mullan,
Kate Bush, Julia Nocciolino, Ed Casey, Marcus Wilson
and Richard Cookson for their invaluable assistance.

BBC WORLDWIDE

DIRECTOR OF EDITORIAL GOVERNANCE
Nicolas Brett

**DIRECTOR OF CONSUMER
PRODUCTS AND PUBLISHING**
Andrew Moultrie

HEAD OF UK PUBLISHING
Chris Kerwin

PUBLISHER
Mandy Thwaites

PUBLISHING CO-ORDINATOR
Eva Abramik

DOCTOR WHO: FOUR DOCTORS

HB ISBN: 9781782765967
SB ISBN: 9781785851063
Published by Titan Comics, a division of
Titan Publishing Group, Ltd. 144 Southwark Street,
London, SE1 0UP.

BBC, DOCTOR WHO (word marks, logos and devices)
and TARDIS are trade marks of the British Broadcasting
Corporation and are used under license.
BBC logo © BBC 1996. Doctor Who logo © BBC 2009.
TARDIS image © BBC 1963. Cybermen image © BBC/
Kit Pedler/Gerry Davis 1966.

A CIP catalogue record for this title is available from
the British Library. First edition: January 2016

10 9 8 7 6 5 4 3 2 1

Printed in China. TC0868

Titan Comics does not read or accept unsolicited
DOCTOR WHO submissions of ideas, stories or artwork.

BBC

DOCTOR WHO

FOUR DOCTORS

WRITER: PAUL CORNELL

ARTIST: NEIL EDWARDS

COLORIST: IVAN NUNES

LETTERS: RICHARD STARKINGS AND
COMICRAFT'S JIMMY BETANCOURT

TITAN COMICS   BBC

www.titan-comics.com

BBC

DOCTOR WHO
FOUR DOCTORS

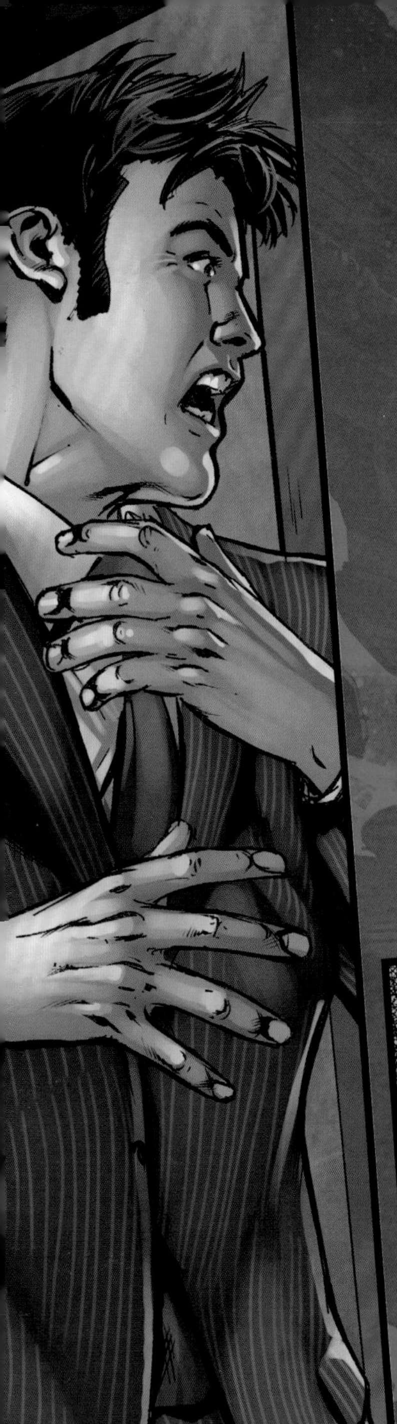

GABBY GONZALEZ

Gabriella Gonzalez is a young would-be artist from Sunset Park, Brooklyn, New York, who is traveling the universe at the Tenth Doctor's side. Her youthful spirit and artistic eye are coupled to an adventurous and quick-witted mind.

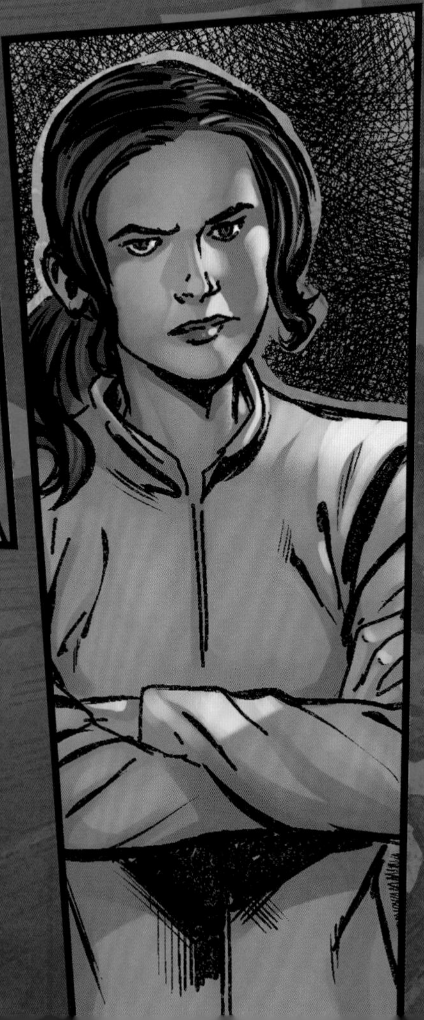

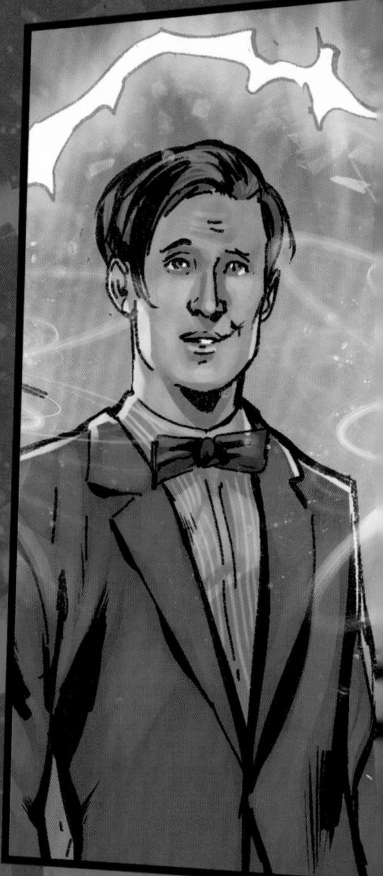

TENTH DOCTOR

The Doctor is an alien who walks like a man. His Tenth incarnation is trying to get over his post-Time War guilt by sprinting along in a happy-go-lucky guise – but he keeps shooting himself in the foot, because all his guilt, rage and frustration is buried just underneath.

ELEVENTH DOCTOR

The Doctor is the last of the Time Lords of Gallifrey. His Eleventh incarnation is a gangly boy professor with an old, old soul. Not guilty or embarrassed about anything, he has made mistakes – some enormous! – but owns each and every one.

PREVIOUSLY...

The Doctor is an immortal time traveler who, when mortally-wounded, regenerates into an entirely new body.

He has worn many faces in his long and adventurous life.

When the fabric of the universe is threatened, when the laws of time, space and all of reality start to break down...

...on those dire days, different incarnations of the Doctor can meet.

It should never happen. But this is one of those days...

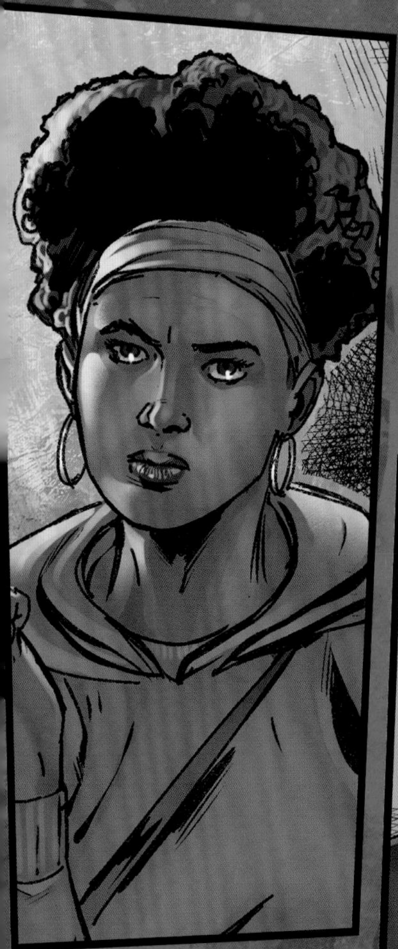

TWELFTH DOCTOR

The Doctor is never cruel or cowardly, he champions the oppressed across time and space. His Twelfth incarnation is done with guilt, wants to fix things, and now he feels he has licence to – and doesn't have to be a happy, fun Manic Pixie Dream Doctor to do so.

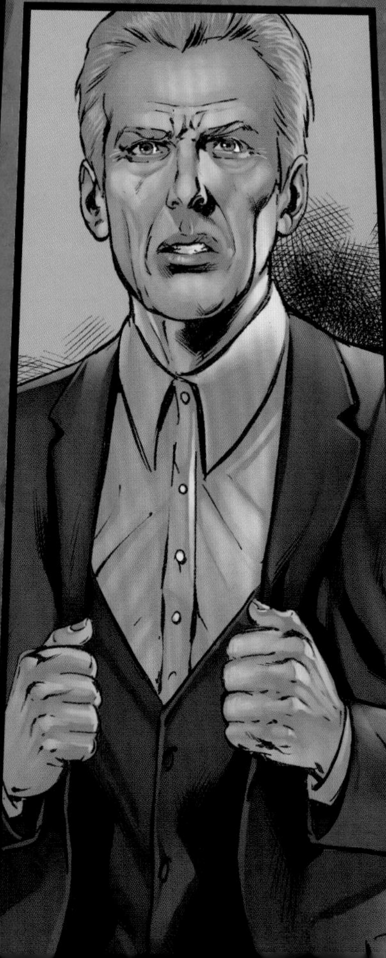

ALICE OBIEFUNE

Former Library Assistant Alice Obiefune has grown into a courageous hero since her travels with the Eleventh Doctor began. Having put the death of her mother behind her, Alice now embraces all that traveling in the TARDIS can offer her.

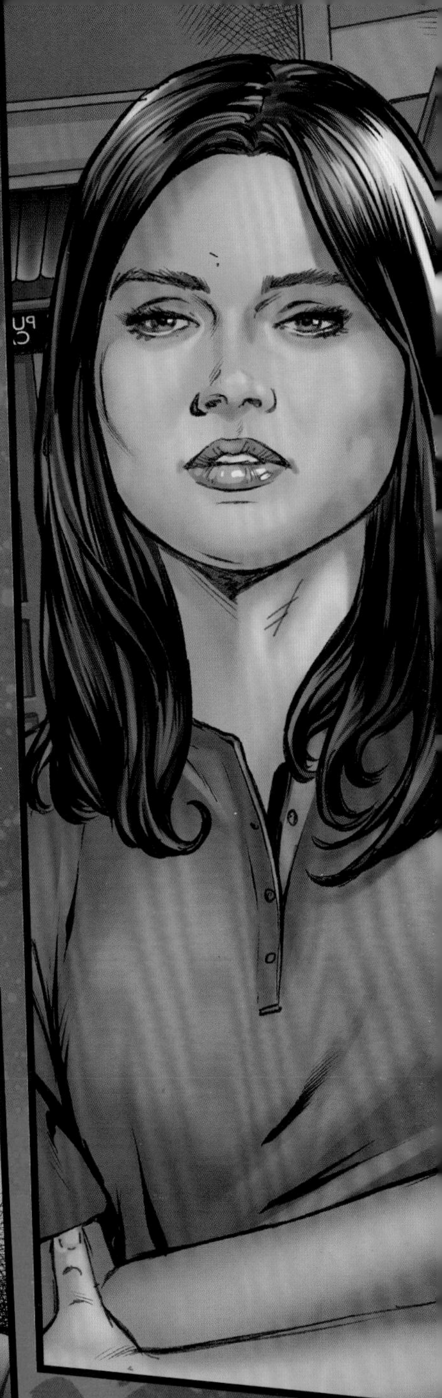

CLARA OSWALD

Clara Oswald has known the Doctor through both his Eleventh and Twelfth incarnations, and has stuck with him through thick and thin, witnessing all manner of strange, wonderful and terrifying things. A teacher at Coal Hill School, she juggles her 'real life' with her secret adventures in the TARDIS!

BBC

DOCTOR WHO

FOUR DOCTORS

WRITER
PAUL CORNELL

ARTIST
NEIL EDWARDS

COLORIST
IVAN NUNES

LETTERER
RICHARD STARKINGS AND COMICRAFT'S
JIMMY BETANCOURT

GABBY'S SKETCHBOOK ARTIST
ARIANNA FLOREAN

EDITOR
ANDREW JAMES

ASSISTANT EDITOR
KIRSTEN MURRAY

DESIGNER
ROB FARMER

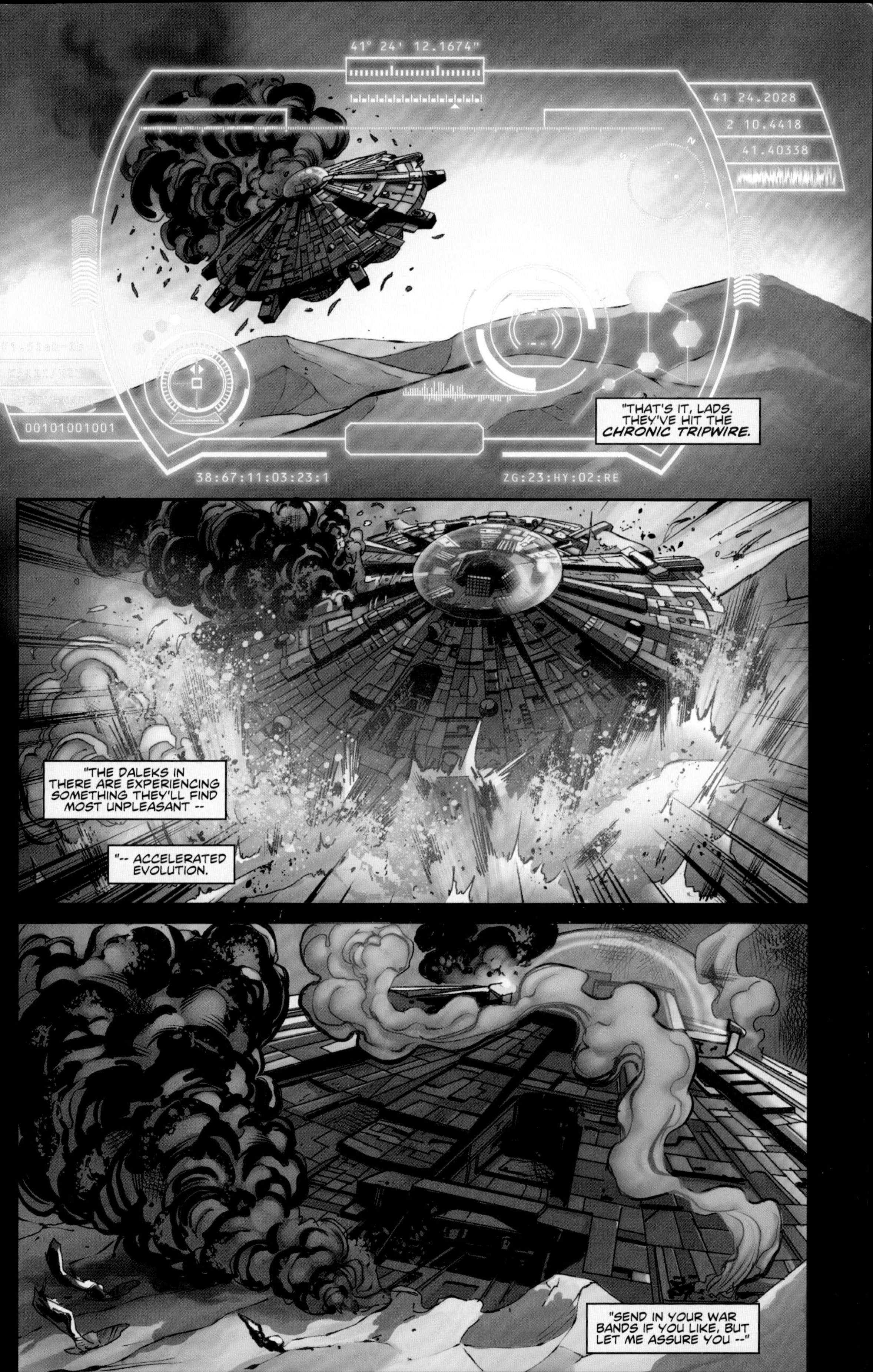
41° 24' 12.1674"
41 24.2028
2 10.4418
41.40338
00101001001
38:67:11:03:23:1
ZG:23:HY:02:RE
"THAT'S IT, LADS. THEY'VE HIT THE *CHRONIC TRIPWIRE.*
"THE DALEKS IN THERE ARE EXPERIENCING SOMETHING THEY'LL FIND MOST UNPLEASANT --
"-- ACCELERATED EVOLUTION.
"SEND IN YOUR WAR BANDS IF YOU LIKE, BUT LET ME ASSURE YOU --"

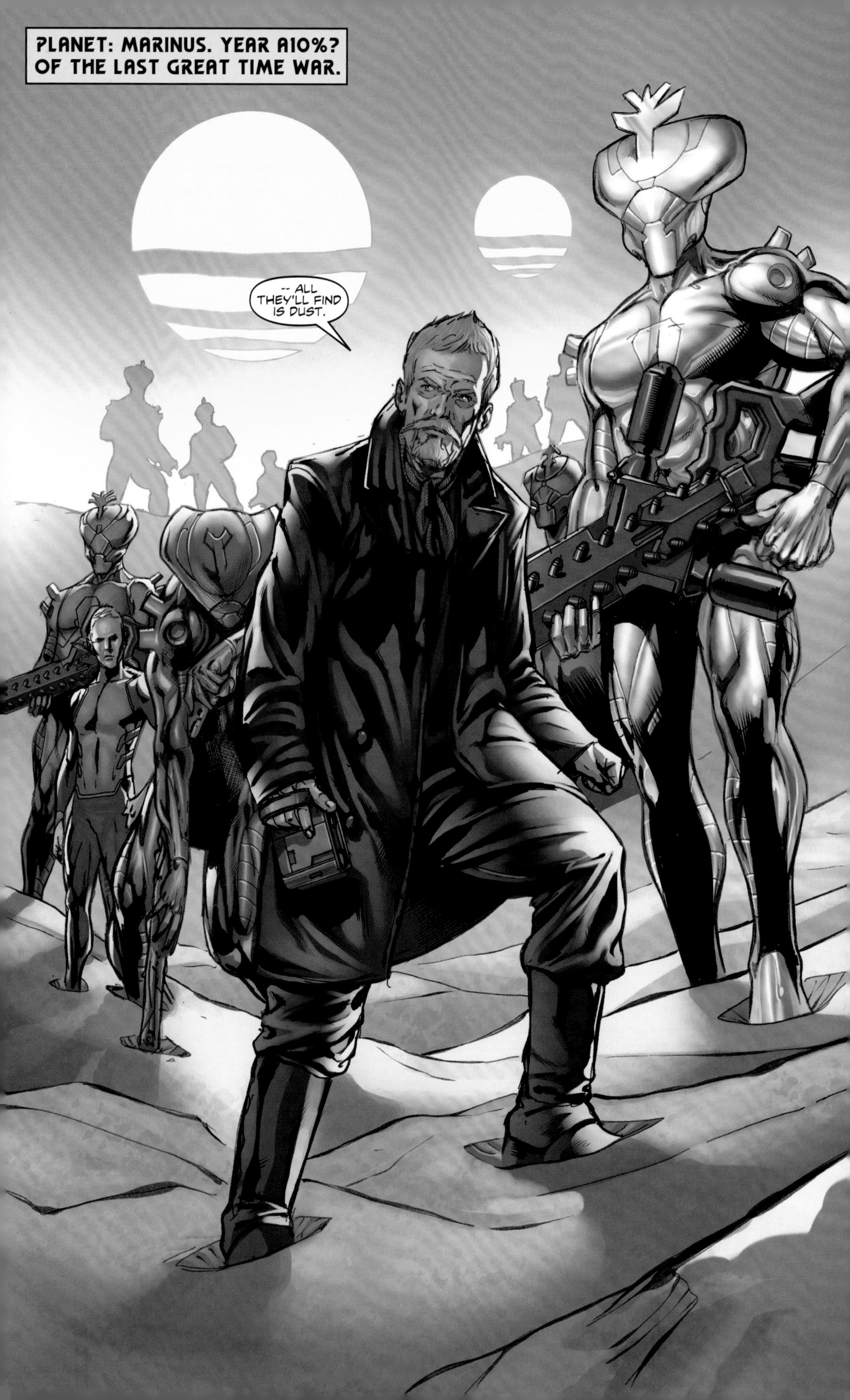
PLANET: MARINUS. YEAR A10%?
OF THE LAST GREAT TIME WAR.
-- ALL THEY'LL FIND IS DUST.

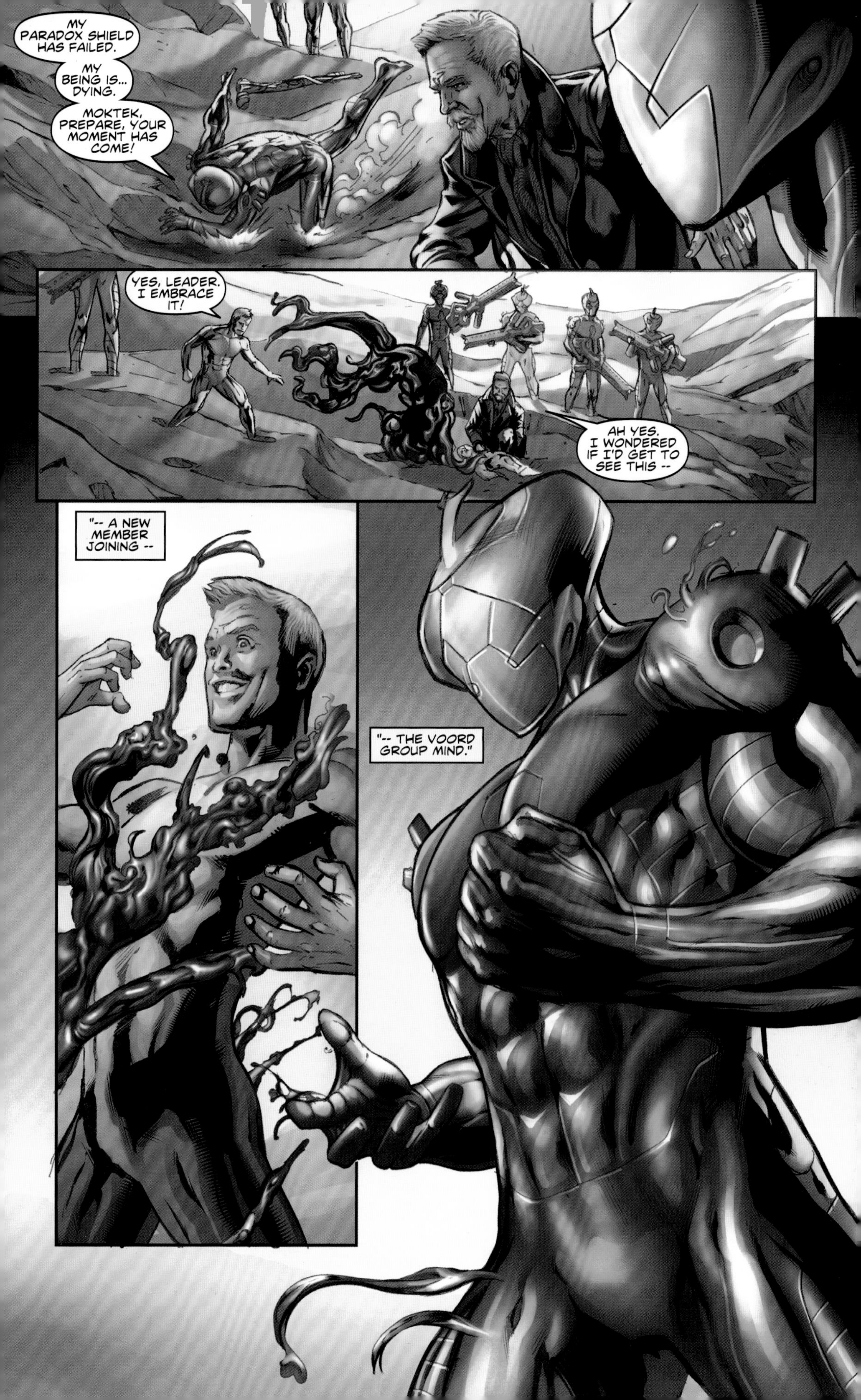
MY PARADOX SHIELD HAS FAILED.
MY BEING IS... DYING.
MOKTEK, PREPARE, YOUR MOMENT HAS COME!
YES, LEADER. I EMBRACE IT!
AH YES. I WONDERED IF I'D GET TO SEE THIS --
"-- A NEW MEMBER JOINING --
"-- THE VOORD GROUP MIND."

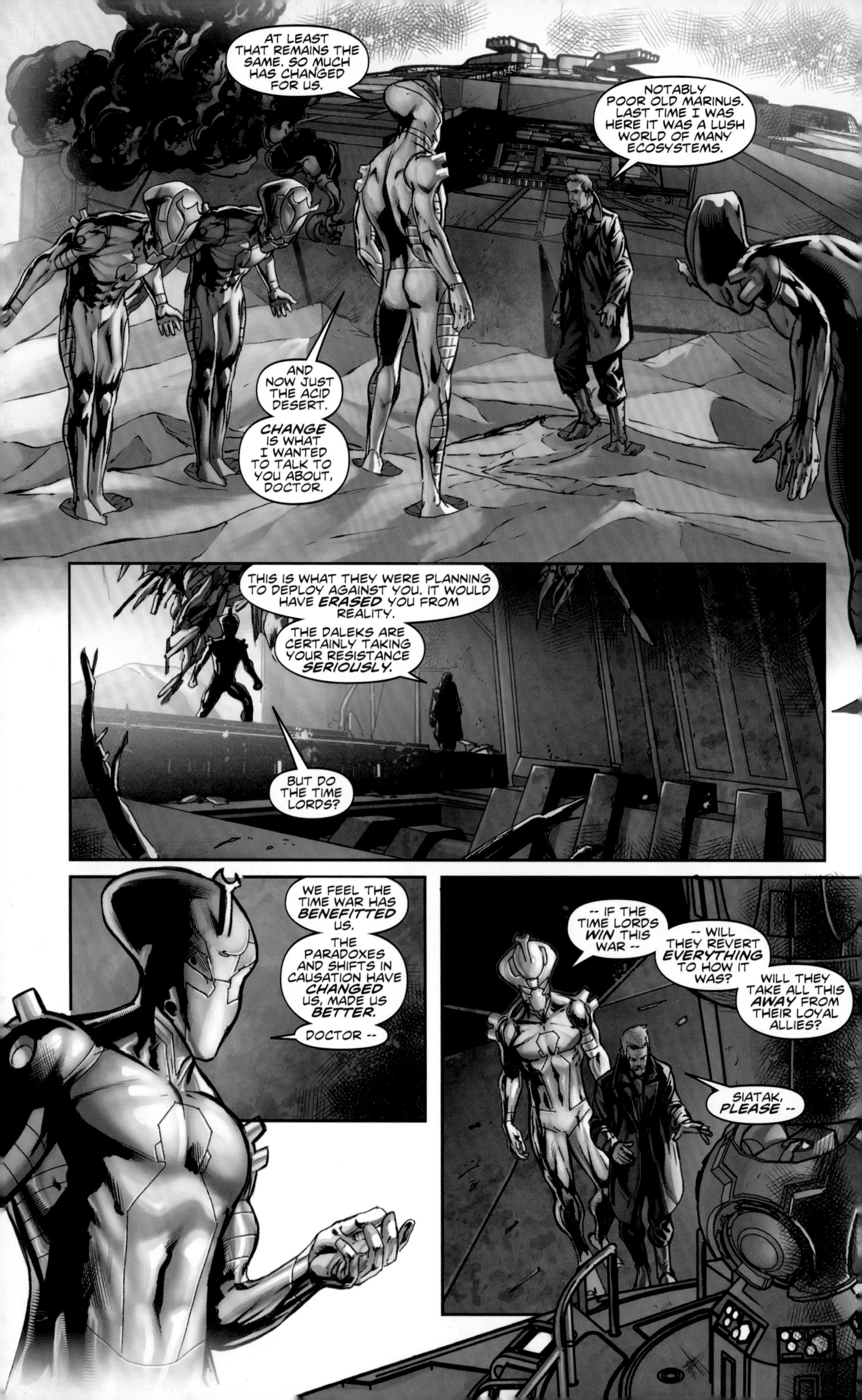
AT LEAST THAT REMAINS THE SAME. SO MUCH HAS CHANGED FOR US.
NOTABLY POOR OLD MARINUS. LAST TIME I WAS HERE IT WAS A LUSH WORLD OF MANY ECOSYSTEMS.
AND NOW JUST THE ACID DESERT.
CHANGE IS WHAT I WANTED TO TALK TO YOU ABOUT, DOCTOR.
THIS IS WHAT THEY WERE PLANNING TO DEPLOY AGAINST YOU. IT WOULD HAVE ERASED YOU FROM REALITY.
THE DALEKS ARE CERTAINLY TAKING YOUR RESISTANCE SERIOUSLY.
BUT DO THE TIME LORDS?
WE FEEL THE TIME WAR HAS BENEFITTED US.
THE PARADOXES AND SHIFTS IN CAUSATION HAVE CHANGED US, MADE US BETTER.
DOCTOR --
-- IF THE TIME LORDS WIN THIS WAR --
-- WILL THEY REVERT EVERYTHING TO HOW IT WAS?
WILL THEY TAKE ALL THIS AWAY FROM THEIR LOYAL ALLIES?
SIATAK, PLEASE --

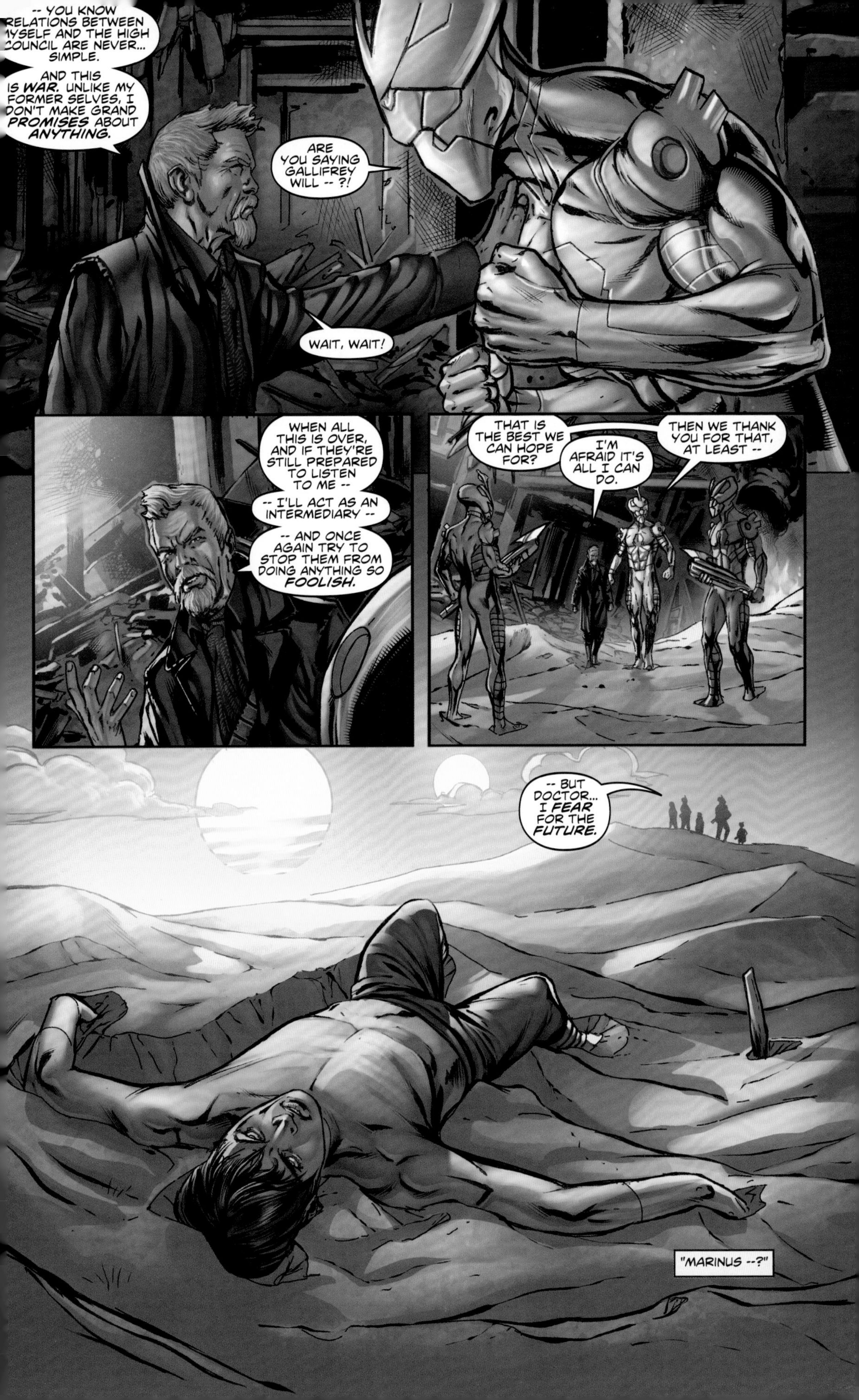
-- YOU KNOW RELATIONS BETWEEN MYSELF AND THE HIGH COUNCIL ARE NEVER... SIMPLE.
AND THIS IS WAR. UNLIKE MY FORMER SELVES, I DON'T MAKE GRAND PROMISES ABOUT ANYTHING.
ARE YOU SAYING GALLIFREY WILL -- ?!
WAIT, WAIT!
WHEN ALL THIS IS OVER, AND IF THEY'RE STILL PREPARED TO LISTEN TO ME --
-- I'LL ACT AS AN INTERMEDIARY --
-- AND ONCE AGAIN TRY TO STOP THEM FROM DOING ANYTHING SO FOOLISH.
THAT IS THE BEST WE CAN HOPE FOR?
I'M AFRAID IT'S ALL I CAN DO.
THEN WE THANK YOU FOR THAT, AT LEAST --
-- BUT DOCTOR... I FEAR FOR THE FUTURE.
"MARINUS --?"

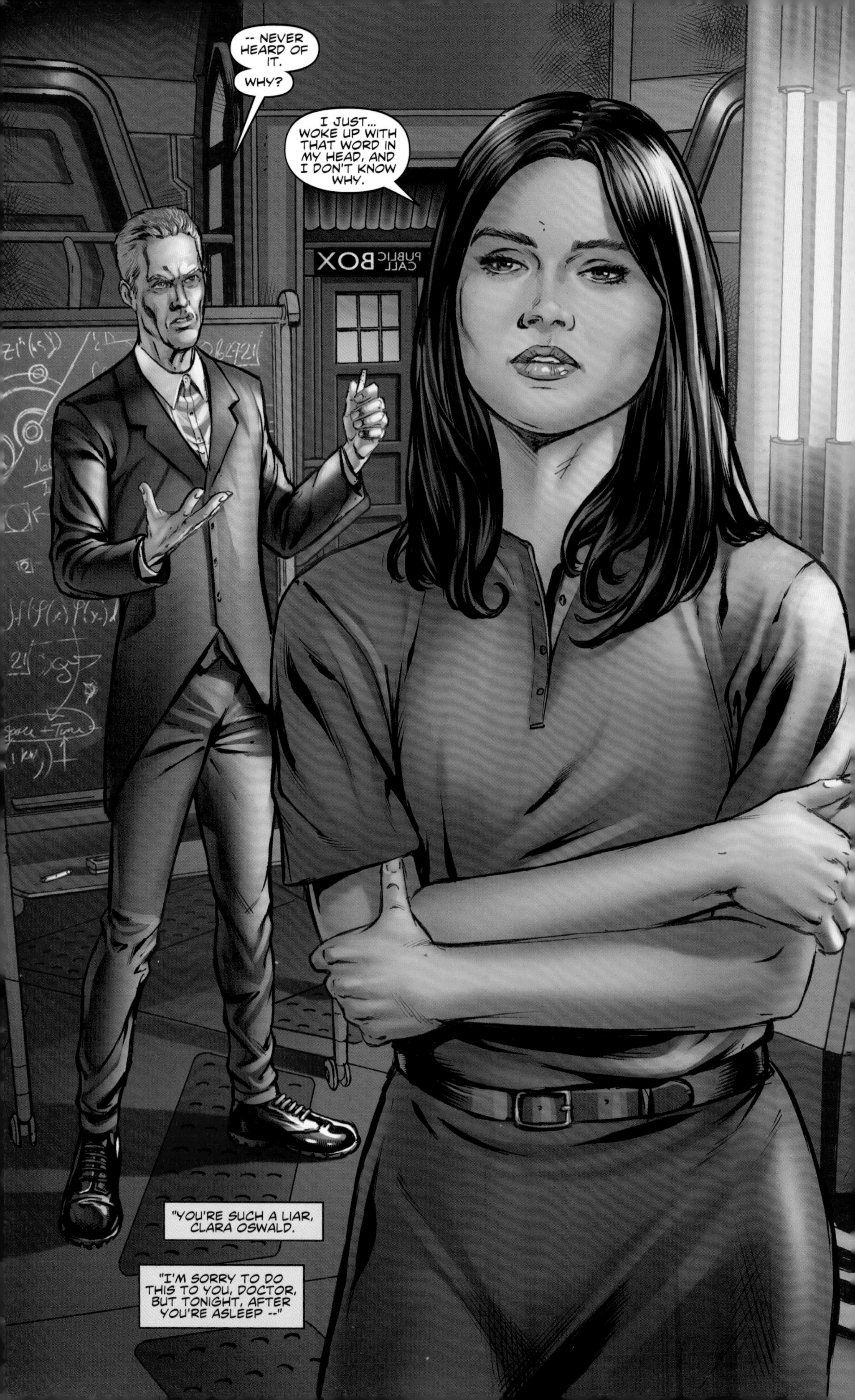
-- NEVER HEARD OF IT.
WHY?
I JUST... WOKE UP WITH THAT WORD IN MY HEAD, AND I DON'T KNOW WHY.
PUBLIC CALL BOX
"YOU'RE SUCH A LIAR, CLARA OSWALD.
"I'M SORRY TO DO THIS TO YOU, DOCTOR, BUT TONIGHT, AFTER YOU'RE ASLEEP --"

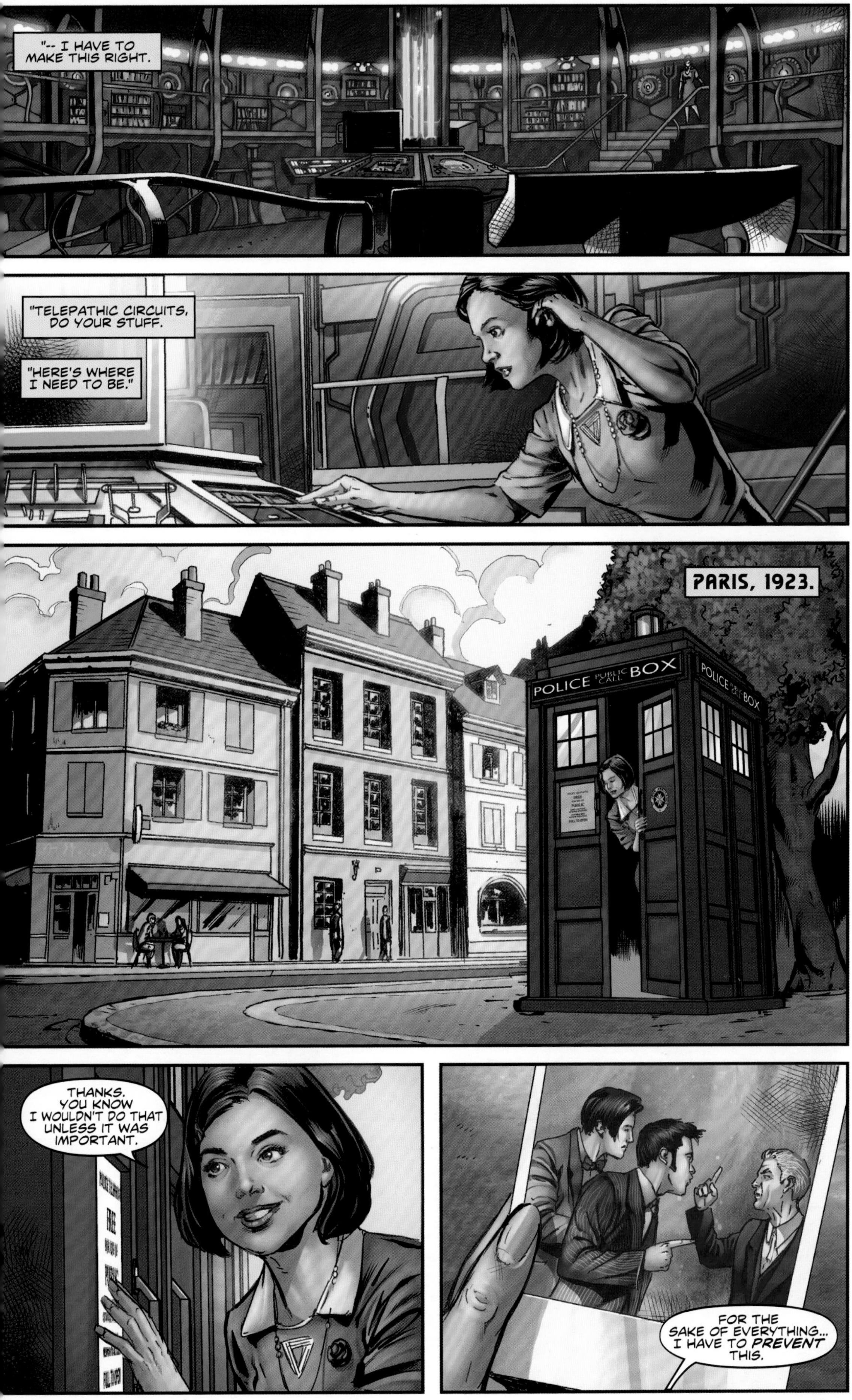
"-- I HAVE TO MAKE THIS RIGHT.
"TELEPATHIC CIRCUITS, DO YOUR STUFF.
"HERE'S WHERE I NEED TO BE."
PARIS, 1923.
POLICE PUBLIC CALL BOX
THANKS. YOU KNOW I WOULDN'T DO THAT UNLESS IT WAS IMPORTANT.
FOR THE SAKE OF EVERYTHING... I HAVE TO *PREVENT* THIS.

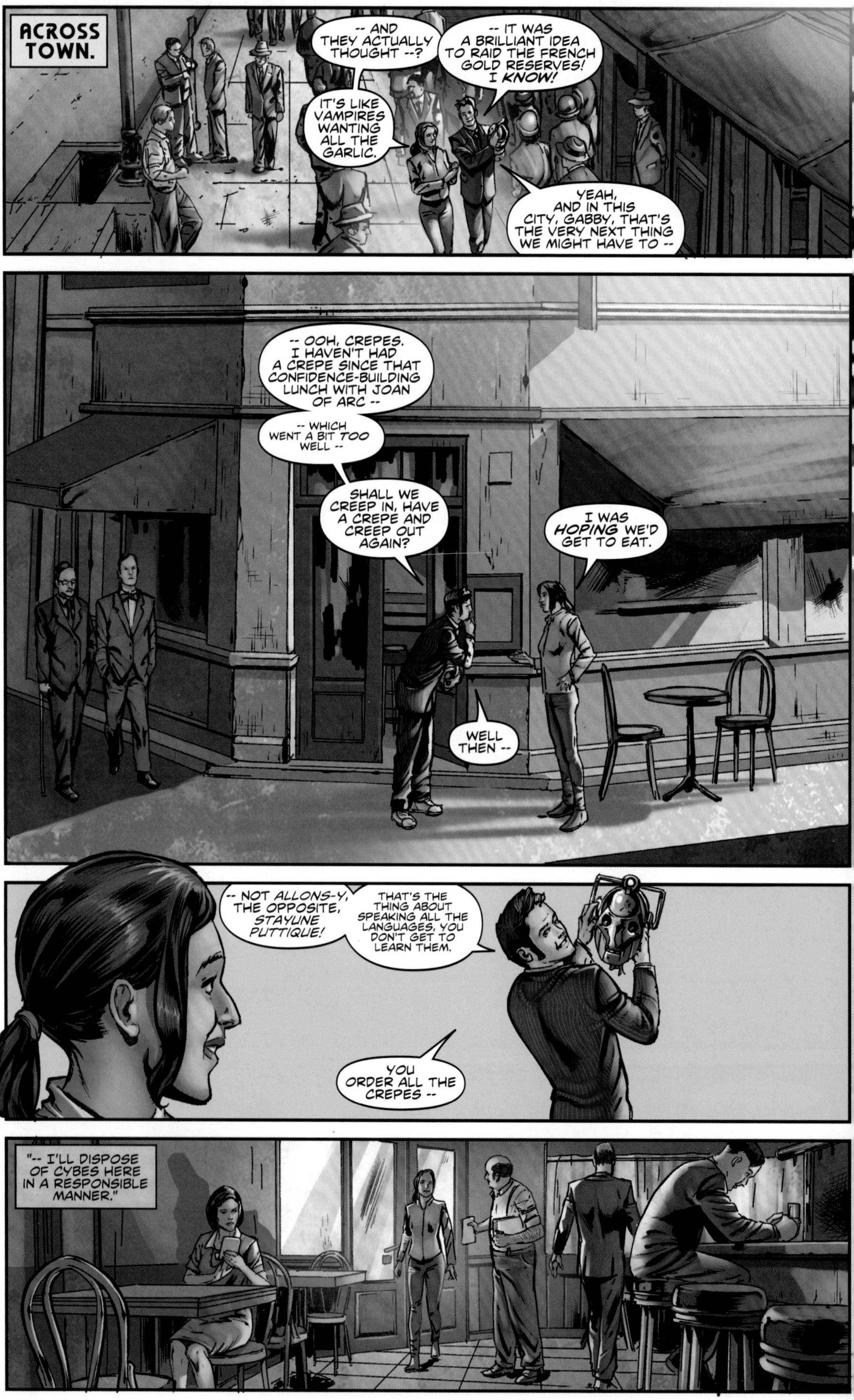
ACROSS TOWN.
-- AND THEY ACTUALLY THOUGHT --?
-- IT WAS A BRILLIANT IDEA TO RAID THE FRENCH GOLD RESERVES! I KNOW!
IT'S LIKE VAMPIRES WANTING ALL THE GARLIC.
YEAH, AND IN THIS CITY, GABBY, THAT'S THE VERY NEXT THING WE MIGHT HAVE TO --
-- OOH, CREPES. I HAVEN'T HAD A CREPE SINCE THAT CONFIDENCE-BUILDING LUNCH WITH JOAN OF ARC --
-- WHICH WENT A BIT TOO WELL --
SHALL WE CREEP IN, HAVE A CREPE AND CREEP OUT AGAIN?
I WAS HOPING WE'D GET TO EAT.
WELL THEN --
-- NOT ALLONS-Y, THE OPPOSITE, STAYUNE PUTTIQUE!
THAT'S THE THING ABOUT SPEAKING ALL THE LANGUAGES, YOU DON'T GET TO LEARN THEM.
YOU ORDER ALL THE CREPES --
"-- I'LL DISPOSE OF CYBES HERE IN A RESPONSIBLE MANNER."

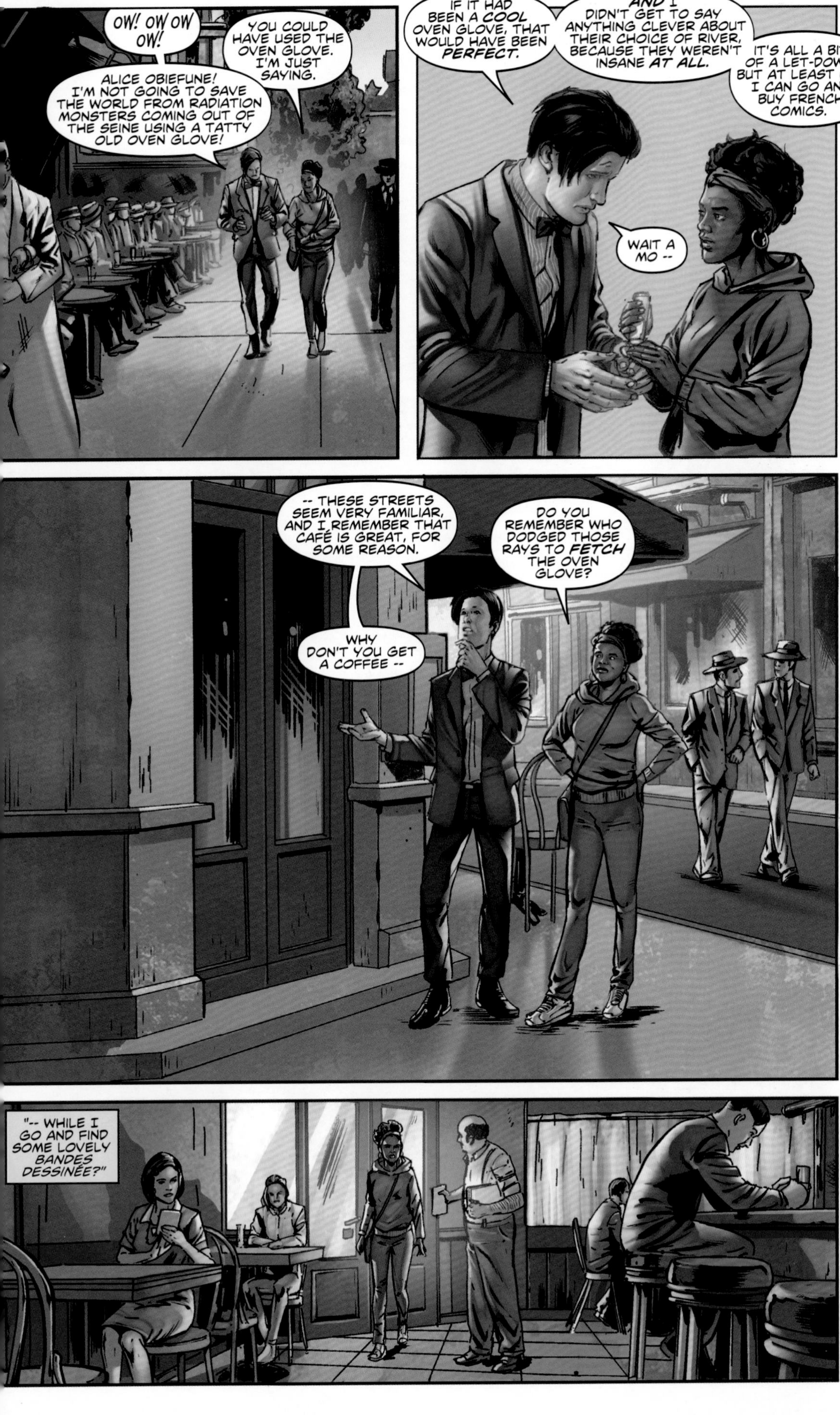
OW! OW OW OW!
YOU COULD HAVE USED THE OVEN GLOVE. I'M JUST SAYING.
ALICE OBIEFUNE! I'M NOT GOING TO SAVE THE WORLD FROM RADIATION MONSTERS COMING OUT OF THE SEINE USING A TATTY OLD OVEN GLOVE!
IF IT HAD BEEN A COOL OVEN GLOVE, THAT WOULD HAVE BEEN PERFECT.
AND I DIDN'T GET TO SAY ANYTHING CLEVER ABOUT THEIR CHOICE OF RIVER, BECAUSE THEY WEREN'T INSANE AT ALL.
IT'S ALL A BIT OF A LET-DOWN. BUT AT LEAST NOW I CAN GO AND BUY FRENCH COMICS.
WAIT A MO --
-- THESE STREETS SEEM VERY FAMILIAR, AND I REMEMBER THAT CAFÉ IS GREAT, FOR SOME REASON.
WHY DON'T YOU GET A COFFEE --
DO YOU REMEMBER WHO DODGED THOSE RAYS TO FETCH THE OVEN GLOVE?
"-- WHILE I GO AND FIND SOME LOVELY BANDES DESSINÉE?"

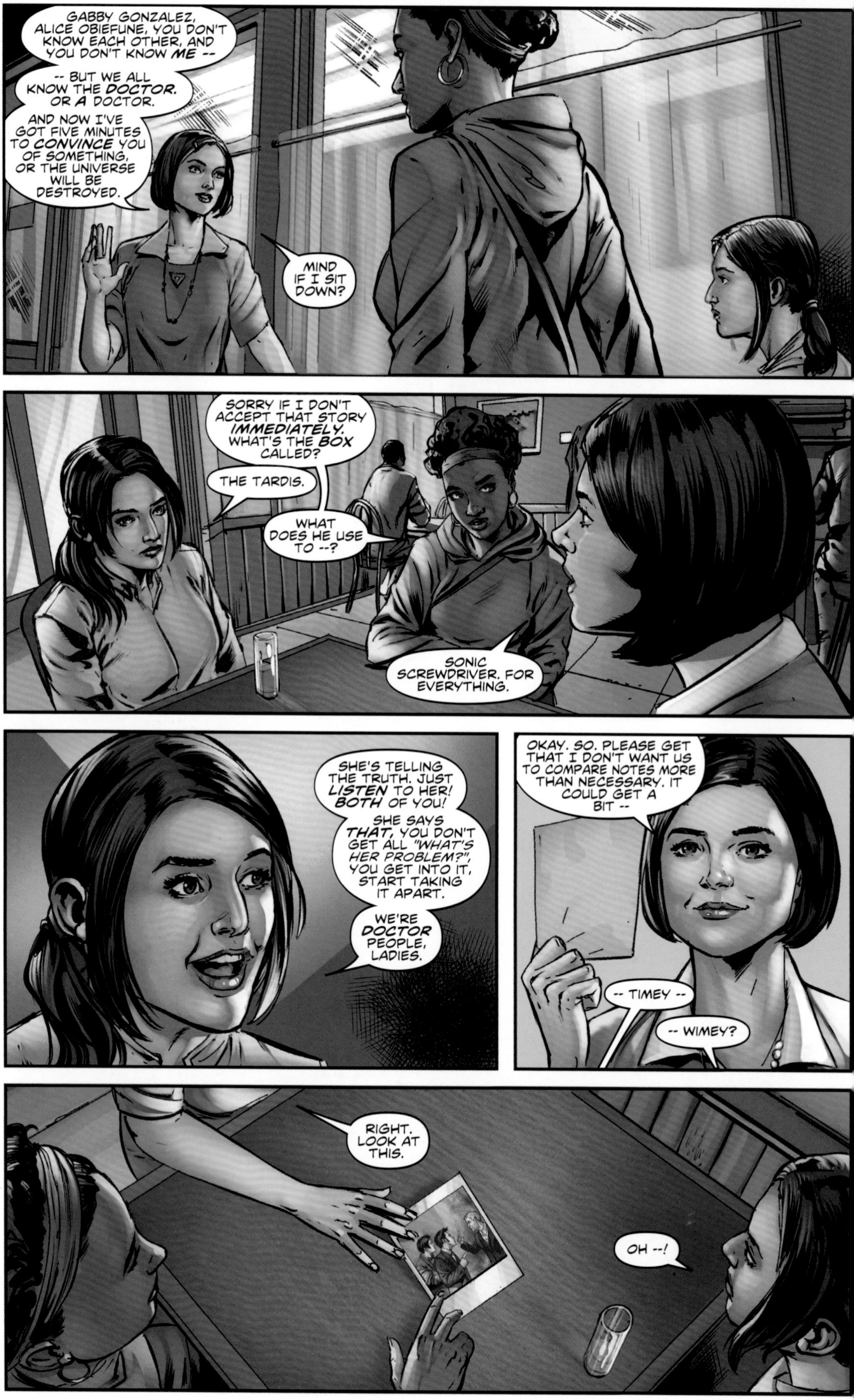
GABBY GONZALEZ, ALICE OBIEFUNE, YOU DON'T KNOW EACH OTHER, AND YOU DON'T KNOW *ME* --
-- BUT WE ALL KNOW THE *DOCTOR.* OR *A* DOCTOR.
AND NOW I'VE GOT FIVE MINUTES TO *CONVINCE* YOU OF SOMETHING, OR THE UNIVERSE WILL BE DESTROYED.
MIND IF I SIT DOWN?
SORRY IF I DON'T ACCEPT THAT STORY *IMMEDIATELY.* WHAT'S THE *BOX* CALLED?
THE TARDIS.
WHAT DOES HE USE TO --?
SONIC SCREWDRIVER. FOR EVERYTHING.
SHE'S TELLING THE TRUTH. JUST *LISTEN* TO HER! *BOTH* OF YOU!
SHE SAYS *THAT,* YOU DON'T GET ALL "*WHAT'S HER PROBLEM?*", YOU GET INTO IT, START TAKING IT APART.
WE'RE *DOCTOR* PEOPLE, LADIES.
OKAY. SO. PLEASE GET THAT I DON'T WANT US TO COMPARE NOTES MORE THAN NECESSARY. IT COULD GET A BIT --
-- TIMEY --
-- WIMEY?
RIGHT. LOOK AT THIS.
OH --!

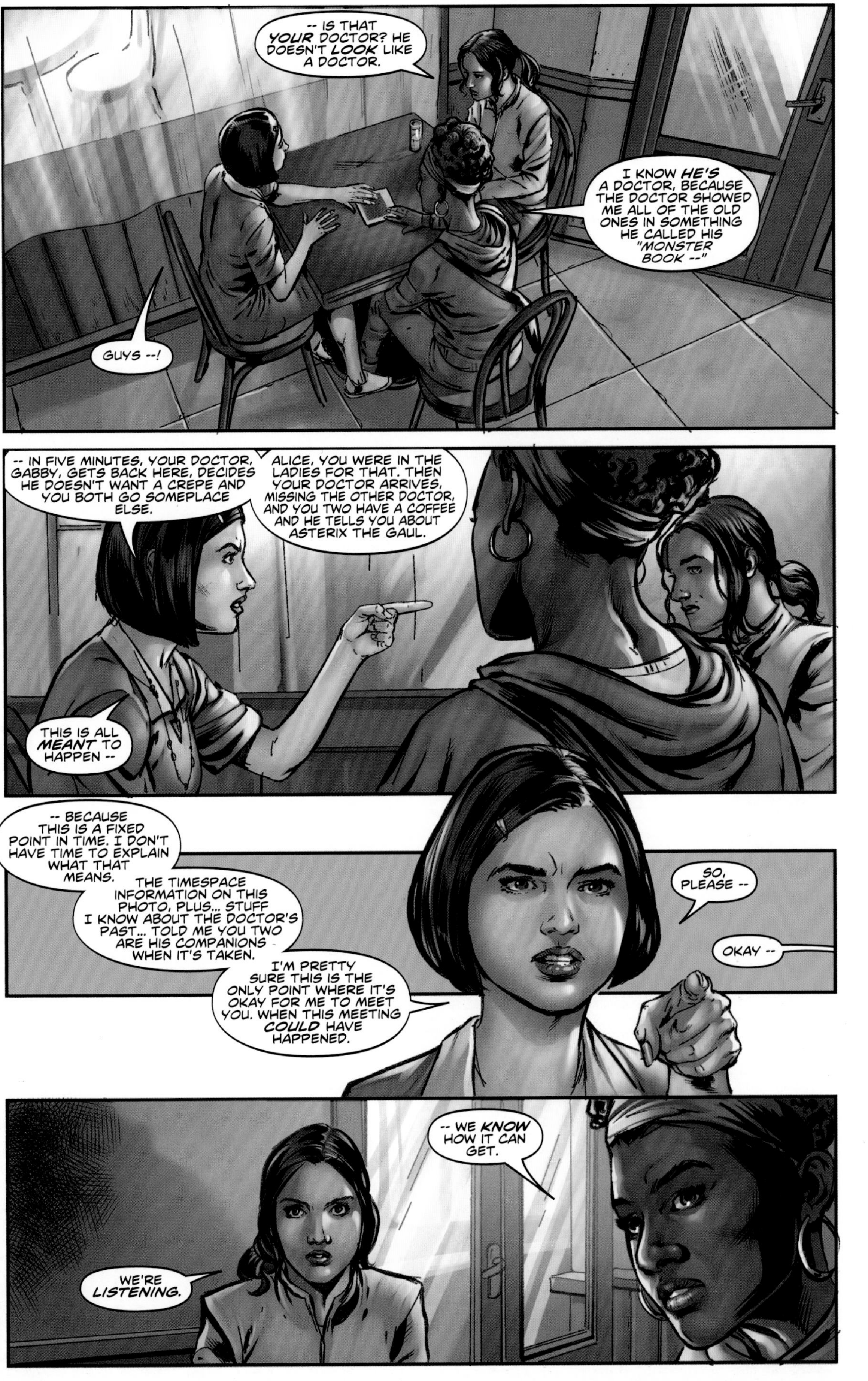
-- IS THAT YOUR DOCTOR? HE DOESN'T LOOK LIKE A DOCTOR.
I KNOW HE'S A DOCTOR, BECAUSE THE DOCTOR SHOWED ME ALL OF THE OLD ONES IN SOMETHING HE CALLED HIS "MONSTER BOOK --"
GUYS --!
-- IN FIVE MINUTES, YOUR DOCTOR, GABBY, GETS BACK HERE, DECIDES HE DOESN'T WANT A CREPE AND YOU BOTH GO SOMEPLACE ELSE.
ALICE, YOU WERE IN THE LADIES FOR THAT. THEN YOUR DOCTOR ARRIVES, MISSING THE OTHER DOCTOR, AND YOU TWO HAVE A COFFEE AND HE TELLS YOU ABOUT ASTERIX THE GAUL.
THIS IS ALL MEANT TO HAPPEN --
-- BECAUSE THIS IS A FIXED POINT IN TIME. I DON'T HAVE TIME TO EXPLAIN WHAT THAT MEANS.
THE TIMESPACE INFORMATION ON THIS PHOTO, PLUS... STUFF I KNOW ABOUT THE DOCTOR'S PAST... TOLD ME YOU TWO ARE HIS COMPANIONS WHEN IT'S TAKEN.
I'M PRETTY SURE THIS IS THE ONLY POINT WHERE IT'S OKAY FOR ME TO MEET YOU. WHEN THIS MEETING COULD HAVE HAPPENED.
SO, PLEASE --
OKAY --
-- WE KNOW HOW IT CAN GET.
WE'RE LISTENING.

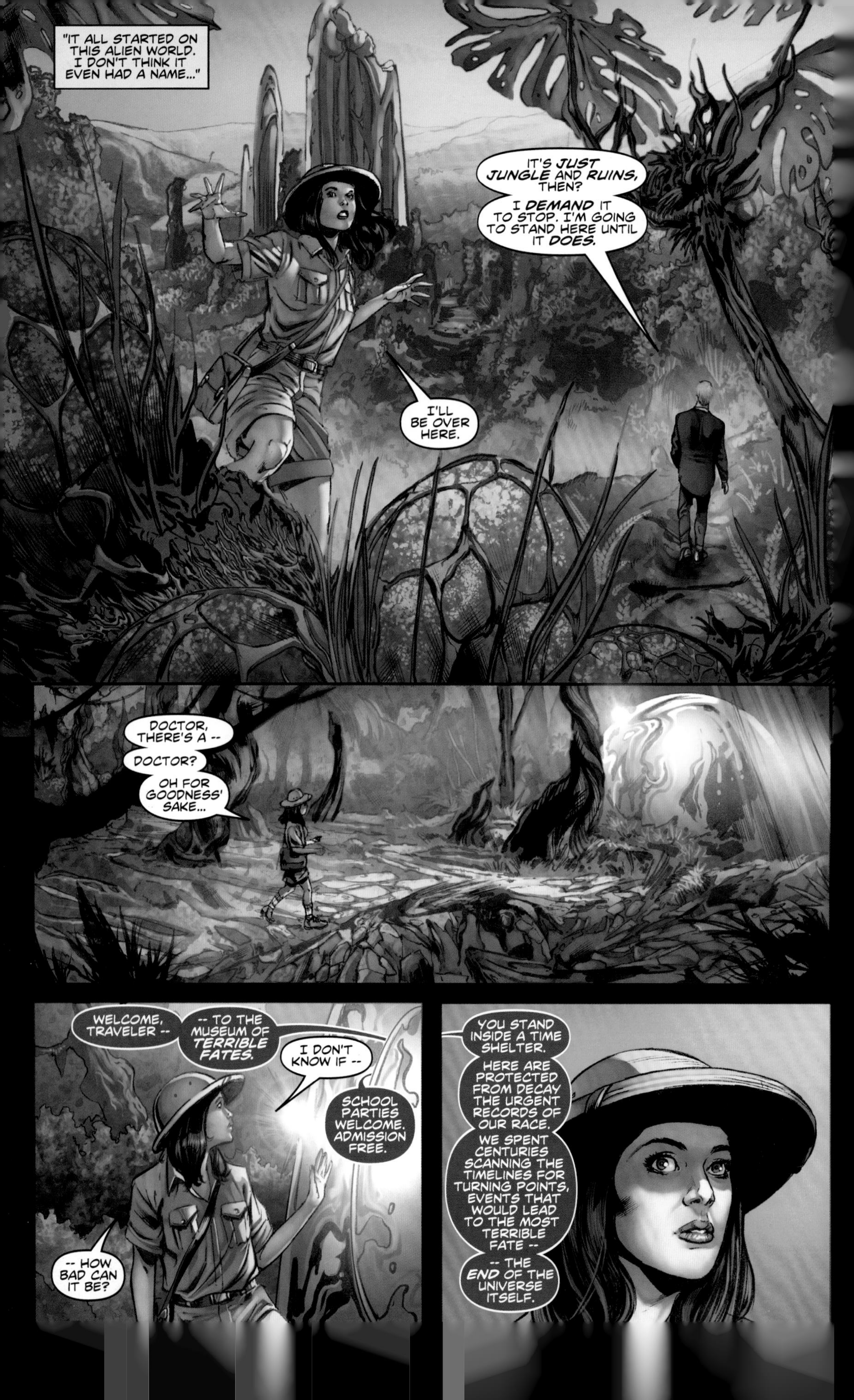
"IT ALL STARTED ON THIS ALIEN WORLD. I DON'T THINK IT EVEN HAD A NAME..."
IT'S JUST JUNGLE AND RUINS, THEN?
I DEMAND IT TO STOP. I'M GOING TO STAND HERE UNTIL IT DOES.
I'LL BE OVER HERE.
DOCTOR, THERE'S A --
DOCTOR?
OH FOR GOODNESS' SAKE...
WELCOME, TRAVELER --
-- TO THE MUSEUM OF TERRIBLE FATES.
I DON'T KNOW IF --
SCHOOL PARTIES WELCOME. ADMISSION FREE.
-- HOW BAD CAN IT BE?
YOU STAND INSIDE A TIME SHELTER.
HERE ARE PROTECTED FROM DECAY THE URGENT RECORDS OF OUR RACE.
WE SPENT CENTURIES SCANNING THE TIMELINES FOR TURNING POINTS, EVENTS THAT WOULD LEAD TO THE MOST TERRIBLE FATE --
-- THE END OF THE UNIVERSE ITSELF.

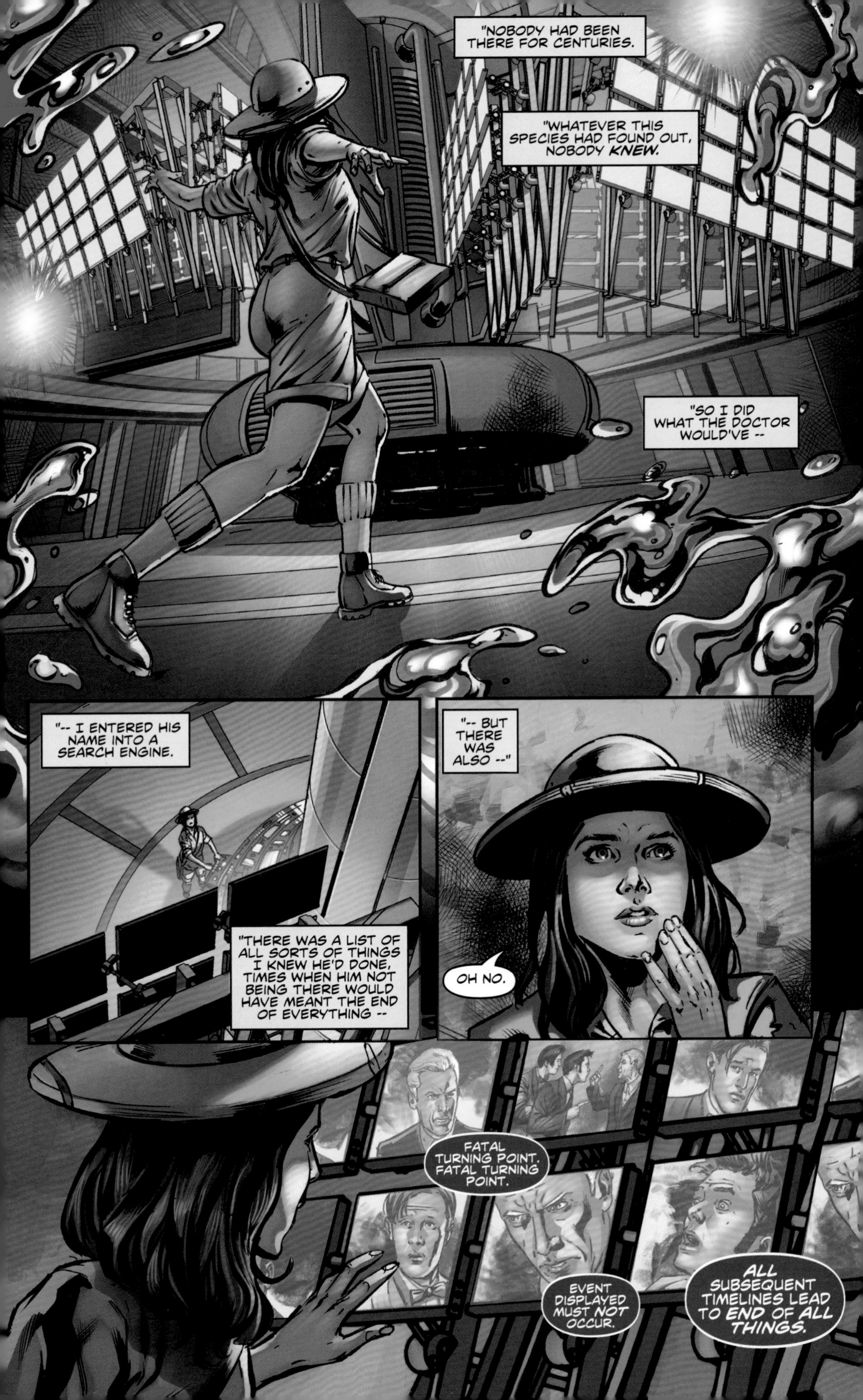
"NOBODY HAD BEEN THERE FOR CENTURIES.
"WHATEVER THIS SPECIES HAD FOUND OUT, NOBODY KNEW.
"SO I DID WHAT THE DOCTOR WOULD'VE --
"-- I ENTERED HIS NAME INTO A SEARCH ENGINE.
"THERE WAS A LIST OF ALL SORTS OF THINGS I KNEW HE'D DONE, TIMES WHEN HIM NOT BEING THERE WOULD HAVE MEANT THE END OF EVERYTHING --
"-- BUT THERE WAS ALSO --"
OH NO.
FATAL TURNING POINT. FATAL TURNING POINT.
EVENT DISPLAYED MUST NOT OCCUR.
ALL SUBSEQUENT TIMELINES LEAD TO END OF ALL THINGS.

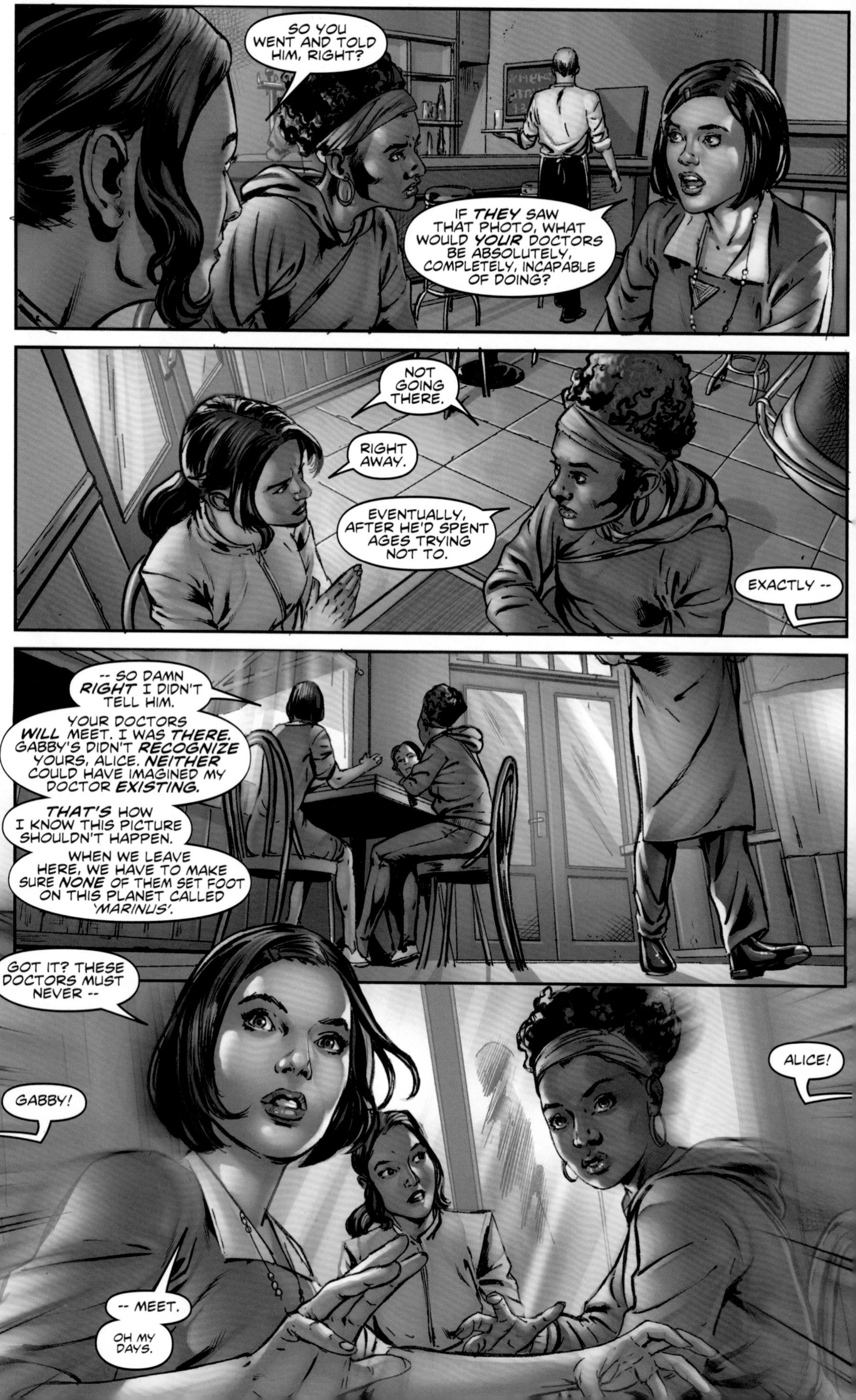
SO YOU WENT AND TOLD HIM, RIGHT?
IF THEY SAW THAT PHOTO, WHAT WOULD YOUR DOCTORS BE ABSOLUTELY, COMPLETELY, INCAPABLE OF DOING?
NOT GOING THERE.
RIGHT AWAY.
EVENTUALLY, AFTER HE'D SPENT AGES TRYING NOT TO.
EXACTLY --
-- SO DAMN RIGHT I DIDN'T TELL HIM.
YOUR DOCTORS WILL MEET. I WAS THERE. GABBY'S DIDN'T RECOGNIZE YOURS, ALICE. NEITHER COULD HAVE IMAGINED MY DOCTOR EXISTING.
THAT'S HOW I KNOW THIS PICTURE SHOULDN'T HAPPEN.
WHEN WE LEAVE HERE, WE HAVE TO MAKE SURE NONE OF THEM SET FOOT ON THIS PLANET CALLED 'MARINUS'.
GOT IT? THESE DOCTORS MUST NEVER --
GABBY!
ALICE!
-- MEET.
OH MY DAYS.

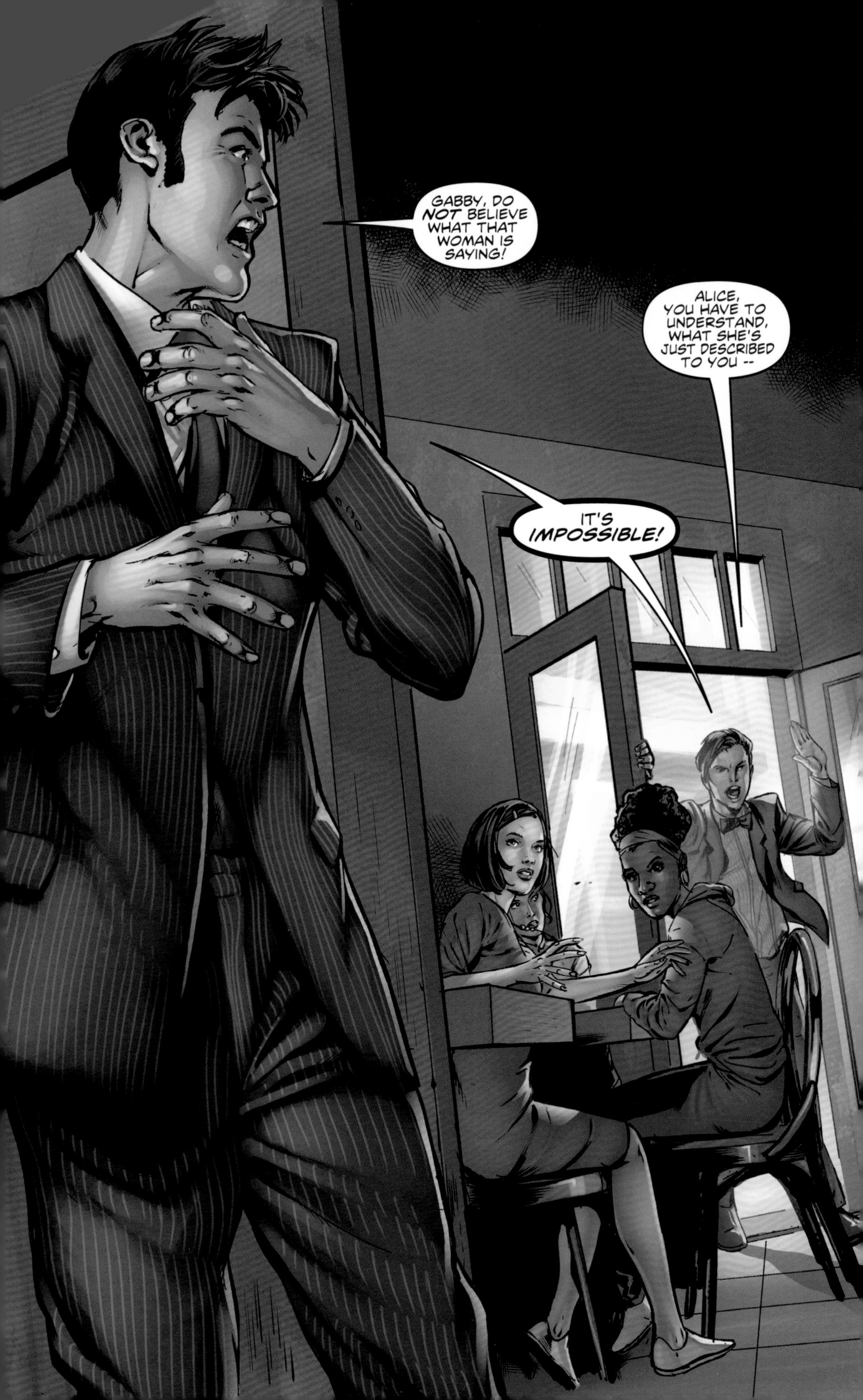
GABBY, DO NOT BELIEVE WHAT THAT WOMAN IS SAYING!
ALICE, YOU HAVE TO UNDERSTAND, WHAT SHE'S JUST DESCRIBED TO YOU --
IT'S IMPOSSIBLE!

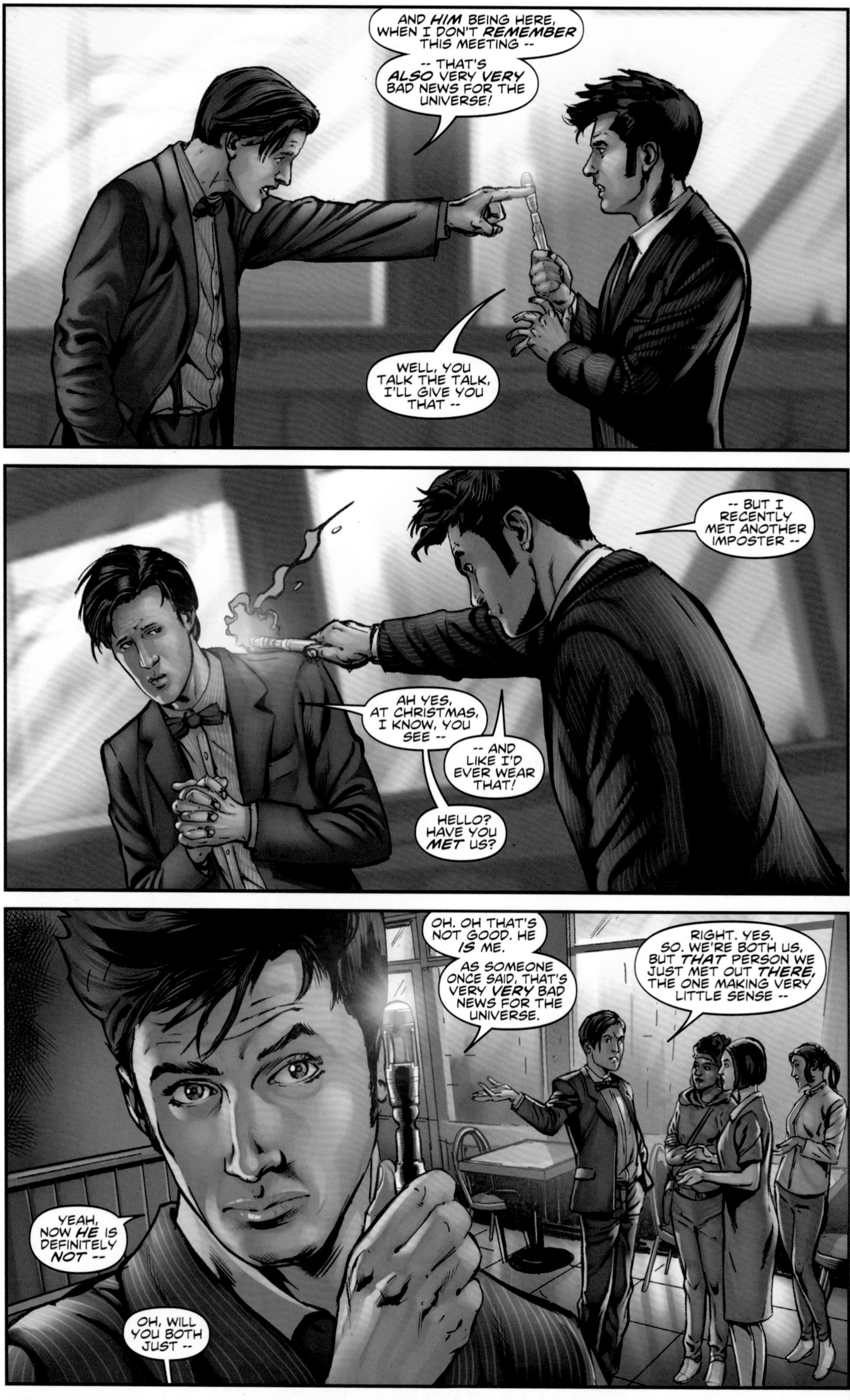
AND HIM BEING HERE, WHEN I DON'T REMEMBER THIS MEETING --
-- THAT'S ALSO VERY VERY BAD NEWS FOR THE UNIVERSE!
WELL, YOU TALK THE TALK, I'LL GIVE YOU THAT --
-- BUT I RECENTLY MET ANOTHER IMPOSTER --
AH YES, AT CHRISTMAS, I KNOW, YOU SEE --
-- AND LIKE I'D EVER WEAR THAT!
HELLO? HAVE YOU MET US?
OH. OH THAT'S NOT GOOD. HE IS ME.
AS SOMEONE ONCE SAID, THAT'S VERY VERY BAD NEWS FOR THE UNIVERSE.
RIGHT. YES. SO. WE'RE BOTH US, BUT THAT PERSON WE JUST MET OUT THERE, THE ONE MAKING VERY LITTLE SENSE --
YEAH, NOW HE IS DEFINITELY NOT --
OH, WILL YOU BOTH JUST --

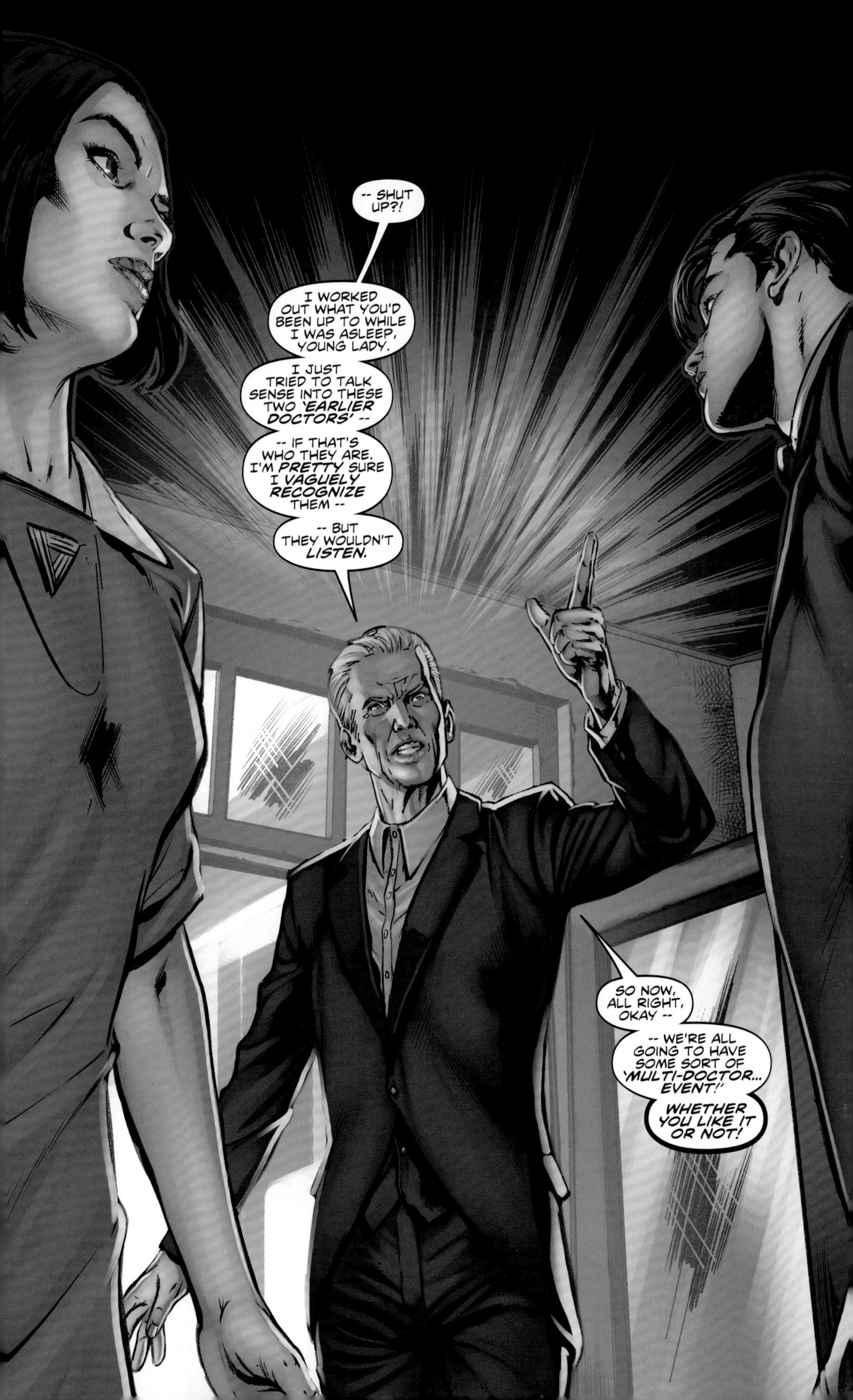
-- SHUT UP?!
I WORKED OUT WHAT YOU'D BEEN UP TO WHILE I WAS ASLEEP, YOUNG LADY.
I JUST TRIED TO TALK SENSE INTO THESE TWO 'EARLIER DOCTORS' --
-- IF THAT'S WHO THEY ARE. I'M PRETTY SURE I VAGUELY RECOGNIZE THEM --
-- BUT THEY WOULDN'T LISTEN.
SO NOW, ALL RIGHT, OKAY --
-- WE'RE ALL GOING TO HAVE SOME SORT OF 'MULTI-DOCTOR... EVENT!'
WHETHER YOU LIKE IT OR NOT!

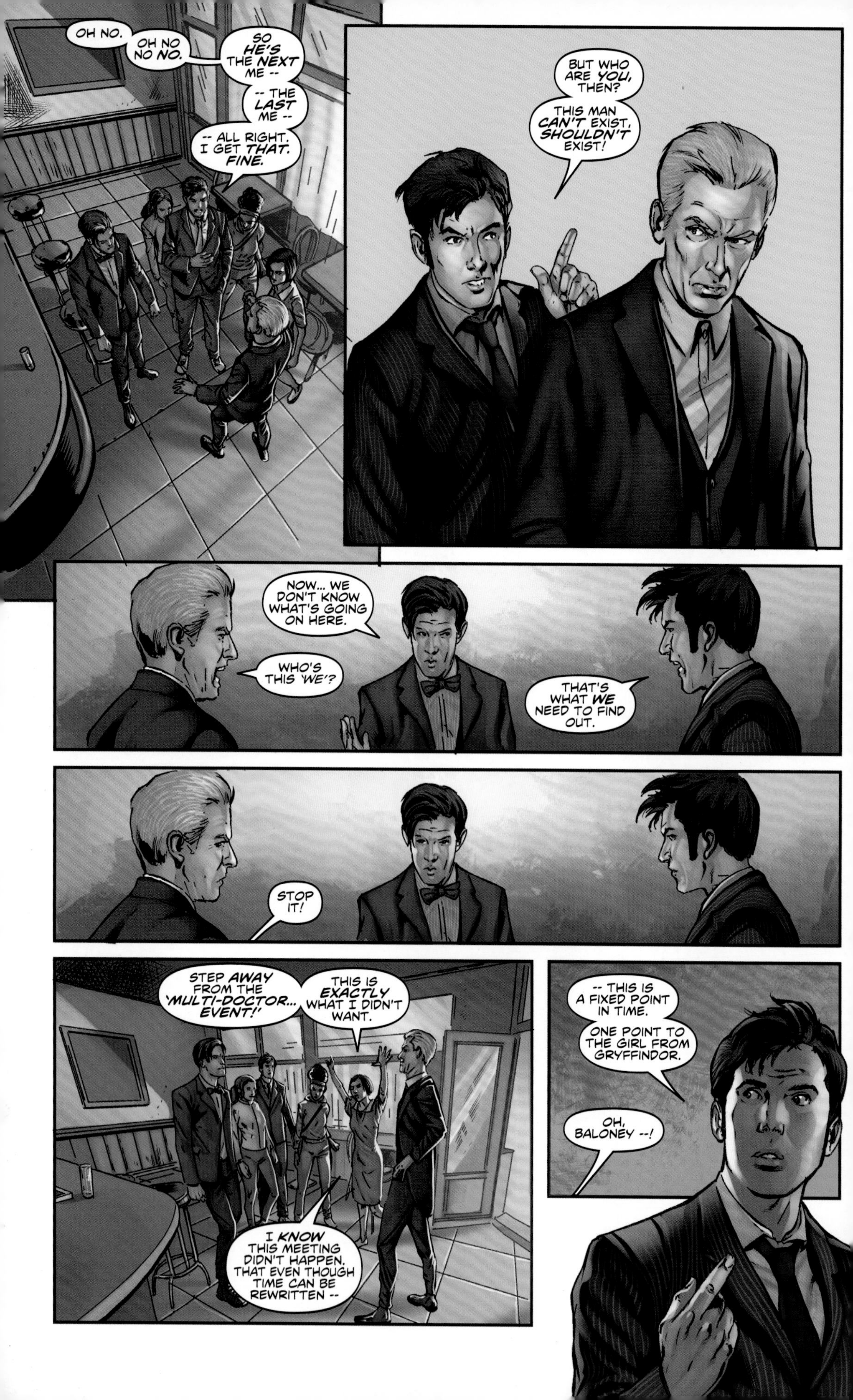
OH NO.
OH NO NO NO.
SO HE'S THE NEXT ME --
-- THE LAST ME --
-- ALL RIGHT. I GET THAT. FINE.
BUT WHO ARE YOU, THEN?
THIS MAN CAN'T EXIST, SHOULDN'T EXIST!
NOW... WE DON'T KNOW WHAT'S GOING ON HERE.
WHO'S THIS 'WE'?
THAT'S WHAT WE NEED TO FIND OUT.
STOP IT!
STEP AWAY FROM THE 'MULTI-DOCTOR... EVENT!'
THIS IS EXACTLY WHAT I DIDN'T WANT.
I KNOW THIS MEETING DIDN'T HAPPEN. THAT EVEN THOUGH TIME CAN BE REWRITTEN --
-- THIS IS A FIXED POINT IN TIME.
ONE POINT TO THE GIRL FROM GRYFFINDOR.
OH, BALONEY --!

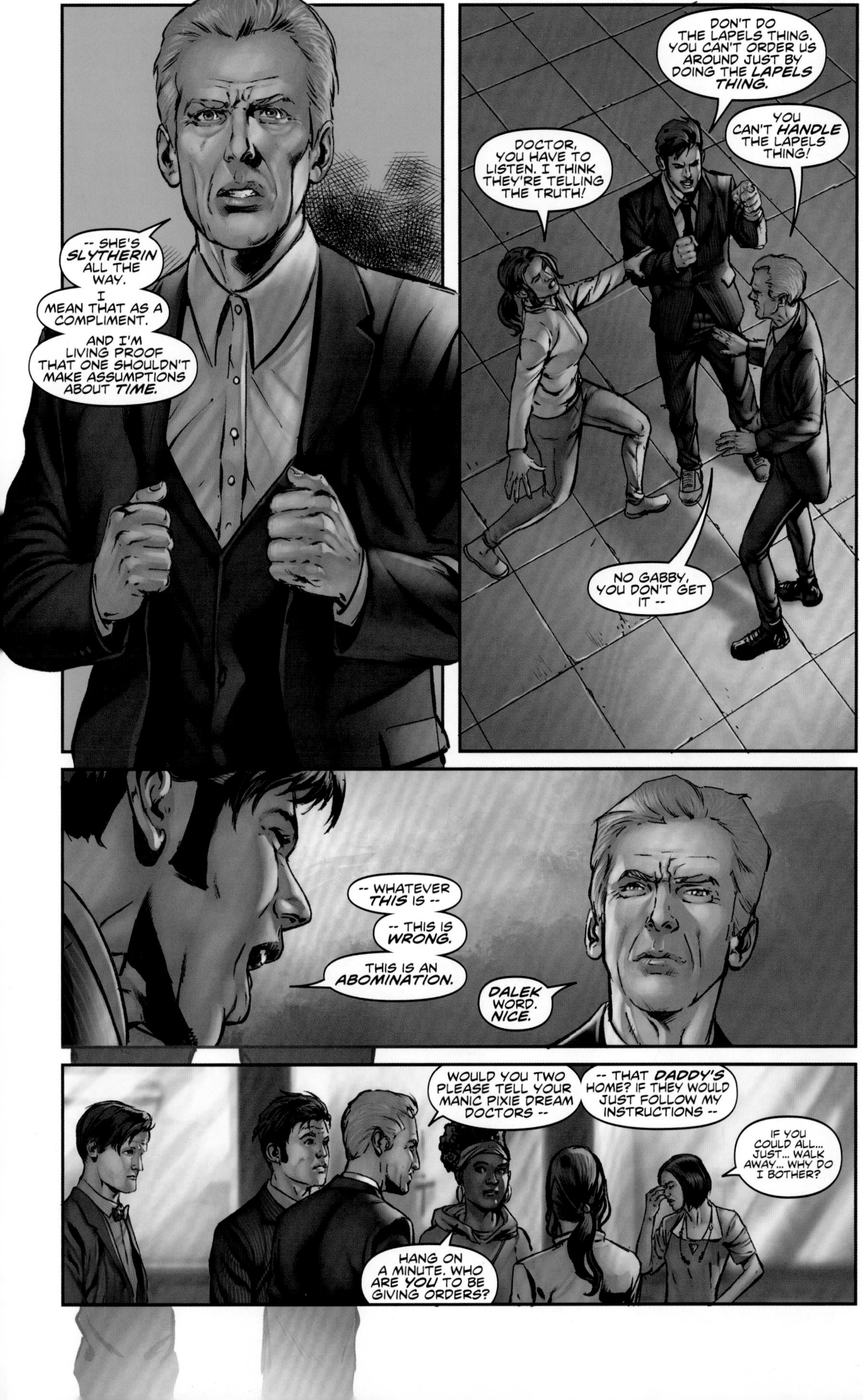
-- SHE'S SLYTHERIN ALL THE WAY.
I MEAN THAT AS A COMPLIMENT.
AND I'M LIVING PROOF THAT ONE SHOULDN'T MAKE ASSUMPTIONS ABOUT TIME.
DON'T DO THE LAPELS THING. YOU CAN'T ORDER US AROUND JUST BY DOING THE LAPELS THING.
DOCTOR, YOU HAVE TO LISTEN. I THINK THEY'RE TELLING THE TRUTH!
YOU CAN'T HANDLE THE LAPELS THING!
NO GABBY, YOU DON'T GET IT --
-- WHATEVER THIS IS --
-- THIS IS WRONG.
THIS IS AN ABOMINATION.
DALEK WORD. NICE.
WOULD YOU TWO PLEASE TELL YOUR MANIC PIXIE DREAM DOCTORS --
-- THAT DADDY'S HOME? IF THEY WOULD JUST FOLLOW MY INSTRUCTIONS --
IF YOU COULD ALL... JUST... WALK AWAY... WHY DO I BOTHER?
HANG ON A MINUTE. WHO ARE YOU TO BE GIVING ORDERS?

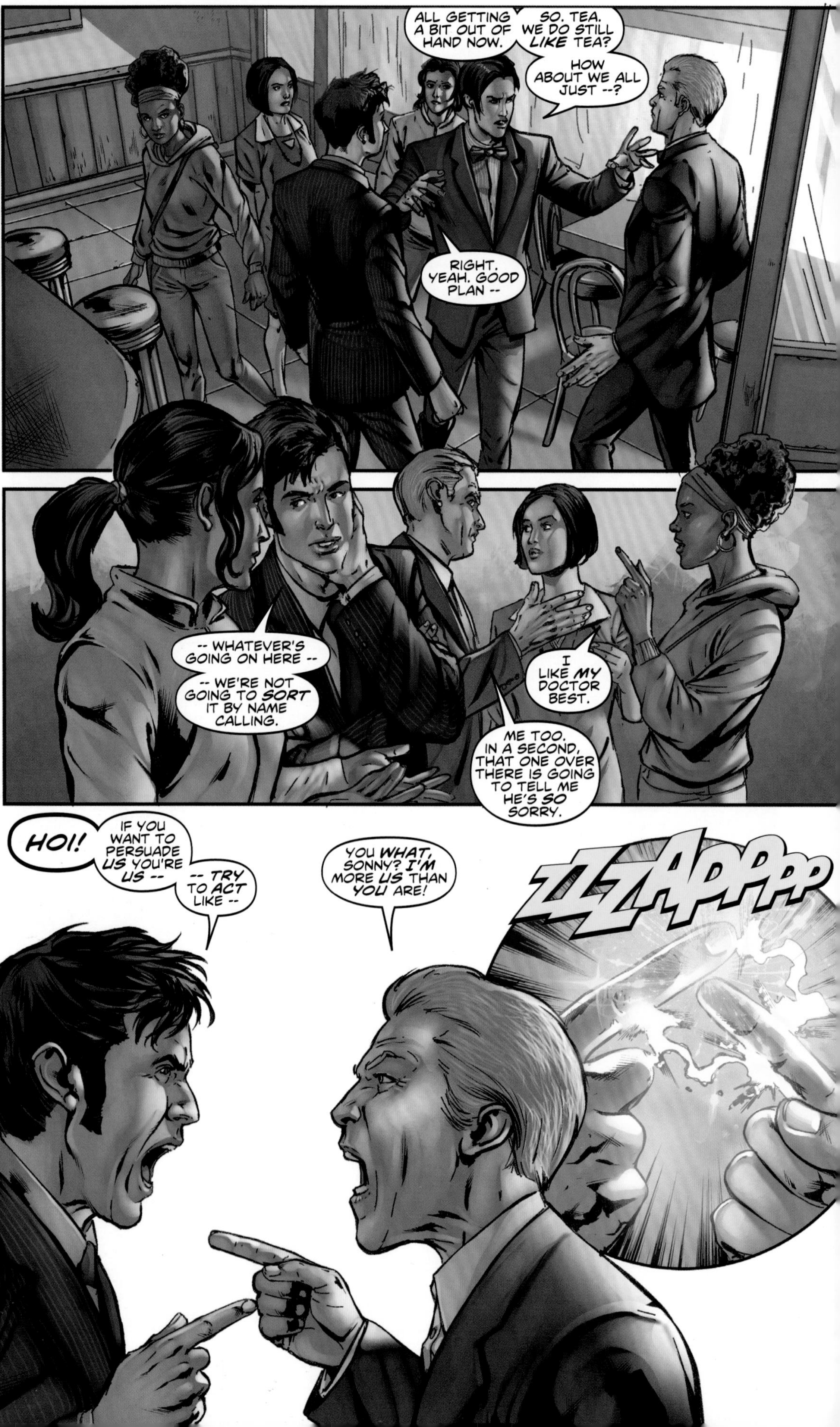

ALL GETTING A BIT OUT OF HAND NOW.
SO. TEA. WE DO STILL LIKE TEA?
HOW ABOUT WE ALL JUST --?
RIGHT. YEAH. GOOD PLAN --
-- WHATEVER'S GOING ON HERE --
-- WE'RE NOT GOING TO SORT IT BY NAME CALLING.
I LIKE MY DOCTOR BEST.
ME TOO. IN A SECOND, THAT ONE OVER THERE IS GOING TO TELL ME HE'S SO SORRY.
HOI!
IF YOU WANT TO PERSUADE US YOU'RE US --
-- TRY TO ACT LIKE --
YOU WHAT, SONNY? I'M MORE US THAN YOU ARE!
ZZZAPPPP

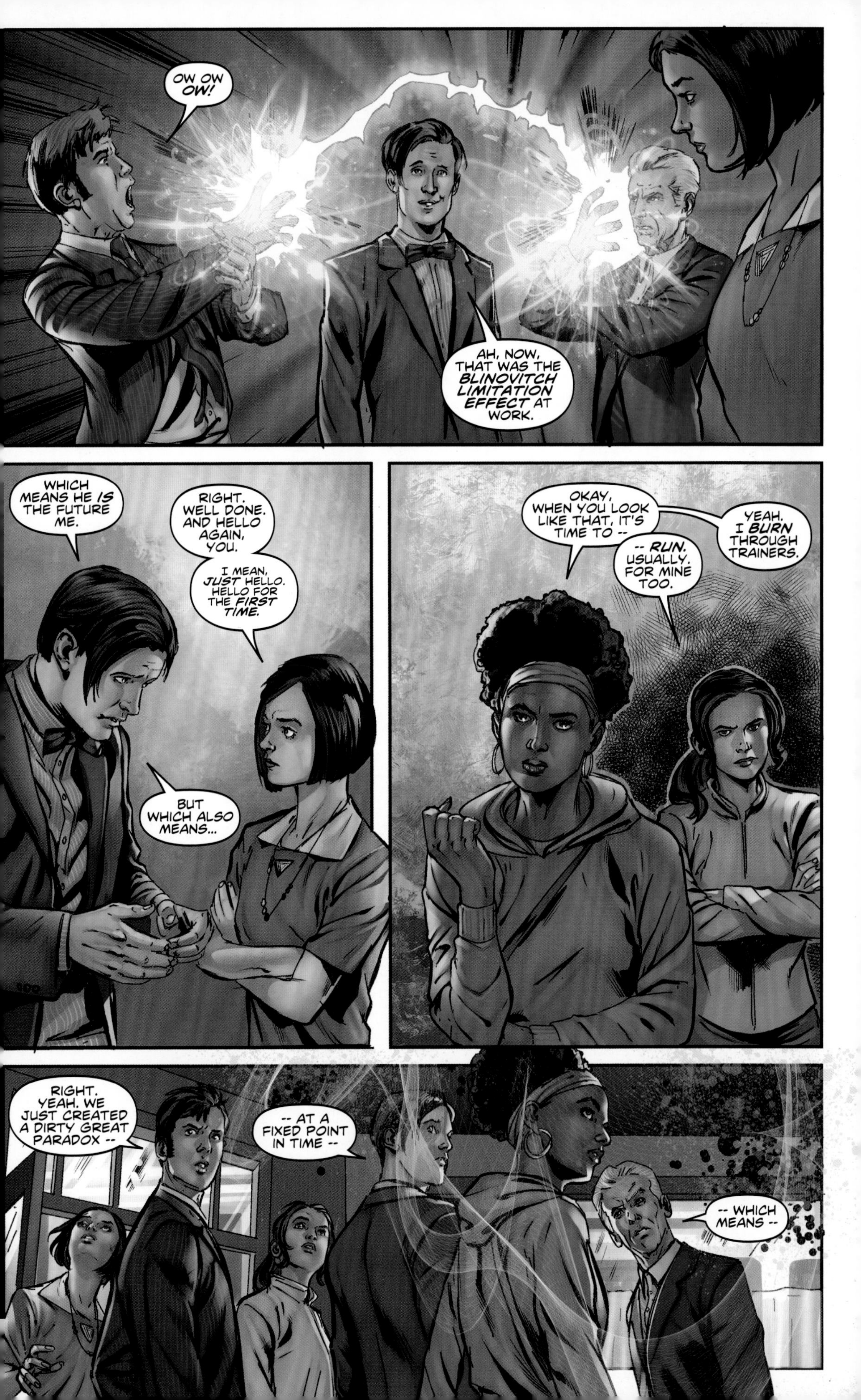
OW OW OW!
AH, NOW, THAT WAS THE BLINOVITCH LIMITATION EFFECT AT WORK.
WHICH MEANS HE IS THE FUTURE ME.
RIGHT. WELL DONE. AND HELLO AGAIN, YOU.
I MEAN, JUST HELLO. HELLO FOR THE FIRST TIME.
BUT WHICH ALSO MEANS...
OKAY, WHEN YOU LOOK LIKE THAT, IT'S TIME TO --
-- RUN. USUALLY. FOR MINE TOO.
YEAH. I BURN THROUGH TRAINERS.
RIGHT. YEAH. WE JUST CREATED A DIRTY GREAT PARADOX --
-- AT A FIXED POINT IN TIME --
-- WHICH MEANS --

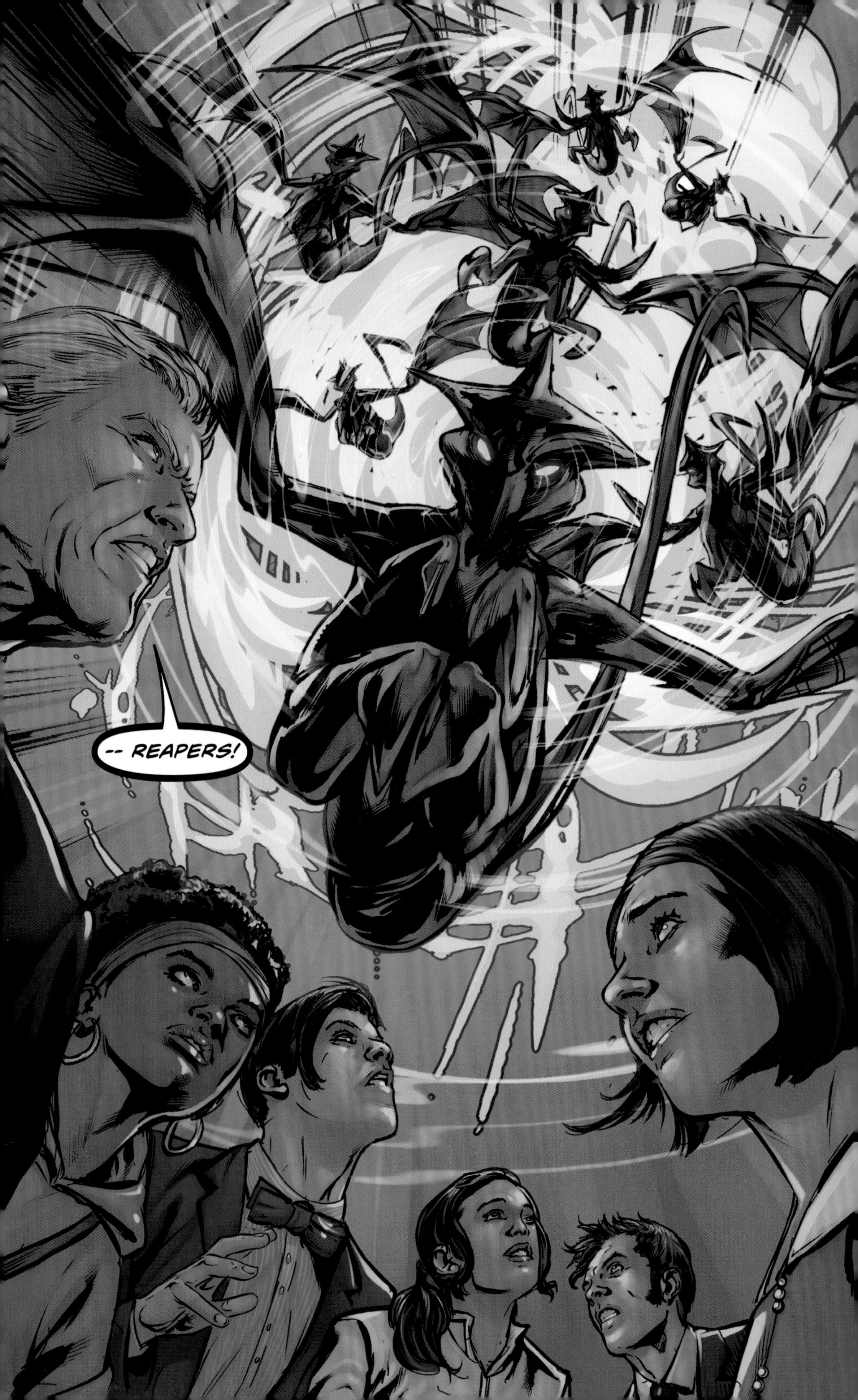
-- REAPERS!

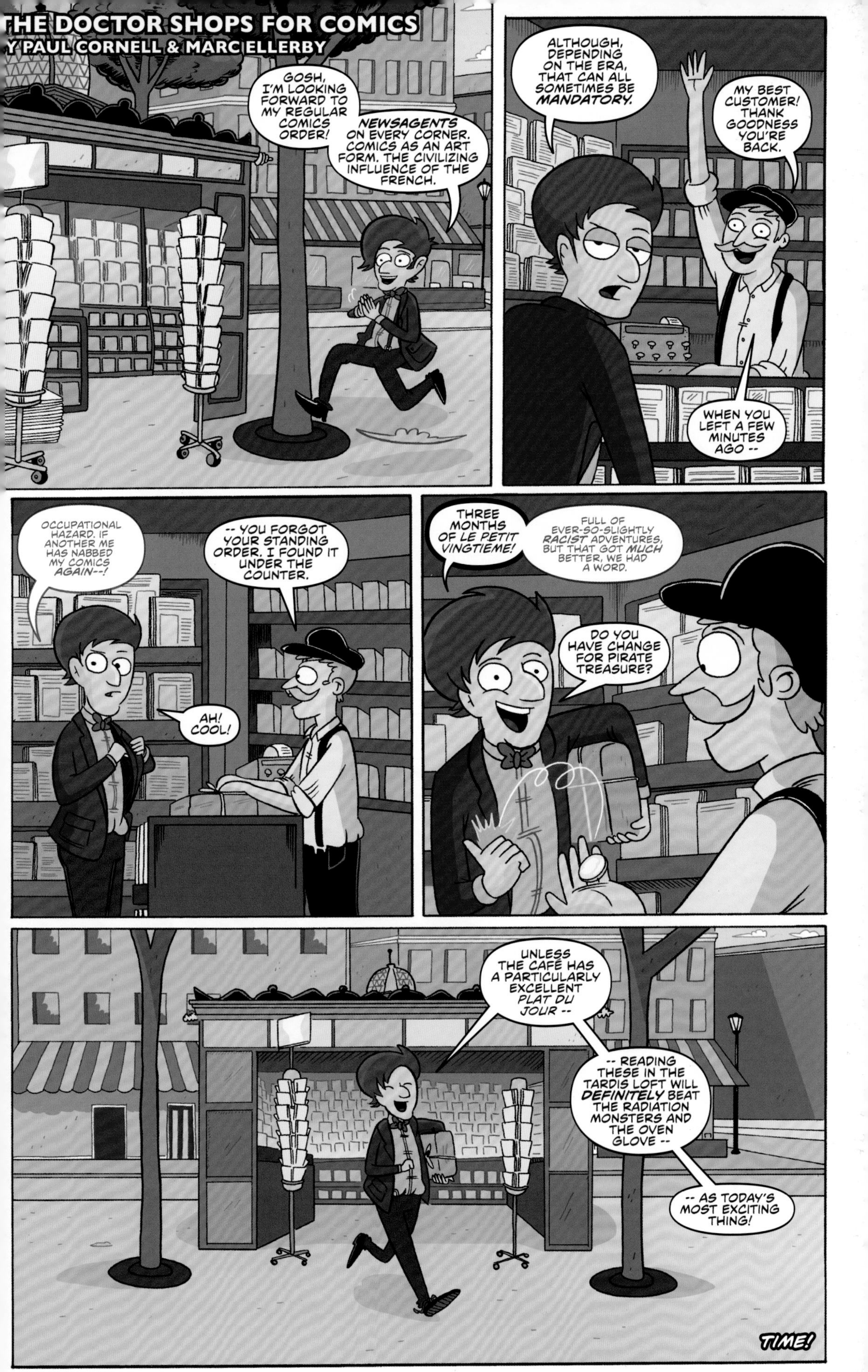
THE DOCTOR SHOPS FOR COMICS
Y PAUL CORNELL & MARC ELLERBY
GOSH, I'M LOOKING FORWARD TO MY REGULAR COMICS ORDER!
NEWSAGENTS ON EVERY CORNER. COMICS AS AN ART FORM. THE CIVILIZING INFLUENCE OF THE FRENCH.
ALTHOUGH, DEPENDING ON THE ERA, THAT CAN ALL SOMETIMES BE MANDATORY.
MY BEST CUSTOMER! THANK GOODNESS YOU'RE BACK.
WHEN YOU LEFT A FEW MINUTES AGO --
OCCUPATIONAL HAZARD. IF ANOTHER ME HAS NABBED MY COMICS AGAIN--!
-- YOU FORGOT YOUR STANDING ORDER. I FOUND IT UNDER THE COUNTER.
AH! COOL!
THREE MONTHS OF LE PETIT VINGTIEME!
FULL OF EVER-SO-SLIGHTLY RACIST ADVENTURES, BUT THAT GOT MUCH BETTER, WE HAD A WORD.
DO YOU HAVE CHANGE FOR PIRATE TREASURE?
UNLESS THE CAFÉ HAS A PARTICULARLY EXCELLENT PLAT DU JOUR --
-- READING THESE IN THE TARDIS LOFT WILL DEFINITELY BEAT THE RADIATION MONSTERS AND THE OVEN GLOVE --
-- AS TODAY'S MOST EXCITING THING!
TIME!

COVER 2

REGULAR Cover by
Neil Edwards
& Ivan Nunes

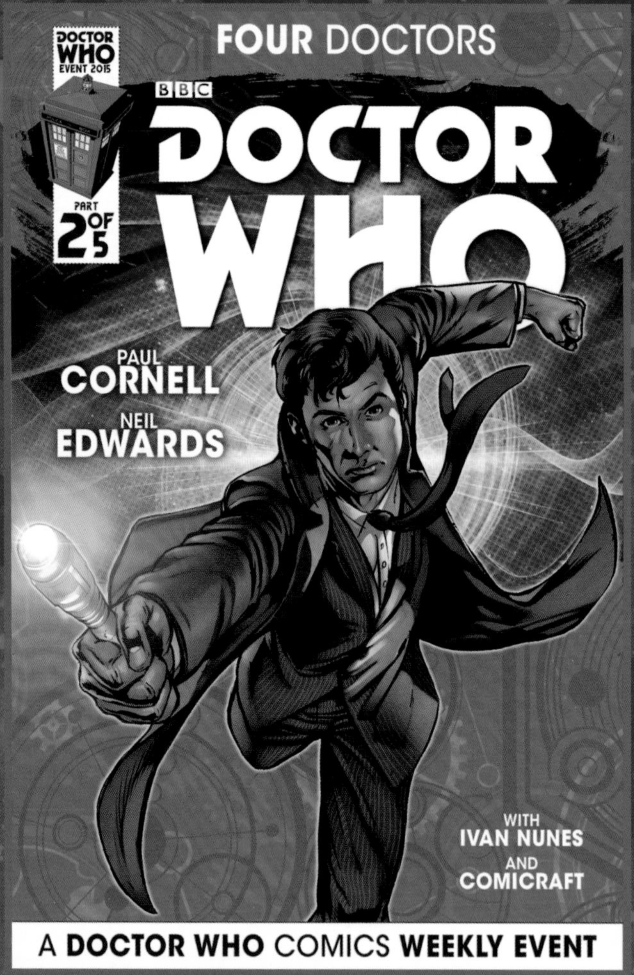

FOUR DOCTORS
DOCTOR WHO EVENT 2015
BBC
DOCTOR WHO
PART 2 OF 5
PAUL CORNELL
NEIL EDWARDS
WITH IVAN NUNES AND COMICRAFT
A DOCTOR WHO COMICS WEEKLY EVENT

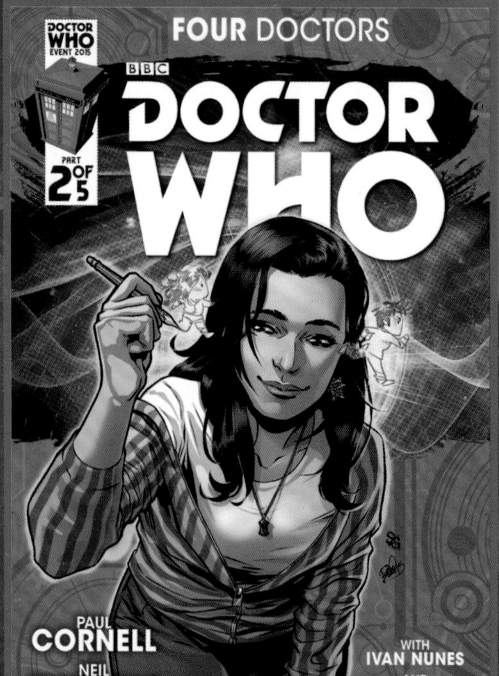

FOUR DOCTORS
DOCTOR WHO EVENT 2015
BBC
DOCTOR WHO
PART 2 OF 5
PAUL CORNELL
NEIL EDWARDS
WITH IVAN NUNES AND COMICRAFT
A DOCTOR WHO COMICS WEEKLY EVENT

COMPANION Cover by Elena Casagrande,
Eleonora Carlini & Claudia SG Iannicello

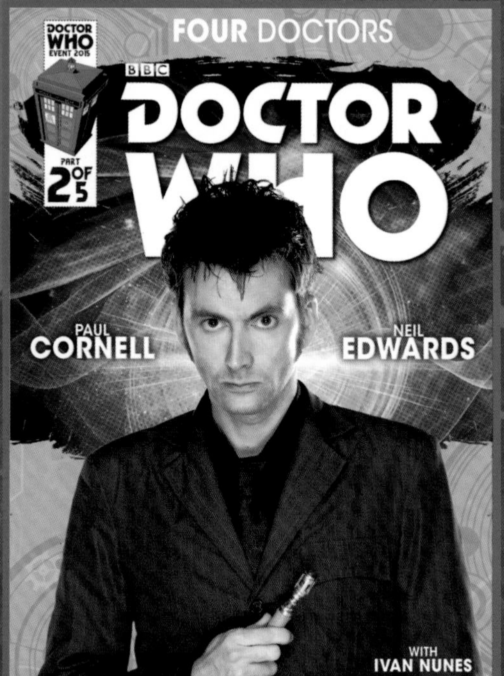

FOUR DOCTORS
DOCTOR WHO EVENT 2015
BBC
DOCTOR WHO
PART 2 OF 5
PAUL CORNELL
NEIL EDWARDS
WITH IVAN NUNES AND COMICRAFT
A DOCTOR WHO COMICS WEEKLY EVENT

SUBSCRIPTION Cover by
AJ & Rob Farmer

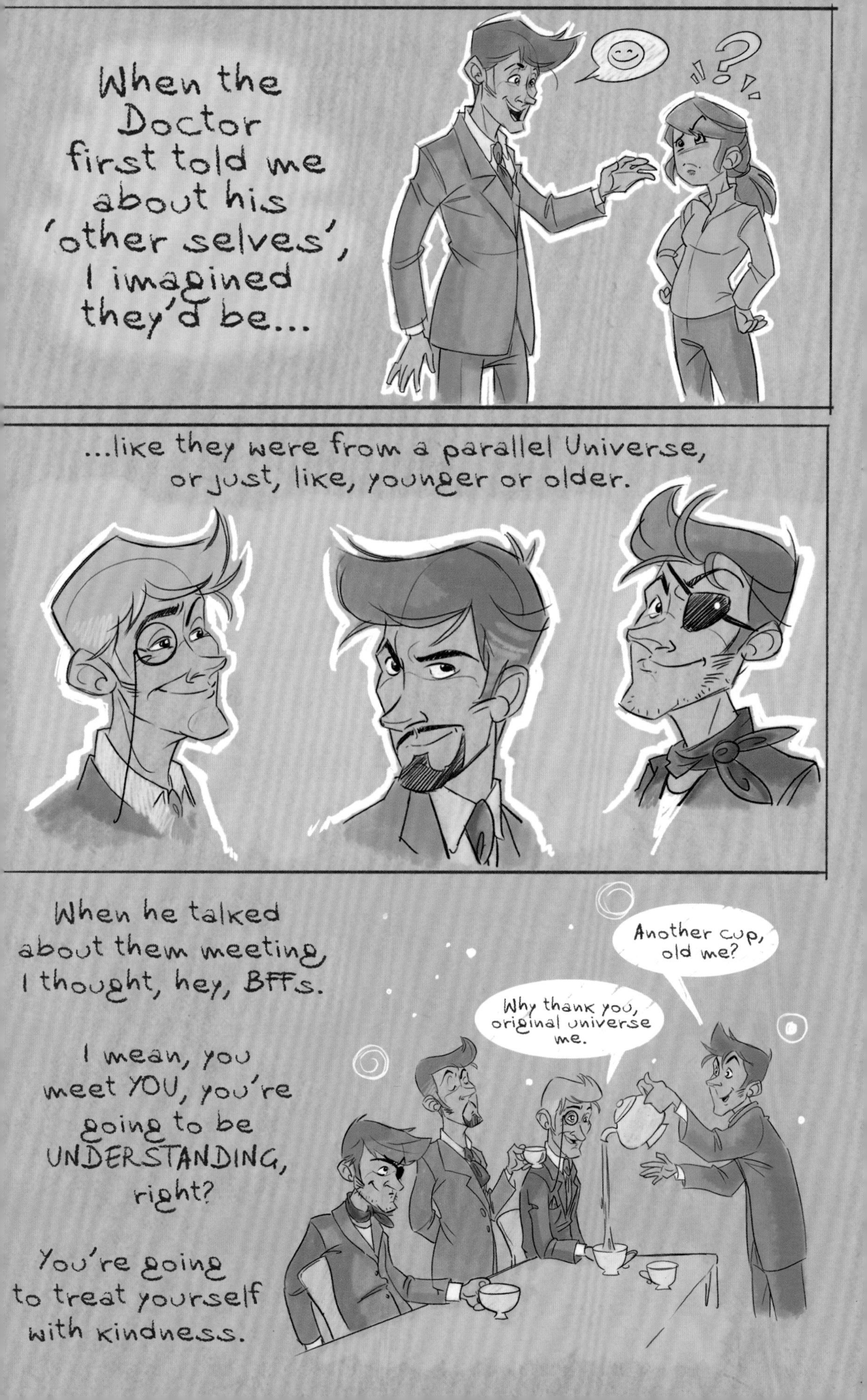
When the Doctor first told me about his 'other selves', I imagined they'd be...
...like they were from a parallel Universe, or just, like, younger or older.
When he talked about them meeting, I thought, hey, BFFs.
Another cup, old me?
Why thank you, original universe me.
I mean, you meet YOU, you're going to be UNDERSTANDING, right?
You're going to treat yourself with kindness.

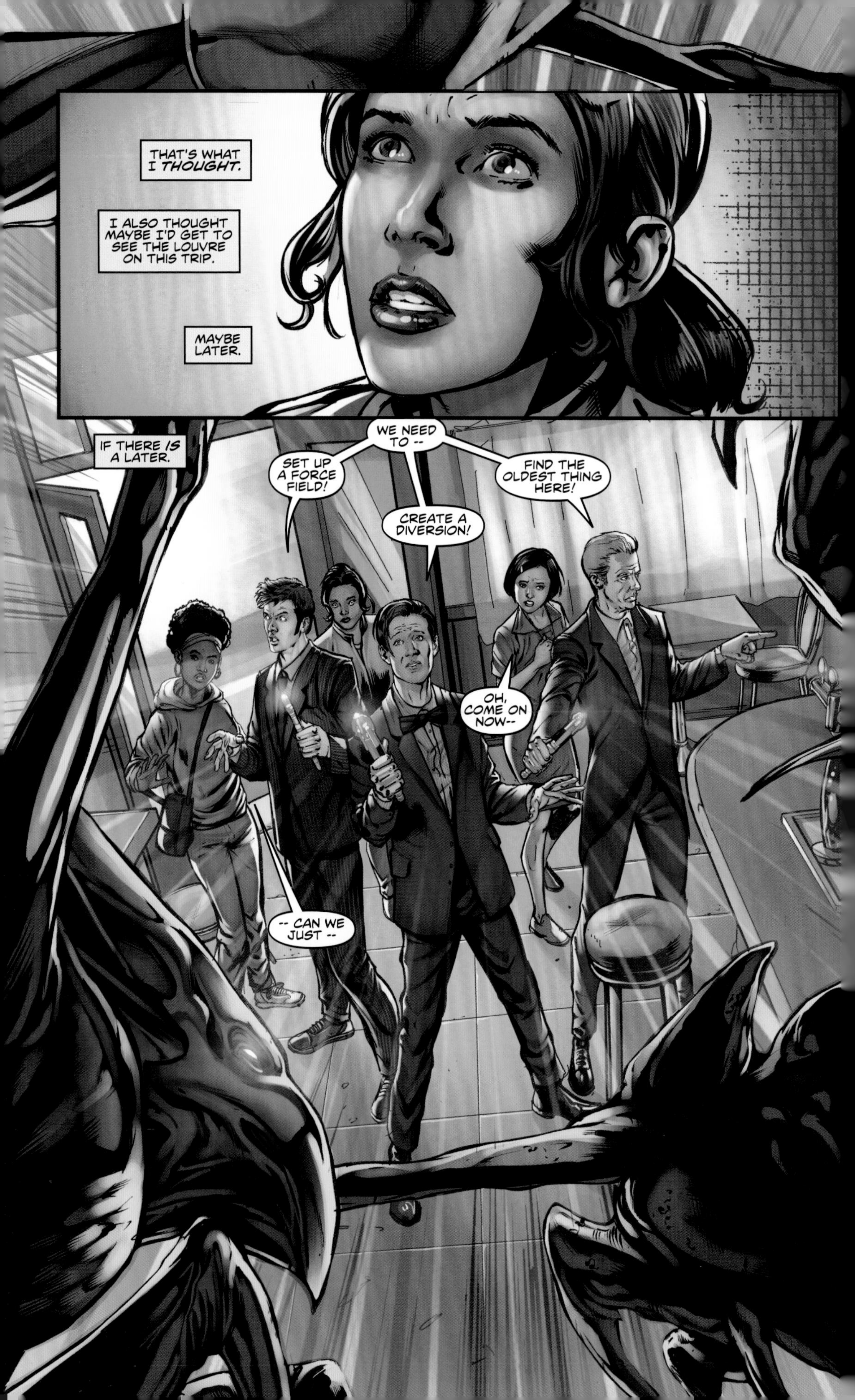
THAT'S WHAT I *THOUGHT*.
I ALSO THOUGHT MAYBE I'D GET TO SEE THE LOUVRE ON THIS TRIP.
MAYBE LATER.
IF THERE *IS* A LATER.
WE NEED TO --
SET UP A FORCE FIELD!
CREATE A DIVERSION!
FIND THE OLDEST THING HERE!
OH, COME ON NOW--
-- CAN WE JUST --

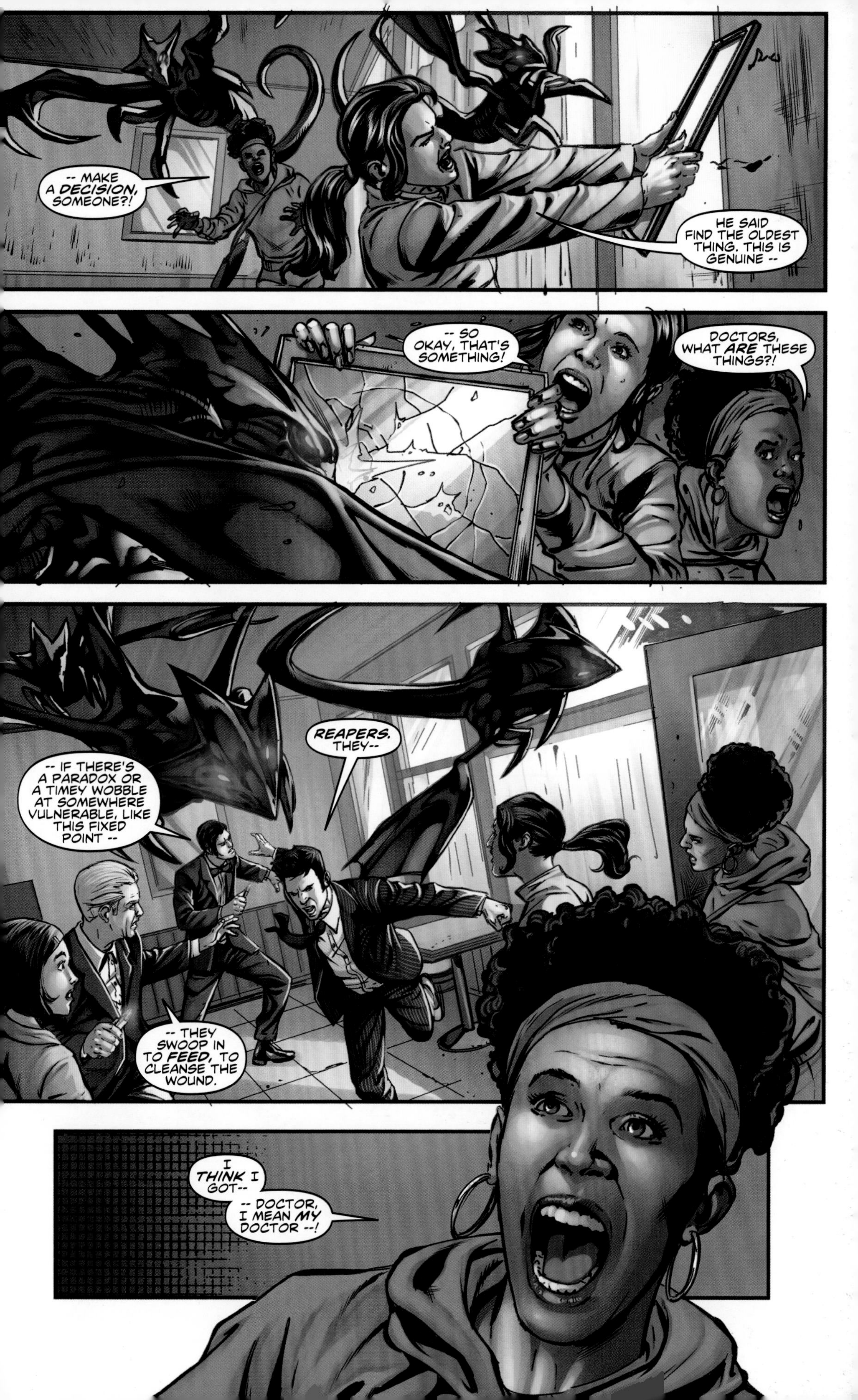

-- MAKE A *DECISION,* SOMEONE?!
HE SAID FIND THE OLDEST THING. THIS IS GENUINE --
-- SO OKAY, THAT'S SOMETHING!
DOCTORS, WHAT *ARE* THESE THINGS?!
REAPERS. THEY--
-- IF THERE'S A PARADOX OR A TIMEY WOBBLE AT SOMEWHERE VULNERABLE, LIKE THIS FIXED POINT --
-- THEY SWOOP IN TO *FEED,* TO CLEANSE THE WOUND.
I *THINK* I GOT--
-- DOCTOR, I MEAN *MY* DOCTOR --!

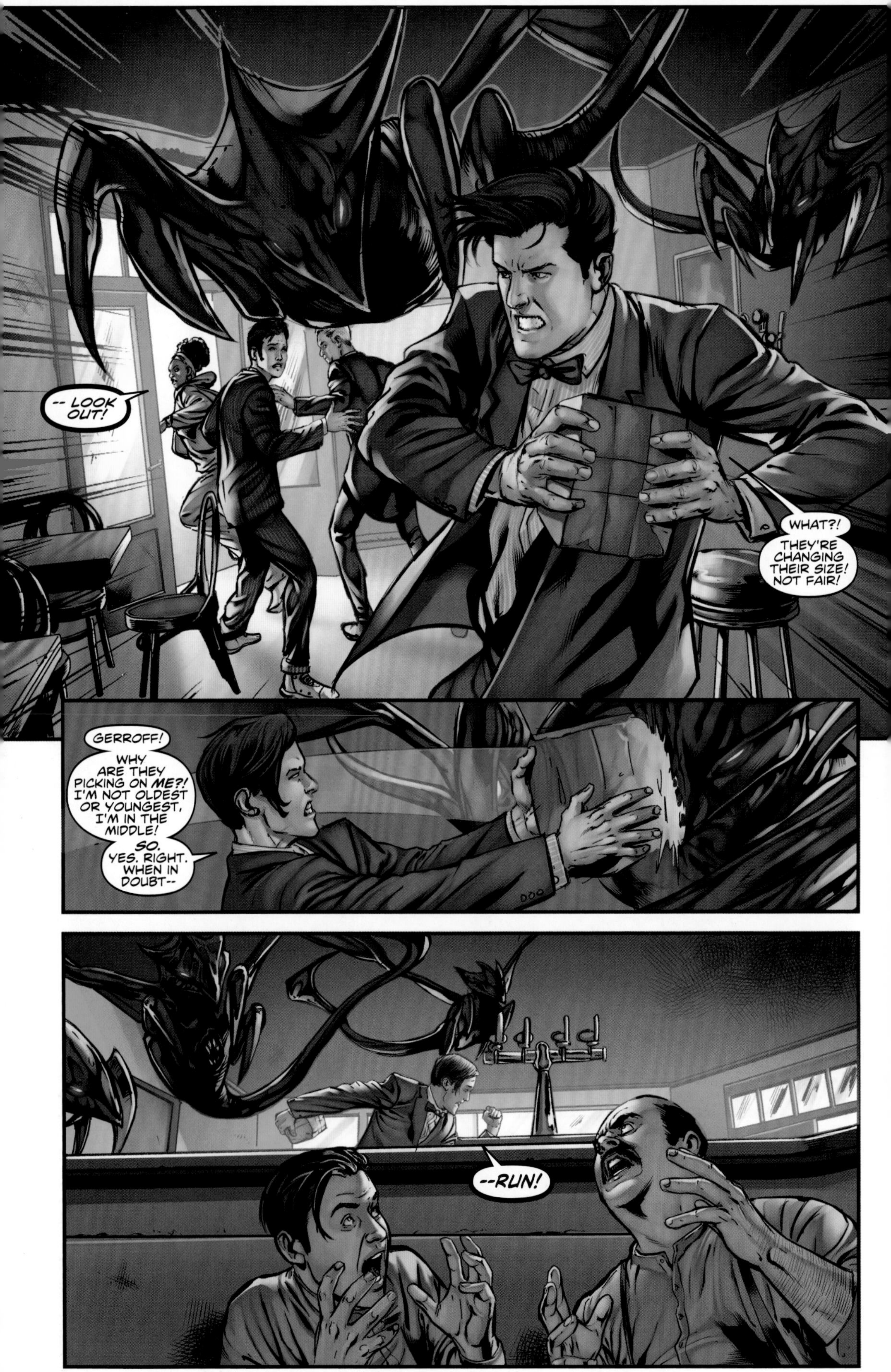

-- LOOK OUT!
WHAT?! THEY'RE CHANGING THEIR SIZE! NOT FAIR!
GERROFF!
WHY ARE THEY PICKING ON *ME?!* I'M NOT OLDEST OR YOUNGEST, I'M IN THE MIDDLE!
SO. YES. RIGHT. WHEN IN DOUBT--
--RUN!

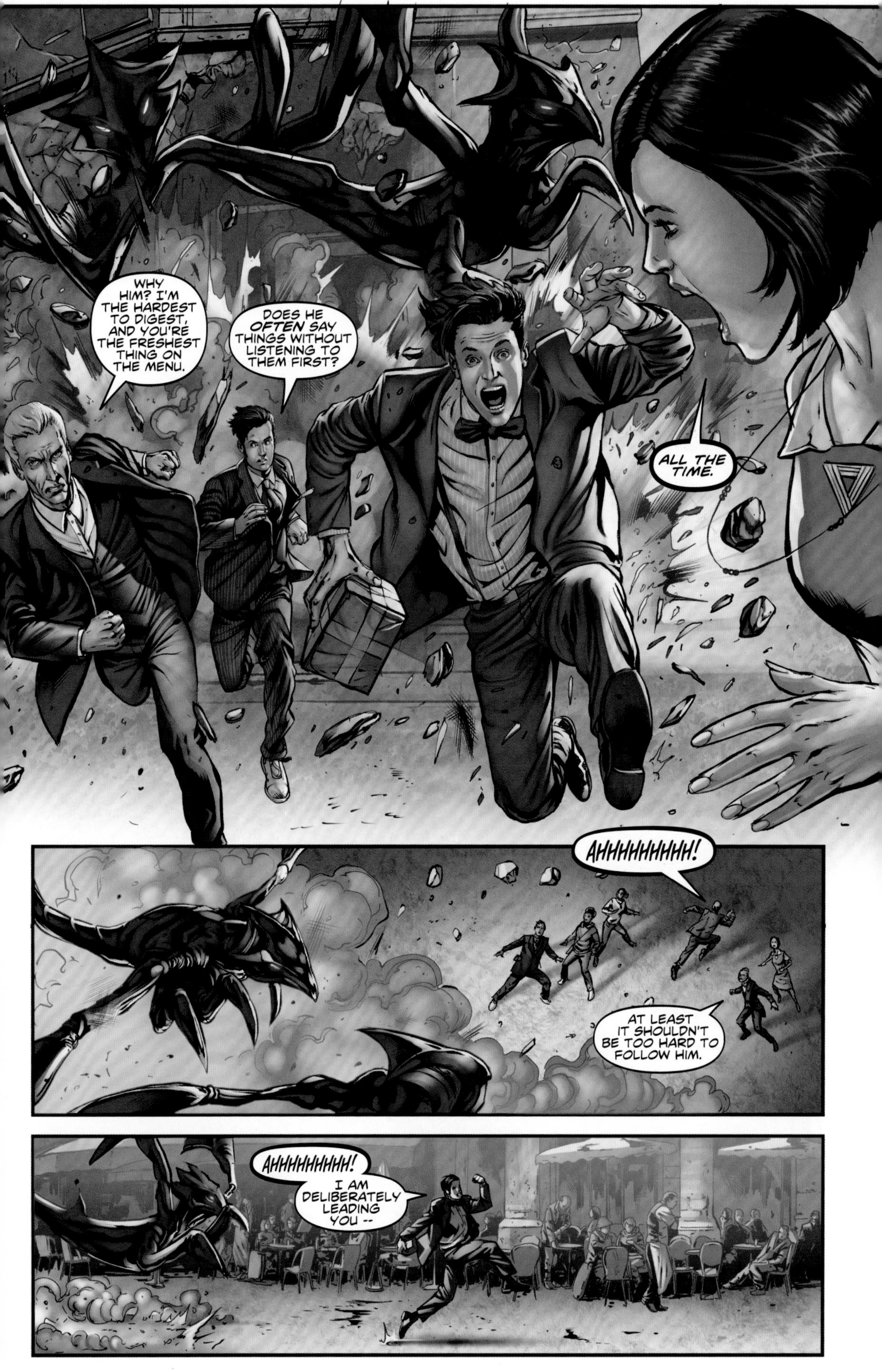
WHY HIM? I'M THE HARDEST TO DIGEST, AND YOU'RE THE FRESHEST THING ON THE MENU.
DOES HE OFTEN SAY THINGS WITHOUT LISTENING TO THEM FIRST?
ALL THE TIME.
AHHHHHHHHH!
AT LEAST IT SHOULDN'T BE TOO HARD TO FOLLOW HIM.
AHHHHHHHHH!
I AM DELIBERATELY LEADING YOU --

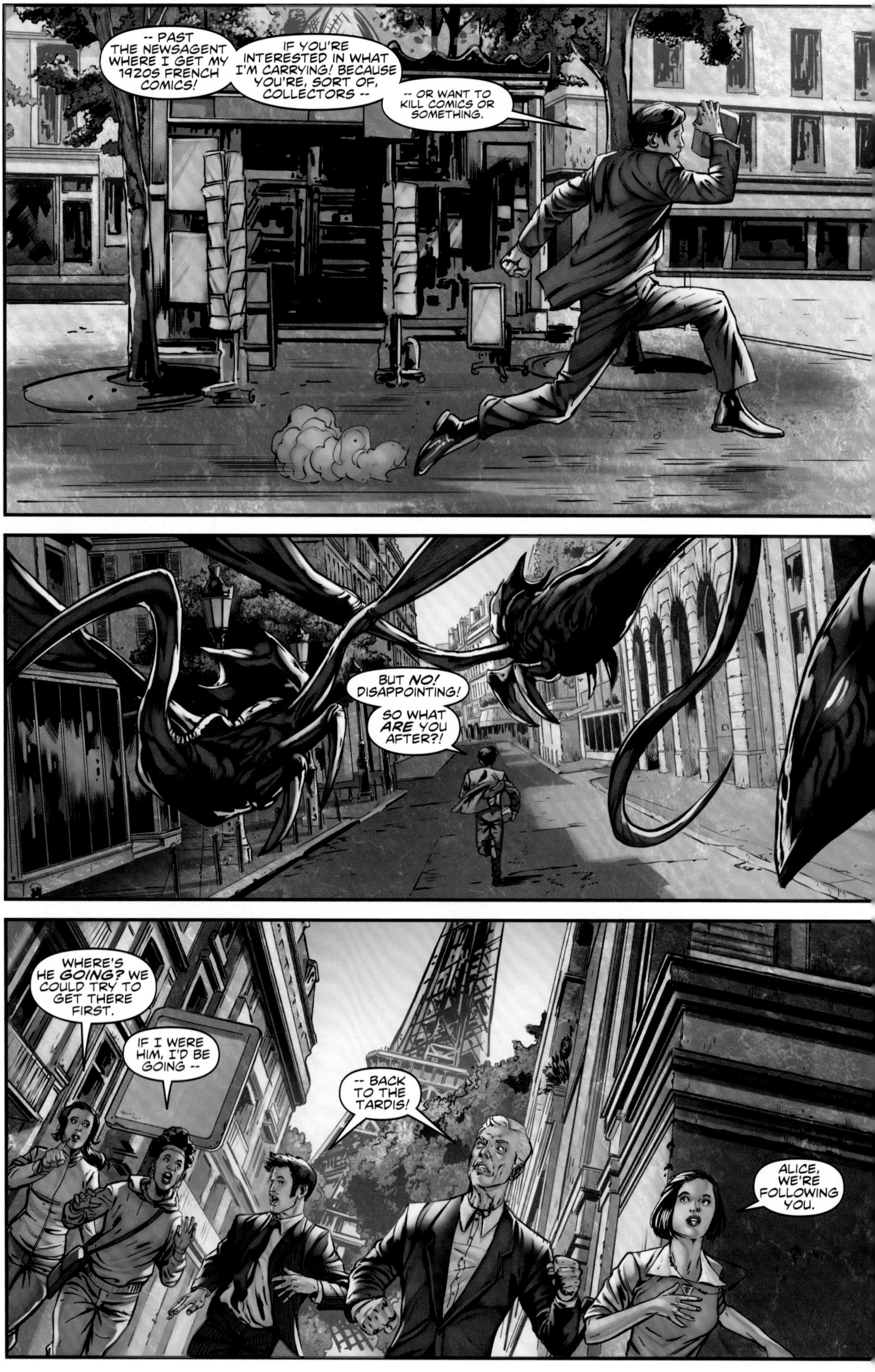
-- PAST THE NEWSAGENT WHERE I GET MY 1920S FRENCH COMICS!
IF YOU'RE INTERESTED IN WHAT I'M CARRYING! BECAUSE YOU'RE, SORT OF, COLLECTORS --
-- OR WANT TO KILL COMICS OR SOMETHING.
BUT NO! DISAPPOINTING!
SO WHAT ARE YOU AFTER?!
WHERE'S HE GOING? WE COULD TRY TO GET THERE FIRST.
IF I WERE HIM, I'D BE GOING --
-- BACK TO THE TARDIS!
ALICE, WE'RE FOLLOWING YOU.

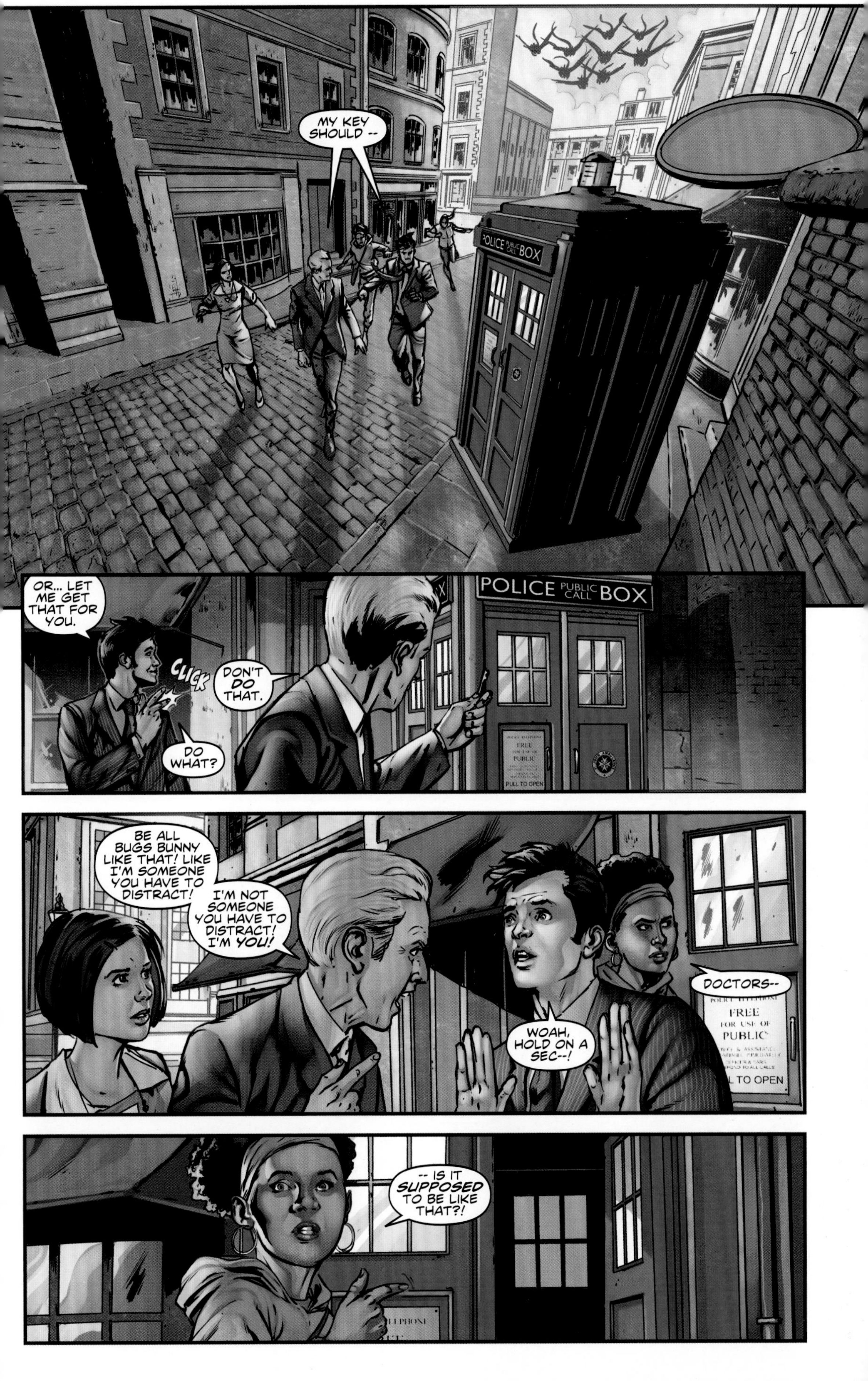
MY KEY SHOULD --
POLICE PUBLIC CALL BOX
OR... LET ME GET THAT FOR YOU.
CLICK
DON'T DO THAT.
DO WHAT?
PULL TO OPEN
BE ALL BUGS BUNNY LIKE THAT! LIKE I'M SOMEONE YOU HAVE TO DISTRACT!
I'M NOT SOMEONE YOU HAVE TO DISTRACT! I'M YOU!
DOCTORS--
WOAH, HOLD ON A SEC--!
-- IS IT SUPPOSED TO BE LIKE THAT?!

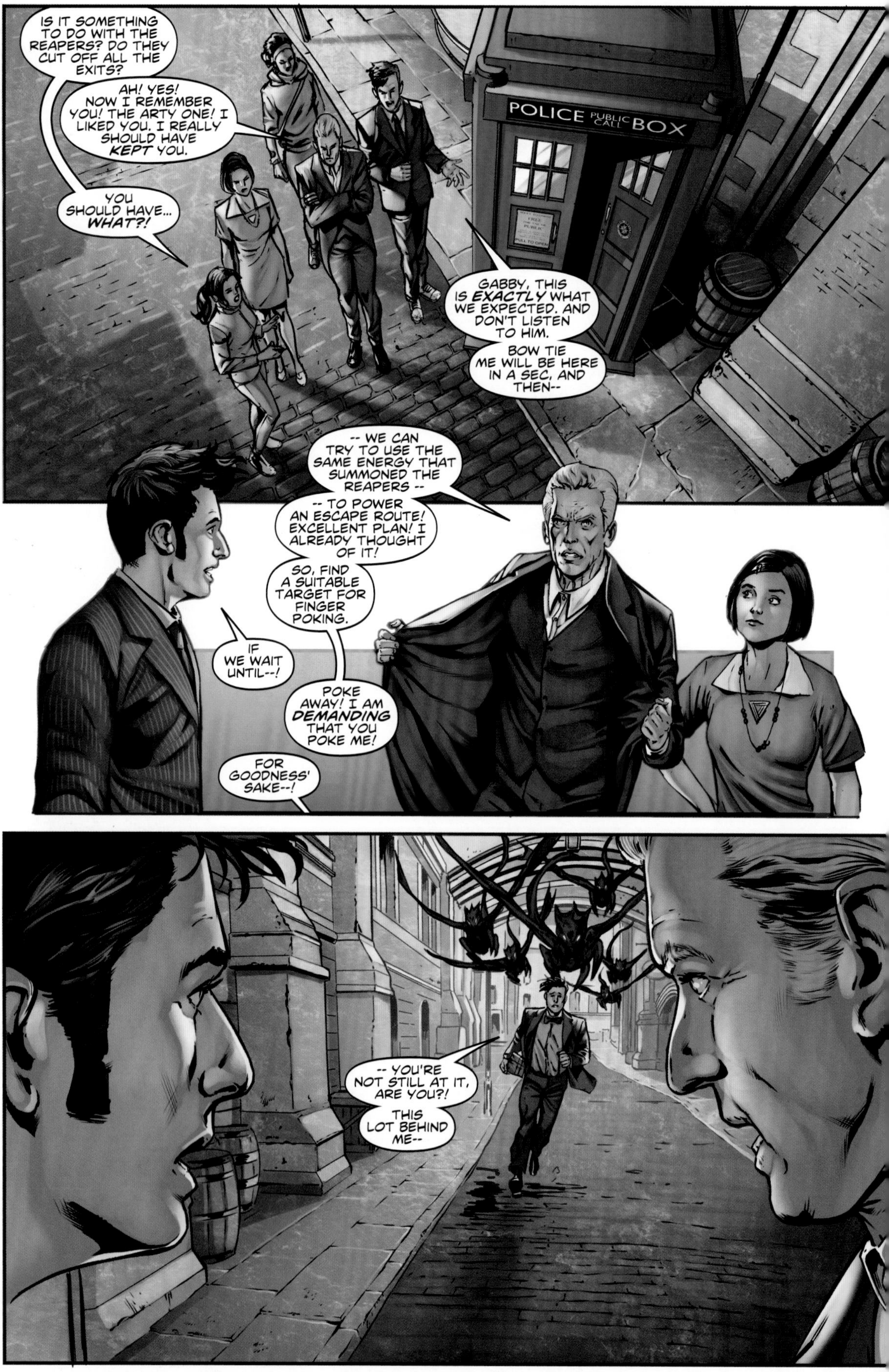
IS IT SOMETHING TO DO WITH THE REAPERS? DO THEY CUT OFF ALL THE EXITS?
AH! YES! NOW I REMEMBER YOU! THE ARTY ONE! I LIKED YOU. I REALLY SHOULD HAVE KEPT YOU.
YOU SHOULD HAVE... WHAT?!
POLICE PUBLIC CALL BOX
PULL TO OPEN
GABBY, THIS IS EXACTLY WHAT WE EXPECTED. AND DON'T LISTEN TO HIM.
BOW TIE ME WILL BE HERE IN A SEC, AND THEN--
-- WE CAN TRY TO USE THE SAME ENERGY THAT SUMMONED THE REAPERS --
-- TO POWER AN ESCAPE ROUTE! EXCELLENT PLAN! I ALREADY THOUGHT OF IT!
SO, FIND A SUITABLE TARGET FOR FINGER POKING.
IF WE WAIT UNTIL--!
POKE AWAY! I AM DEMANDING THAT YOU POKE ME!
FOR GOODNESS' SAKE--!
-- YOU'RE NOT STILL AT IT, ARE YOU?!
THIS LOT BEHIND ME--

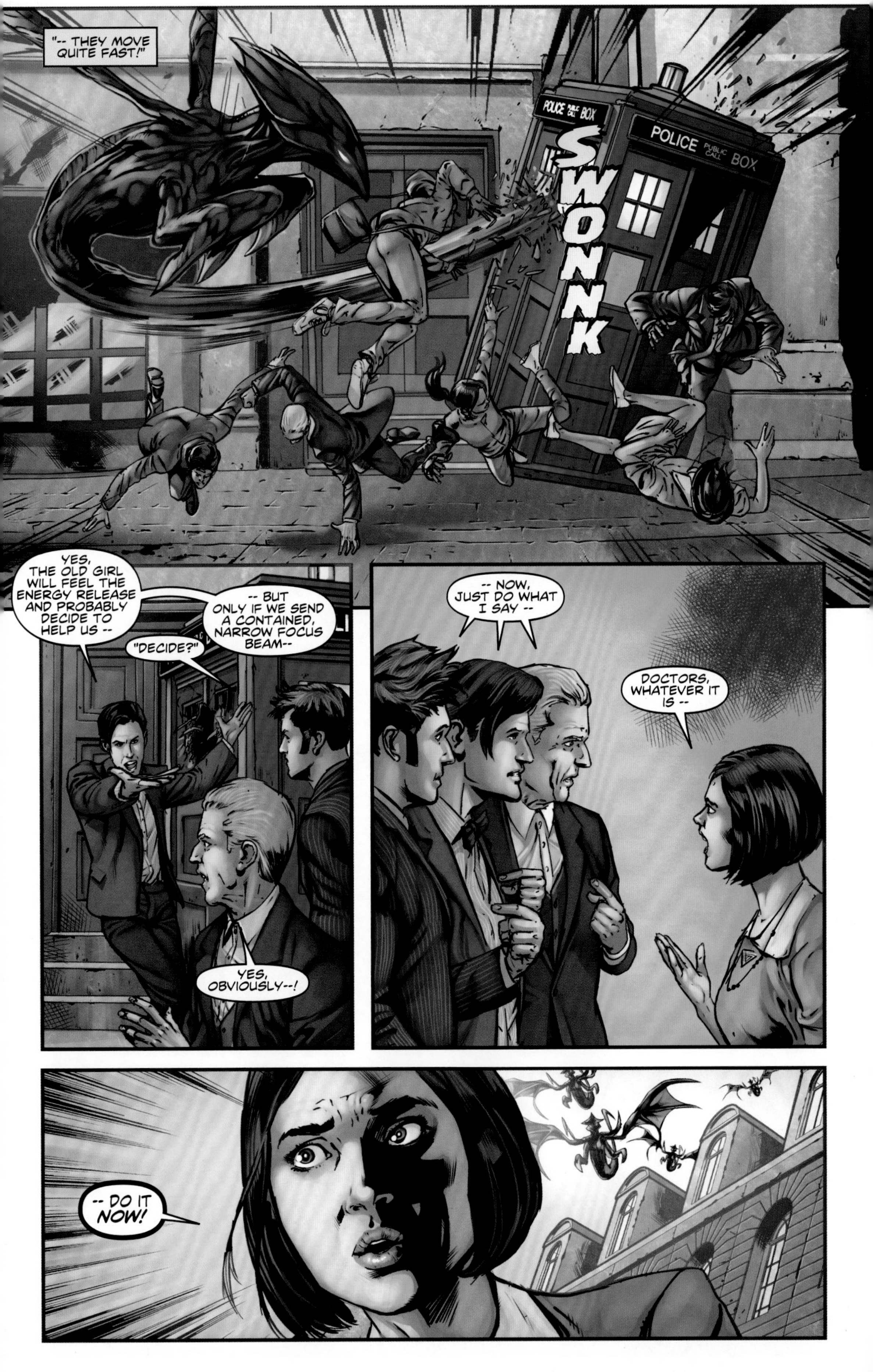
"-- THEY MOVE QUITE FAST!"
POLICE PUBLIC CALL BOX
POLICE PUBLIC CALL BOX
SWONNK
YES, THE OLD GIRL WILL FEEL THE ENERGY RELEASE AND PROBABLY DECIDE TO HELP US --
-- BUT ONLY IF WE SEND A CONTAINED, NARROW FOCUS BEAM--
"DECIDE?"
YES, OBVIOUSLY--!
-- NOW, JUST DO WHAT I SAY --
DOCTORS, WHATEVER IT IS --
-- DO IT NOW!

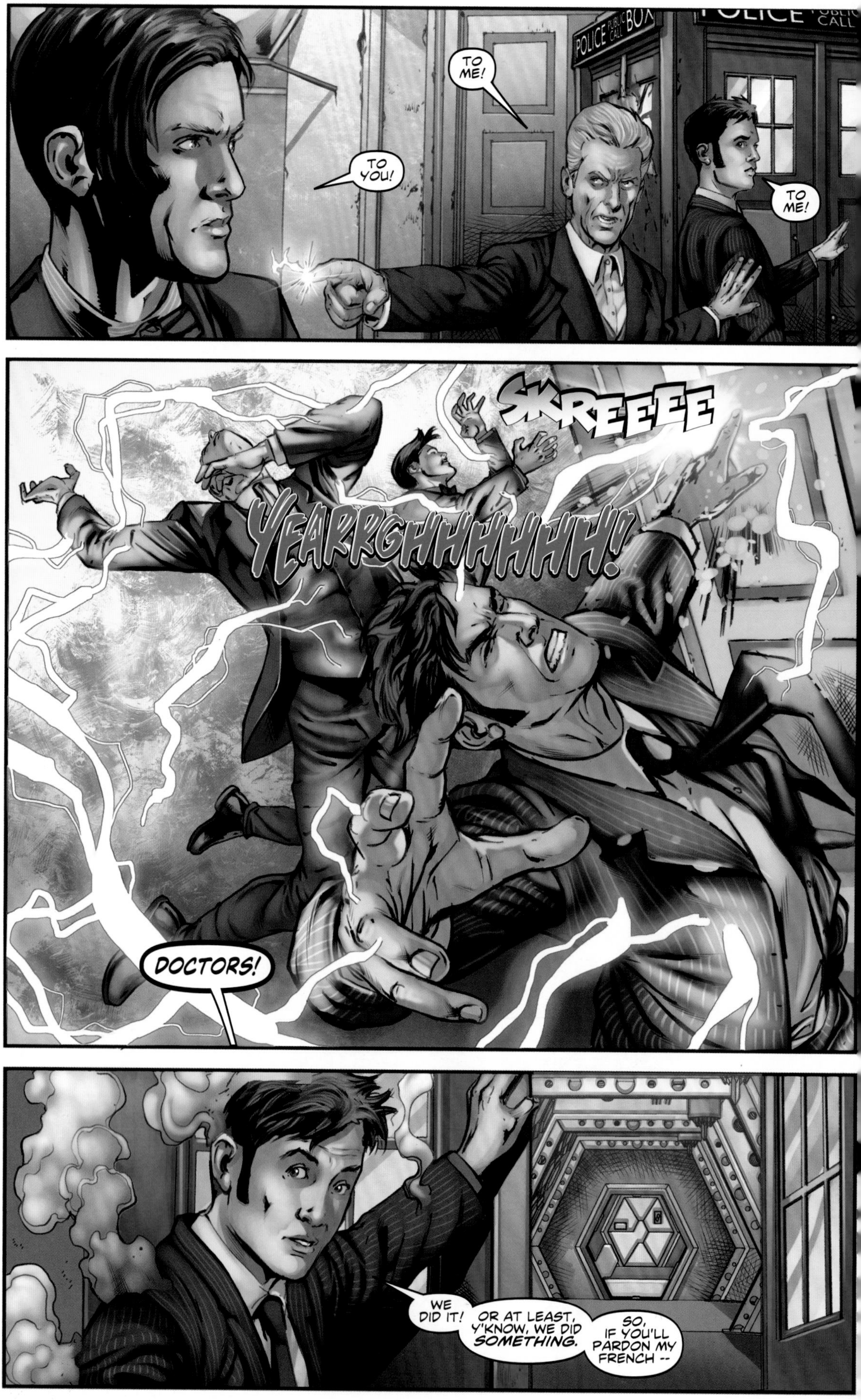
POLICE PUBLIC CALL BOX
TO ME!
TO YOU!
TO ME!
SKREEEE
YEARRGHHHHHHH!
DOCTORS!
WE DID IT!
OR AT LEAST, Y'KNOW, WE DID SOMETHING.
SO, IF YOU'LL PARDON MY FRENCH --

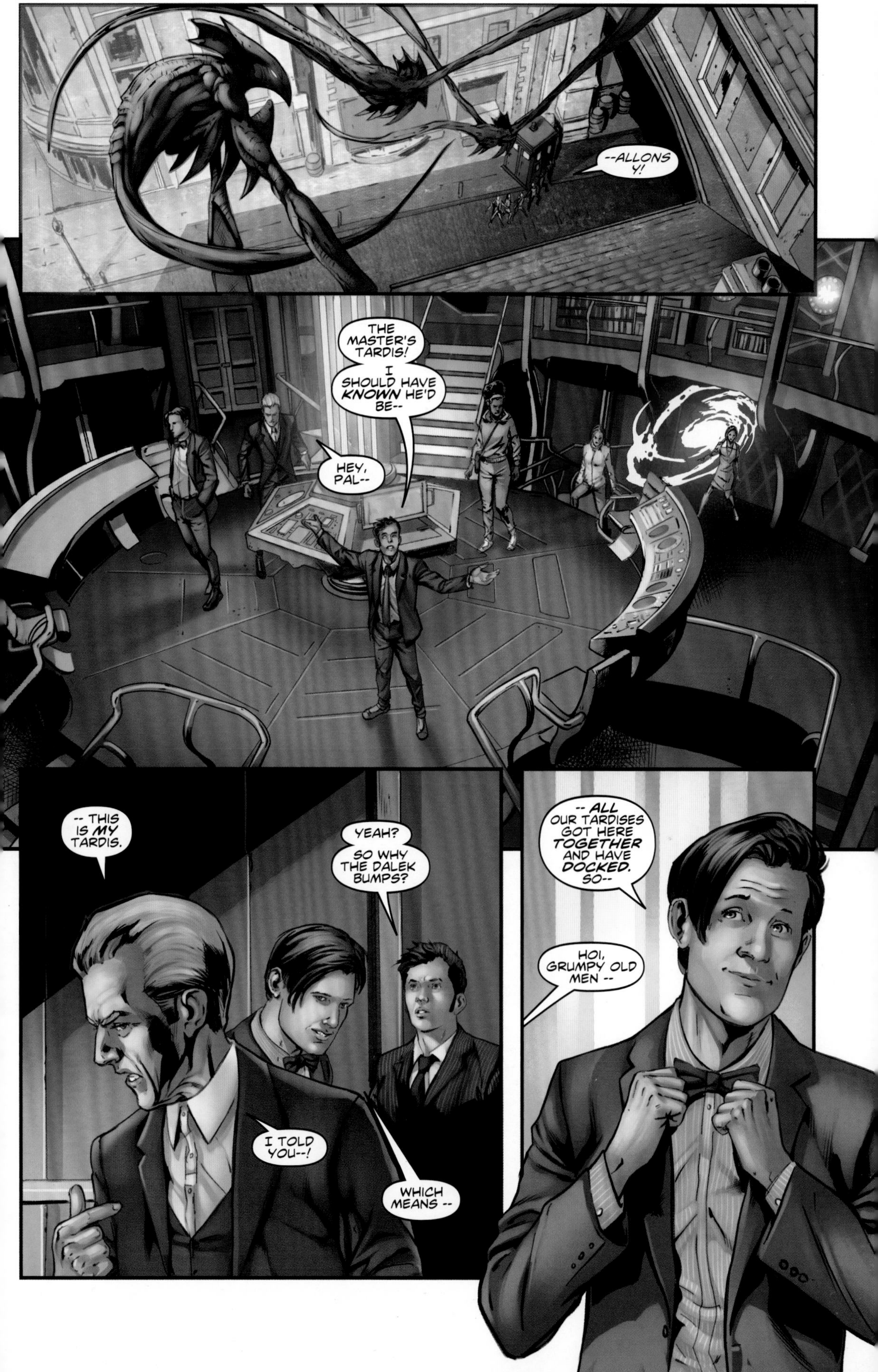
--ALLONS Y!
THE MASTER'S TARDIS!
I SHOULD HAVE KNOWN HE'D BE--
HEY, PAL--
-- THIS IS MY TARDIS.
YEAH? SO WHY THE DALEK BUMPS?
I TOLD YOU--!
WHICH MEANS --
-- ALL OUR TARDISES GOT HERE TOGETHER AND HAVE DOCKED. SO--
HOI, GRUMPY OLD MEN --

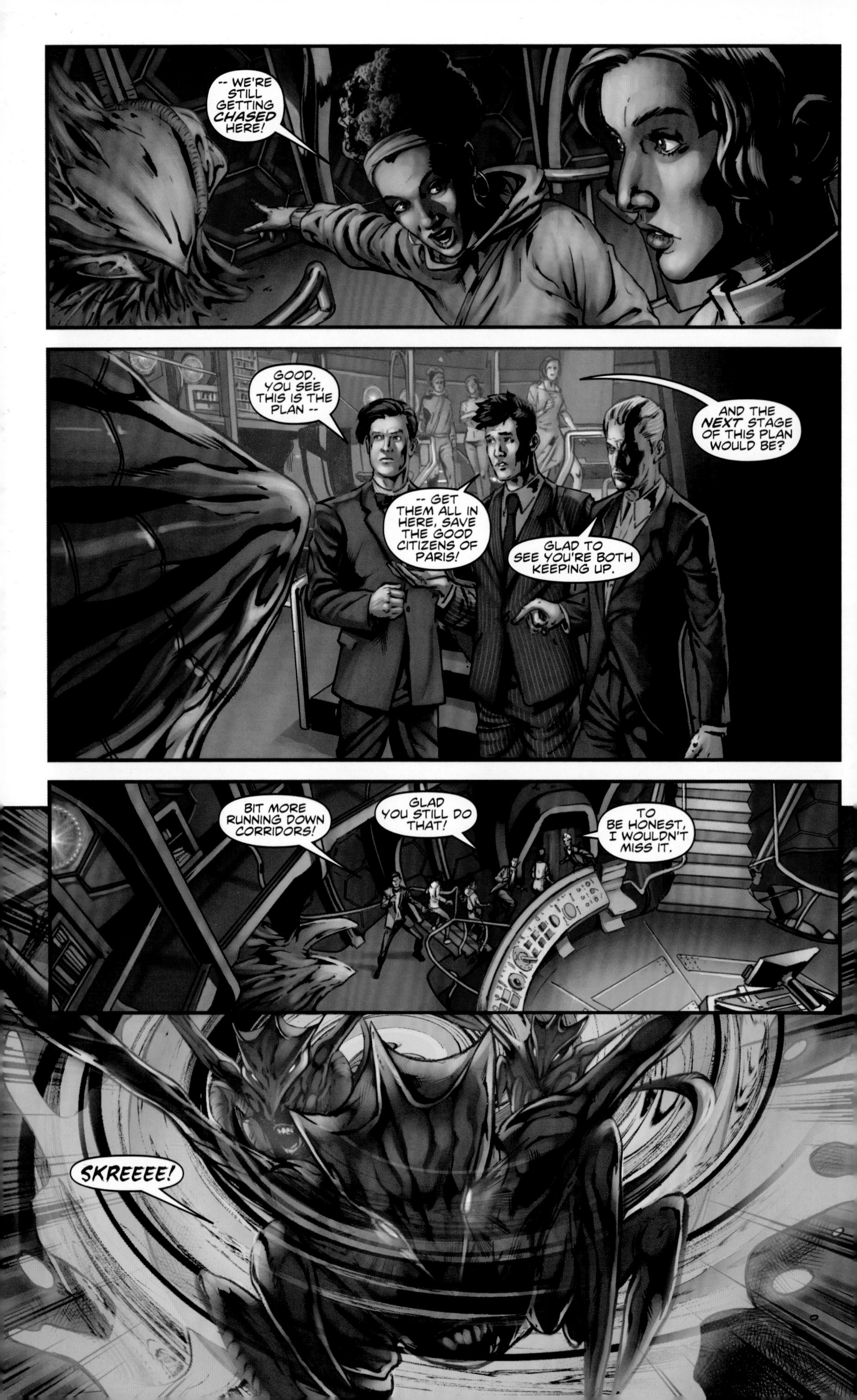
-- WE'RE STILL GETTING CHASED HERE!
GOOD. YOU SEE, THIS IS THE PLAN --
AND THE NEXT STAGE OF THIS PLAN WOULD BE?
-- GET THEM ALL IN HERE, SAVE THE GOOD CITIZENS OF PARIS!
GLAD TO SEE YOU'RE BOTH KEEPING UP.
BIT MORE RUNNING DOWN CORRIDORS!
GLAD YOU STILL DO THAT!
TO BE HONEST, I WOULDN'T MISS IT.
SKREEEE!

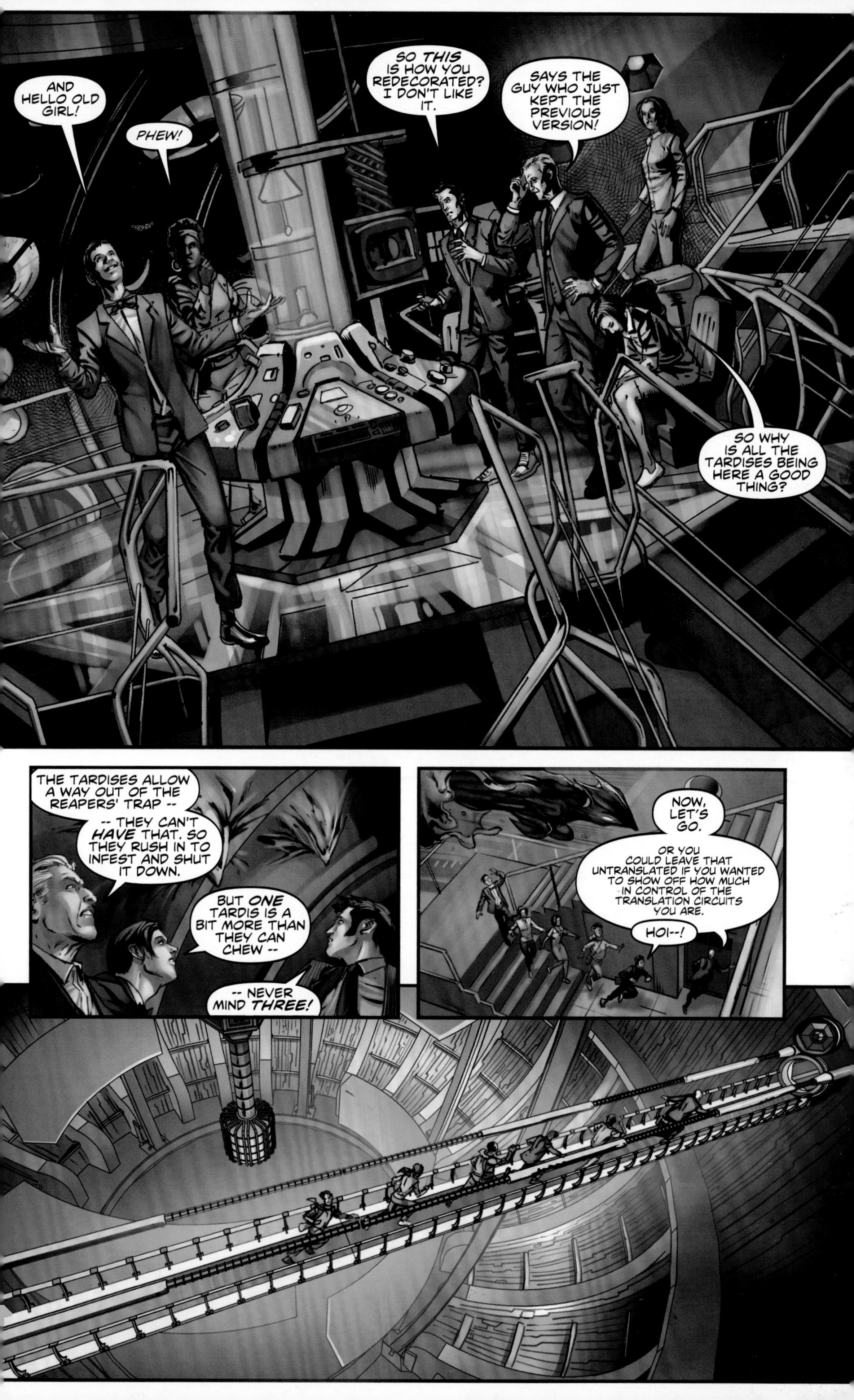
AND HELLO OLD GIRL!
PHEW!
SO *THIS* IS HOW YOU REDECORATED? I DON'T LIKE IT.
SAYS THE GUY WHO JUST KEPT THE PREVIOUS VERSION!
SO WHY IS ALL THE TARDISES BEING HERE A GOOD THING?
THE TARDISES ALLOW A WAY OUT OF THE REAPERS' TRAP --
-- THEY CAN'T ***HAVE*** THAT. SO THEY RUSH IN TO INFEST AND SHUT IT DOWN.
BUT ***ONE*** TARDIS IS A BIT MORE THAN THEY CAN CHEW --
-- NEVER MIND ***THREE!***
NOW, LET'S GO.
OR YOU COULD LEAVE THAT UNTRANSLATED IF YOU WANTED TO SHOW OFF HOW MUCH IN CONTROL OF THE TRANSLATION CIRCUITS YOU ARE.
HOI--!

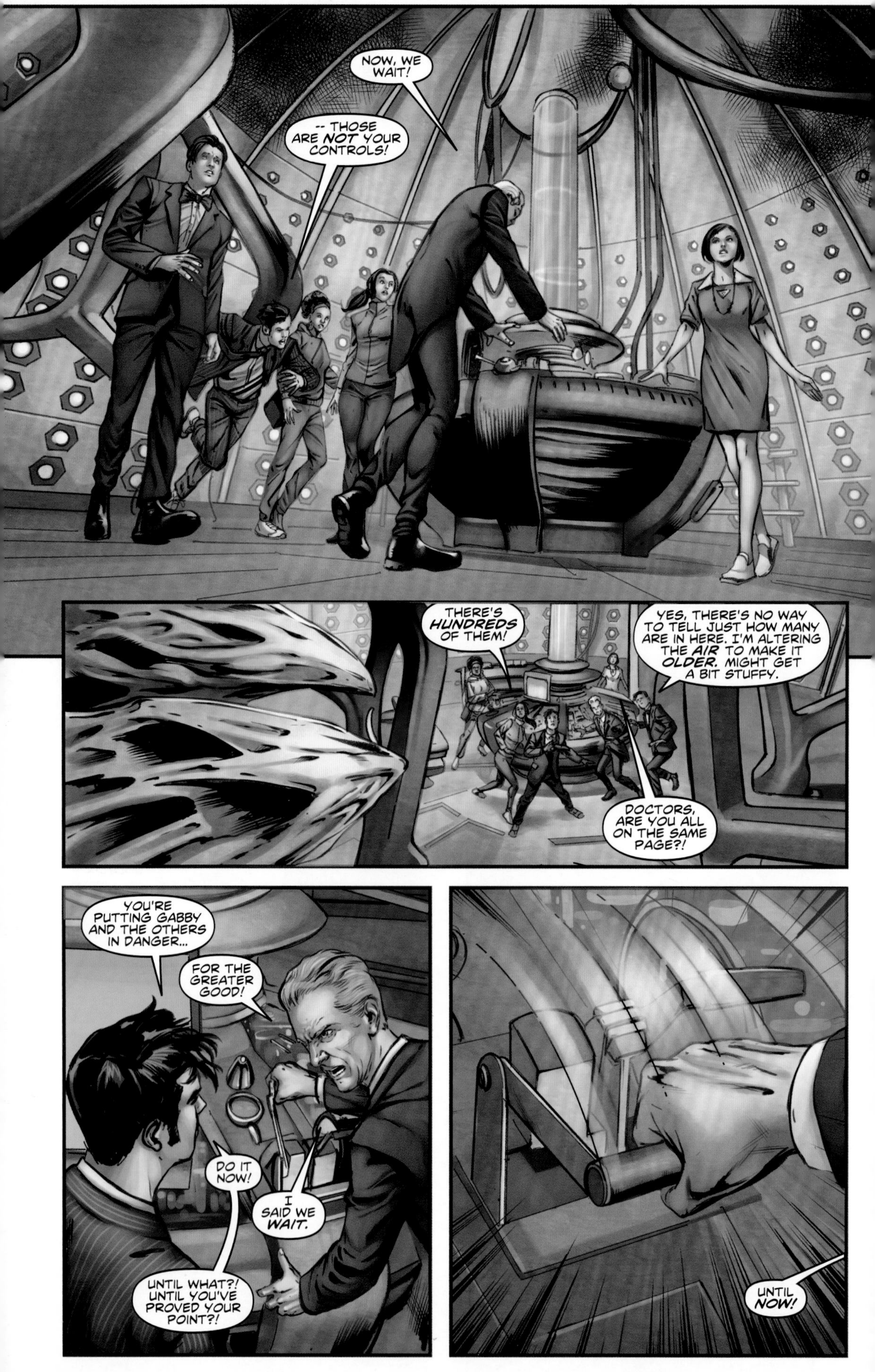
NOW, WE WAIT!
-- THOSE ARE NOT YOUR CONTROLS!
THERE'S HUNDREDS OF THEM!
YES, THERE'S NO WAY TO TELL JUST HOW MANY ARE IN HERE. I'M ALTERING THE AIR TO MAKE IT OLDER. MIGHT GET A BIT STUFFY.
DOCTORS, ARE YOU ALL ON THE SAME PAGE?!
YOU'RE PUTTING GABBY AND THE OTHERS IN DANGER...
FOR THE GREATER GOOD!
DO IT NOW!
I SAID WE WAIT.
UNTIL WHAT?! UNTIL YOU'VE PROVED YOUR POINT?!
UNTIL NOW!

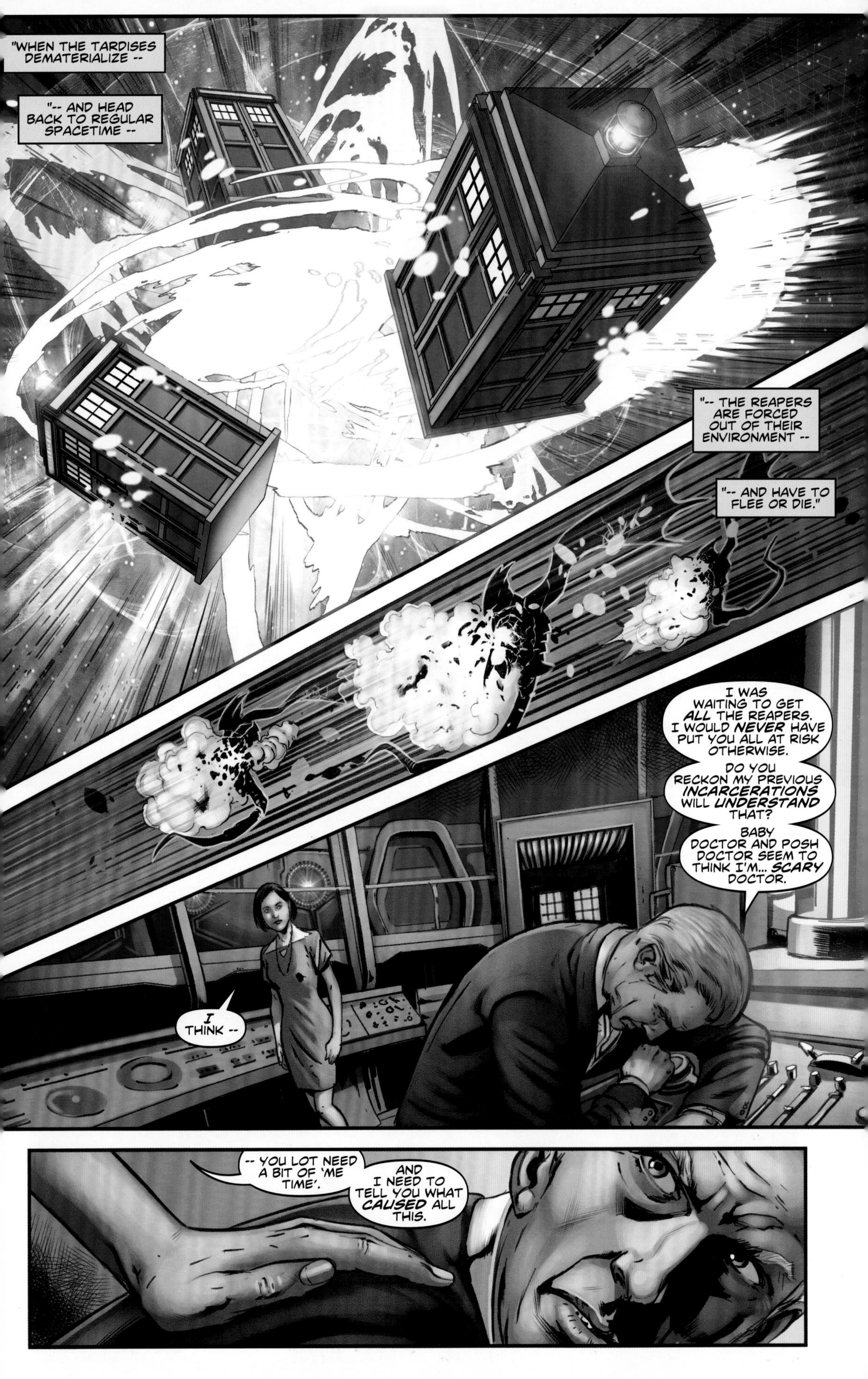
"WHEN THE TARDISES DEMATERIALIZE --
"-- AND HEAD BACK TO REGULAR SPACETIME --
"-- THE REAPERS ARE FORCED OUT OF THEIR ENVIRONMENT --
"-- AND HAVE TO FLEE OR DIE."
I WAS WAITING TO GET ALL THE REAPERS. I WOULD NEVER HAVE PUT YOU ALL AT RISK OTHERWISE.
DO YOU RECKON MY PREVIOUS INCARCERATIONS WILL UNDERSTAND THAT?
BABY DOCTOR AND POSH DOCTOR SEEM TO THINK I'M... SCARY DOCTOR.
I THINK --
-- YOU LOT NEED A BIT OF 'ME TIME'.
AND I NEED TO TELL YOU WHAT CAUSED ALL THIS.

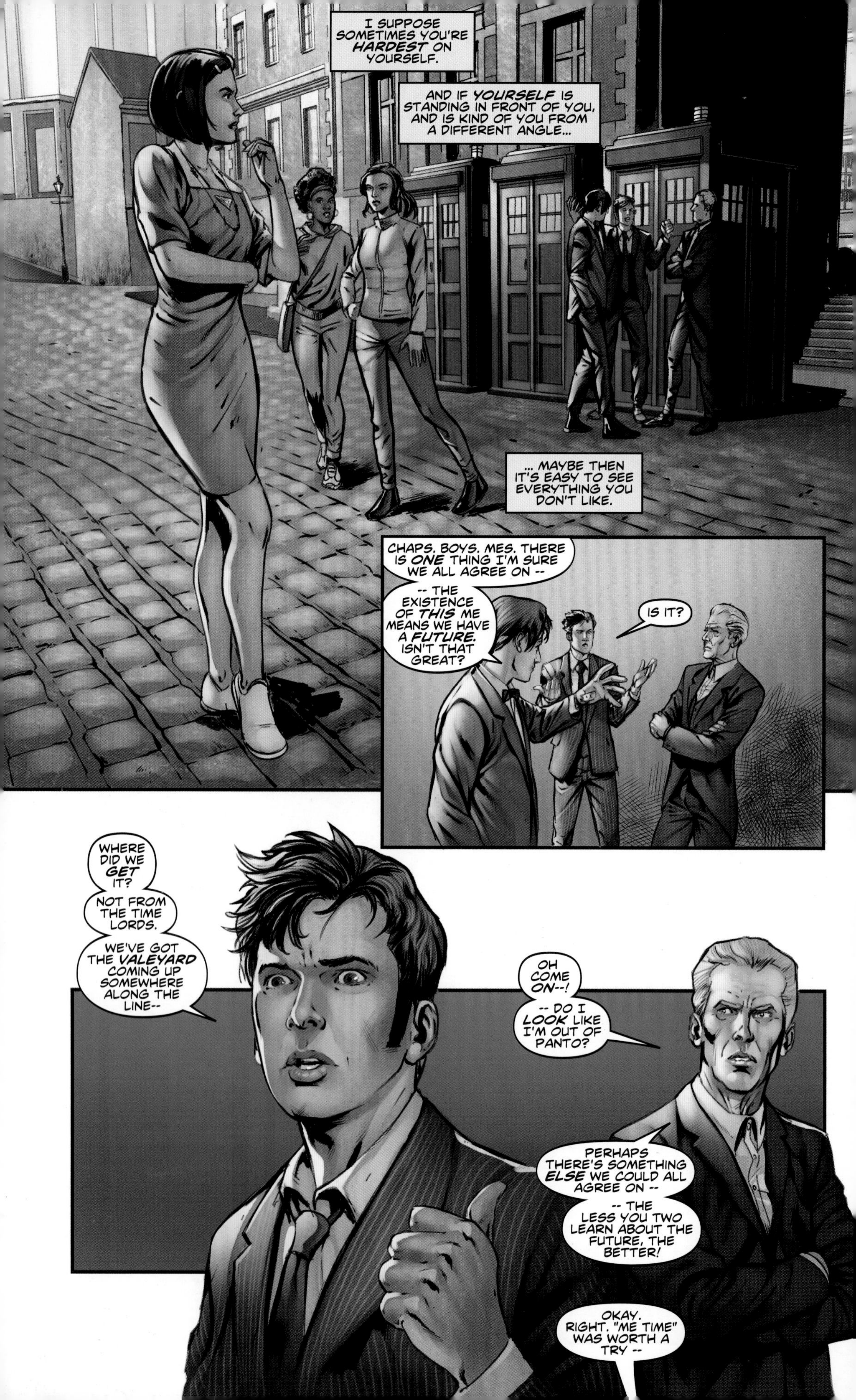
I SUPPOSE SOMETIMES YOU'RE HARDEST ON YOURSELF.
AND IF YOURSELF IS STANDING IN FRONT OF YOU, AND IS KIND OF YOU FROM A DIFFERENT ANGLE...
... MAYBE THEN IT'S EASY TO SEE EVERYTHING YOU DON'T LIKE.
CHAPS. BOYS. MES. THERE IS ONE THING I'M SURE WE ALL AGREE ON --
-- THE EXISTENCE OF THIS ME MEANS WE HAVE A FUTURE. ISN'T THAT GREAT?
IS IT?
WHERE DID WE GET IT?
NOT FROM THE TIME LORDS.
WE'VE GOT THE VALEYARD COMING UP SOMEWHERE ALONG THE LINE--
OH COME ON--!
-- DO I LOOK LIKE I'M OUT OF PANTO?
PERHAPS THERE'S SOMETHING ELSE WE COULD ALL AGREE ON --
-- THE LESS YOU TWO LEARN ABOUT THE FUTURE, THE BETTER!
OKAY. RIGHT. "ME TIME" WAS WORTH A TRY --

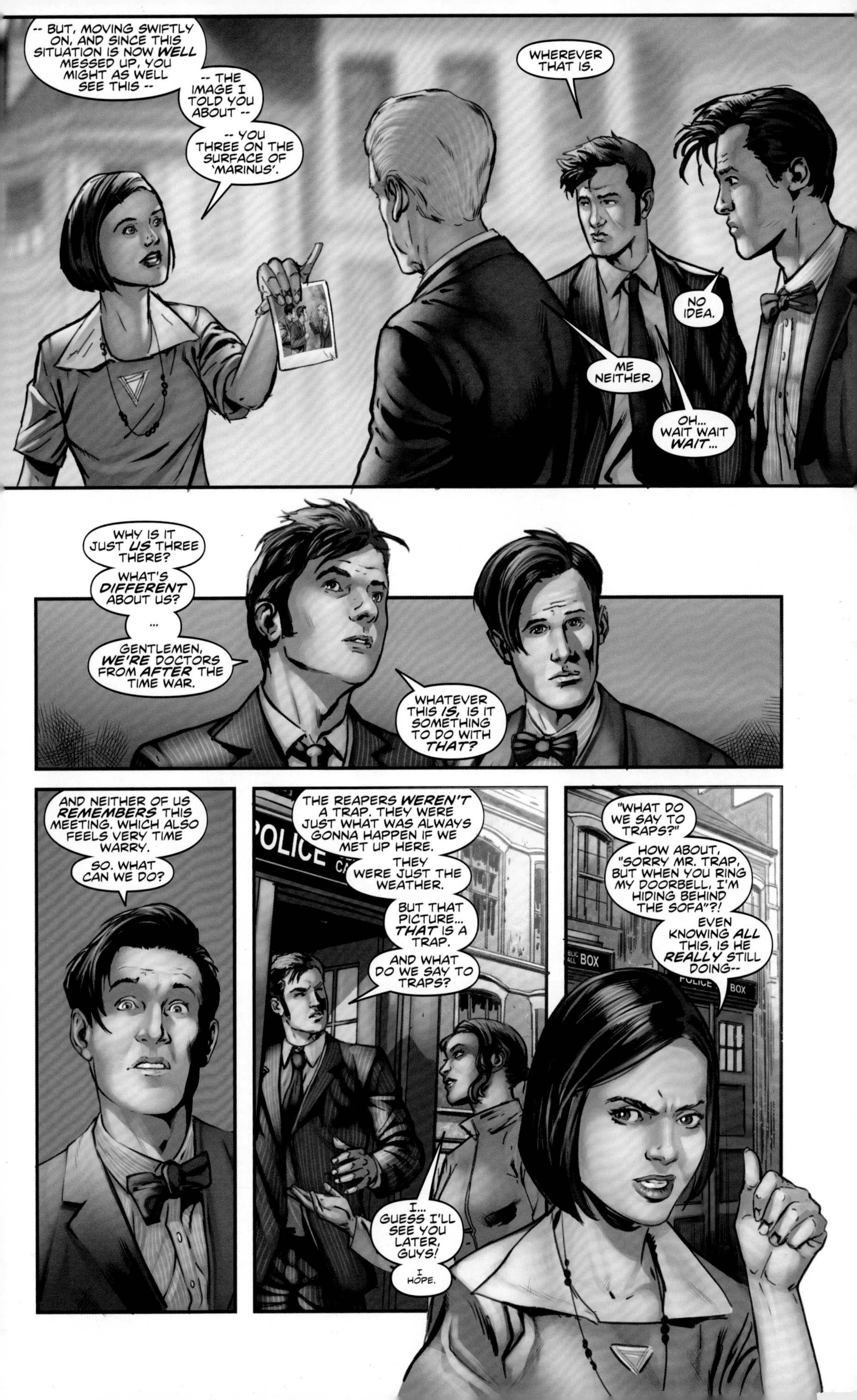
-- BUT, MOVING SWIFTLY ON, AND SINCE THIS SITUATION IS NOW WELL MESSED UP, YOU MIGHT AS WELL SEE THIS --
-- THE IMAGE I TOLD YOU ABOUT --
-- YOU THREE ON THE SURFACE OF 'MARINUS'.
WHEREVER THAT IS.
NO IDEA.
ME NEITHER.
OH... WAIT WAIT WAIT...
WHY IS IT JUST US THREE THERE?
WHAT'S DIFFERENT ABOUT US?
...
GENTLEMEN, WE'RE DOCTORS FROM AFTER THE TIME WAR.
WHATEVER THIS IS, IS IT SOMETHING TO DO WITH THAT?
AND NEITHER OF US REMEMBERS THIS MEETING. WHICH ALSO FEELS VERY TIME WARRY.
SO. WHAT CAN WE DO?
THE REAPERS WEREN'T A TRAP. THEY WERE JUST WHAT WAS ALWAYS GONNA HAPPEN IF WE MET UP HERE.
THEY WERE JUST THE WEATHER.
BUT THAT PICTURE... THAT IS A TRAP.
AND WHAT DO WE SAY TO TRAPS?
POLICE
I... GUESS I'LL SEE YOU LATER, GUYS!
I HOPE.
"WHAT DO WE SAY TO TRAPS?"
HOW ABOUT, "SORRY MR. TRAP, BUT WHEN YOU RING MY DOORBELL, I'M HIDING BEHIND THE SOFA"?!
EVEN KNOWING ALL THIS, IS HE REALLY STILL DOING--
POLICE BOX

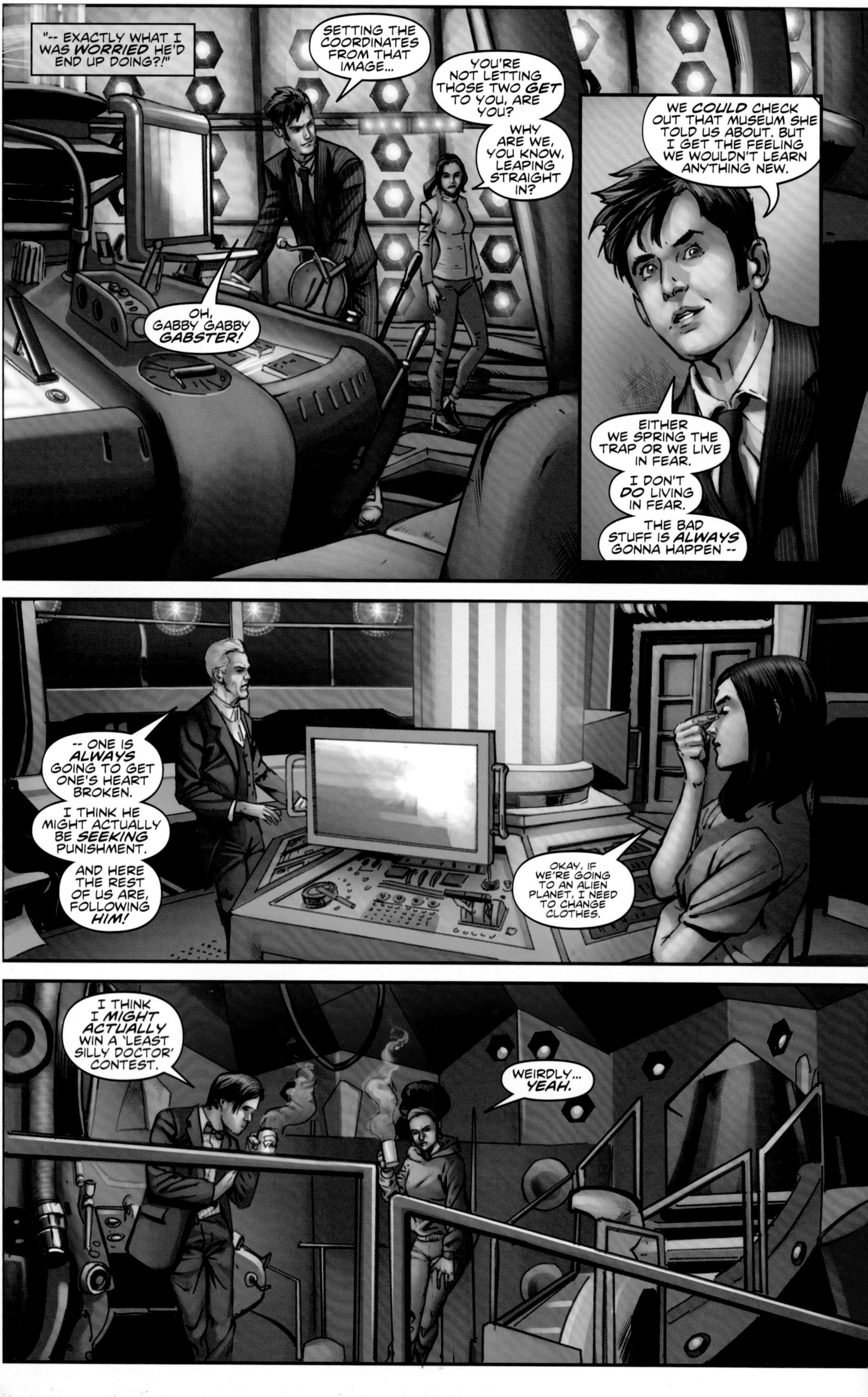
"-- EXACTLY WHAT I WAS WORRIED HE'D END UP DOING?!"
SETTING THE COORDINATES FROM THAT IMAGE...
YOU'RE NOT LETTING THOSE TWO GET TO YOU, ARE YOU?
WHY ARE WE, YOU KNOW, LEAPING STRAIGHT IN?
OH, GABBY GABBY GABSTER!
WE COULD CHECK OUT THAT MUSEUM SHE TOLD US ABOUT. BUT I GET THE FEELING WE WOULDN'T LEARN ANYTHING NEW.
EITHER WE SPRING THE TRAP OR WE LIVE IN FEAR.
I DON'T DO LIVING IN FEAR.
THE BAD STUFF IS ALWAYS GONNA HAPPEN --
-- ONE IS ALWAYS GOING TO GET ONE'S HEART BROKEN.
I THINK HE MIGHT ACTUALLY BE SEEKING PUNISHMENT.
AND HERE THE REST OF US ARE, FOLLOWING HIM!
OKAY, IF WE'RE GOING TO AN ALIEN PLANET, I NEED TO CHANGE CLOTHES.
I THINK I MIGHT ACTUALLY WIN A 'LEAST SILLY DOCTOR' CONTEST.
WEIRDLY... YEAH.

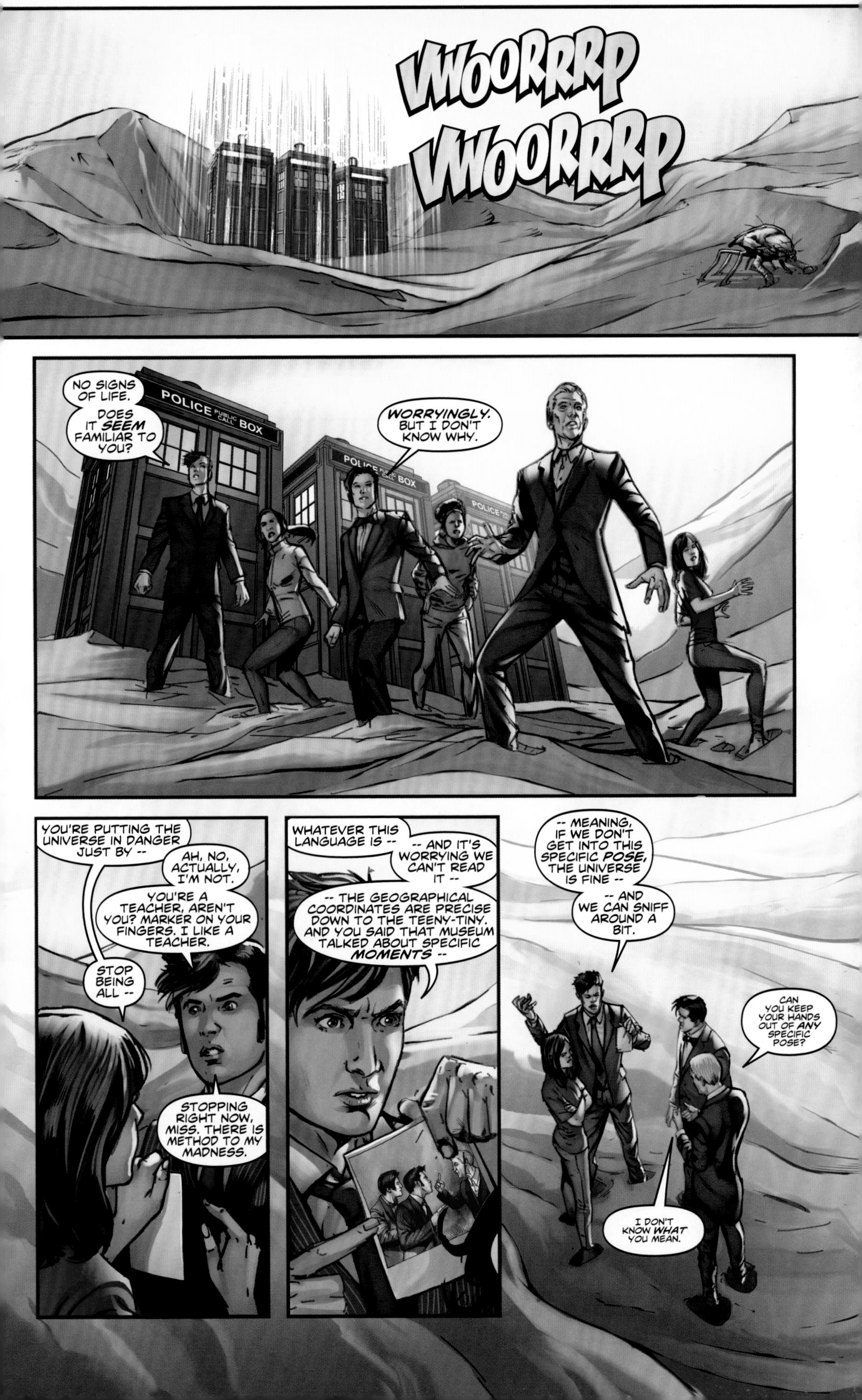
VWOORRRP
VWOORRRP
NO SIGNS OF LIFE. DOES IT SEEM FAMILIAR TO YOU?
POLICE PUBLIC CALL BOX
WORRYINGLY. BUT I DON'T KNOW WHY.
YOU'RE PUTTING THE UNIVERSE IN DANGER JUST BY --
AH, NO, ACTUALLY, I'M NOT.
YOU'RE A TEACHER, AREN'T YOU? MARKER ON YOUR FINGERS. I LIKE A TEACHER.
STOP BEING ALL --
STOPPING RIGHT NOW, MISS. THERE IS METHOD TO MY MADNESS.
WHATEVER THIS LANGUAGE IS --
-- AND IT'S WORRYING WE CAN'T READ IT --
-- THE GEOGRAPHICAL COORDINATES ARE PRECISE DOWN TO THE TEENY-TINY. AND YOU SAID THAT MUSEUM TALKED ABOUT SPECIFIC MOMENTS --
-- MEANING, IF WE DON'T GET INTO THIS SPECIFIC POSE, THE UNIVERSE IS FINE --
-- AND WE CAN SNIFF AROUND A BIT.
CAN YOU KEEP YOUR HANDS OUT OF ANY SPECIFIC POSE?
I DON'T KNOW WHAT YOU MEAN.

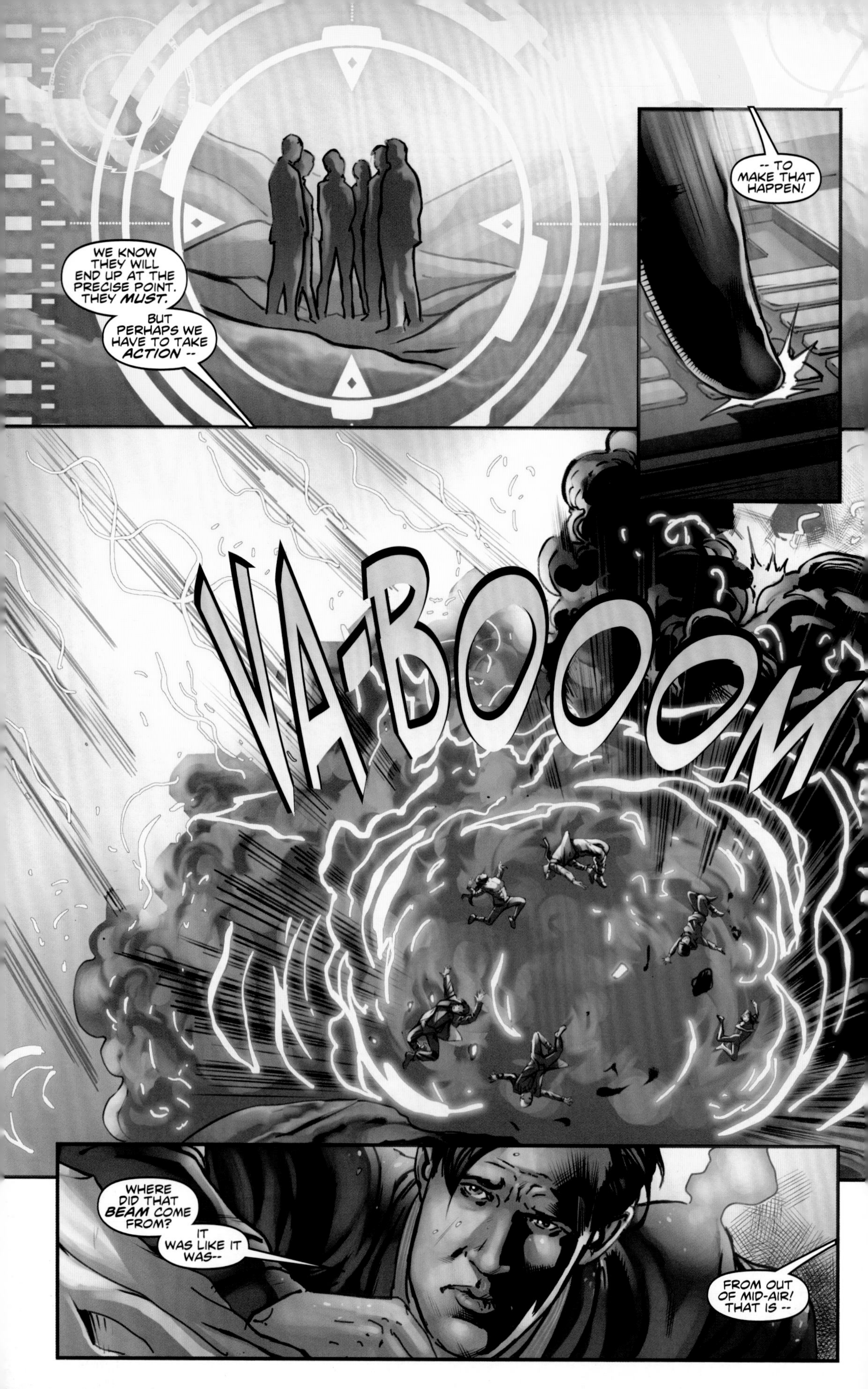

WE KNOW THEY WILL END UP AT THE PRECISE POINT. THEY MUST.
BUT PERHAPS WE HAVE TO TAKE ACTION --
-- TO MAKE THAT HAPPEN!
VA-BOOOM
WHERE DID THAT BEAM COME FROM?
IT WAS LIKE IT WAS--
FROM OUT OF MID-AIR! THAT IS --

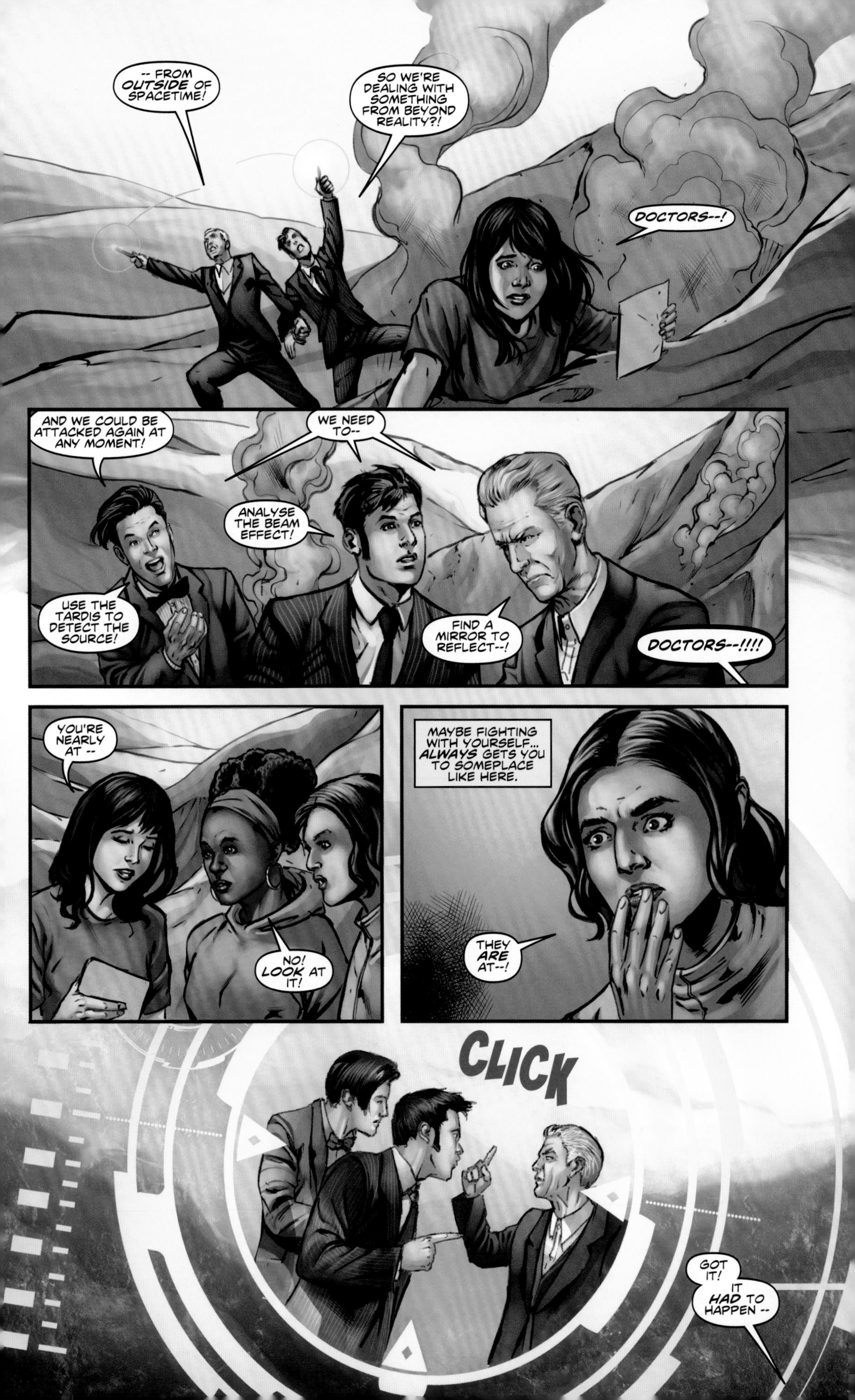

-- FROM OUTSIDE OF SPACETIME!
SO WE'RE DEALING WITH SOMETHING FROM BEYOND REALITY?!
DOCTORS--!
AND WE COULD BE ATTACKED AGAIN AT ANY MOMENT!
WE NEED TO--
ANALYSE THE BEAM EFFECT!
USE THE TARDIS TO DETECT THE SOURCE!
FIND A MIRROR TO REFLECT--!
DOCTORS--!!!!
YOU'RE NEARLY AT --
NO! LOOK AT IT!
MAYBE FIGHTING WITH YOURSELF... ALWAYS GETS YOU TO SOMEPLACE LIKE HERE.
THEY ARE AT--!
CLICK
GOT IT!
IT HAD TO HAPPEN --

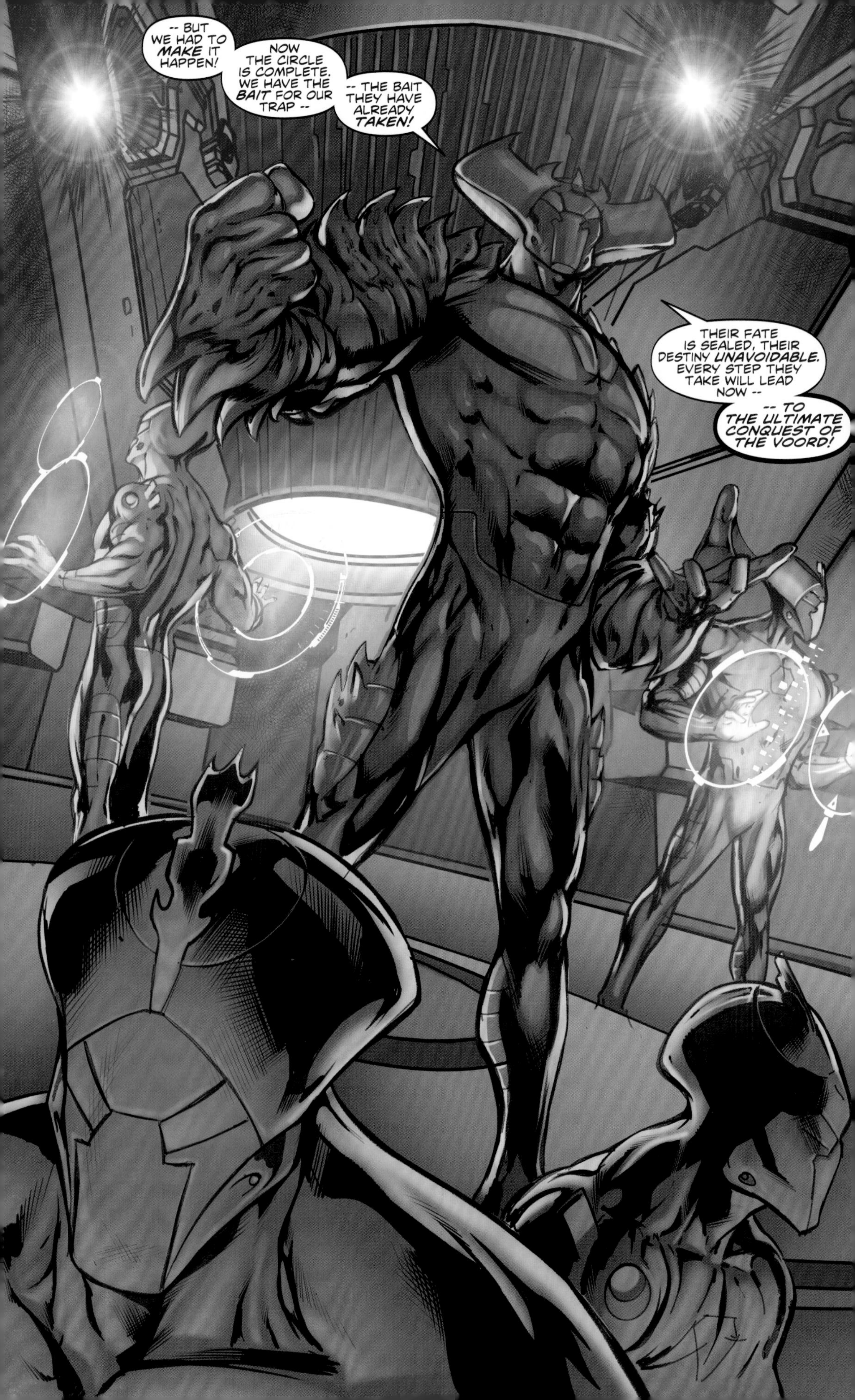
-- BUT WE HAD TO MAKE IT HAPPEN!
NOW THE CIRCLE IS COMPLETE. WE HAVE THE BAIT FOR OUR TRAP --
-- THE BAIT THEY HAVE ALREADY TAKEN!
THEIR FATE IS SEALED, THEIR DESTINY UNAVOIDABLE. EVERY STEP THEY TAKE WILL LEAD NOW --
-- TO THE ULTIMATE CONQUEST OF THE VOORD!

'OPEN MIC NIGHT'

BY PAUL CORNELL & RACHAEL SMITH

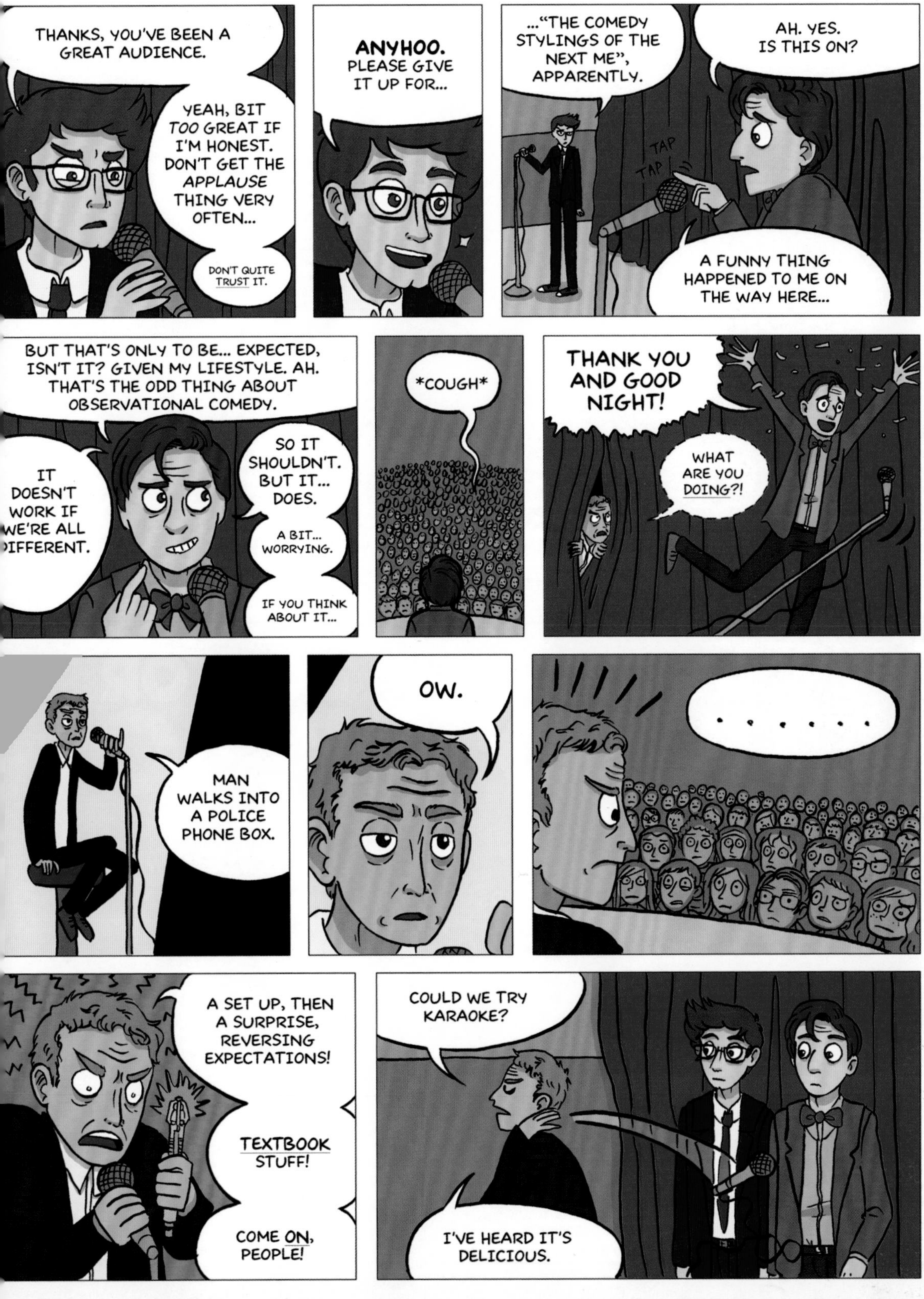
THANKS, YOU'VE BEEN A GREAT AUDIENCE.
YEAH, BIT TOO GREAT IF I'M HONEST. DON'T GET THE APPLAUSE THING VERY OFTEN...
DON'T QUITE TRUST IT.
ANYHOO. PLEASE GIVE IT UP FOR...
..."THE COMEDY STYLINGS OF THE NEXT ME", APPARENTLY.
AH. YES. IS THIS ON?
TAP TAP
A FUNNY THING HAPPENED TO ME ON THE WAY HERE...
BUT THAT'S ONLY TO BE... EXPECTED, ISN'T IT? GIVEN MY LIFESTYLE. AH. THAT'S THE ODD THING ABOUT OBSERVATIONAL COMEDY.
IT DOESN'T WORK IF WE'RE ALL DIFFERENT.
SO IT SHOULDN'T. BUT IT... DOES.
A BIT... WORRYING.
IF YOU THINK ABOUT IT...
COUGH
THANK YOU AND GOOD NIGHT!
WHAT ARE YOU DOING?!
MAN WALKS INTO A POLICE PHONE BOX.
OW.
. . . .
A SET UP, THEN A SURPRISE, REVERSING EXPECTATIONS!
TEXTBOOK STUFF!
COME ON, PEOPLE!
COULD WE TRY KARAOKE?
I'VE HEARD IT'S DELICIOUS.

COVER 3

REGULAR Cover by Neil Edwards & Ivan Nunes

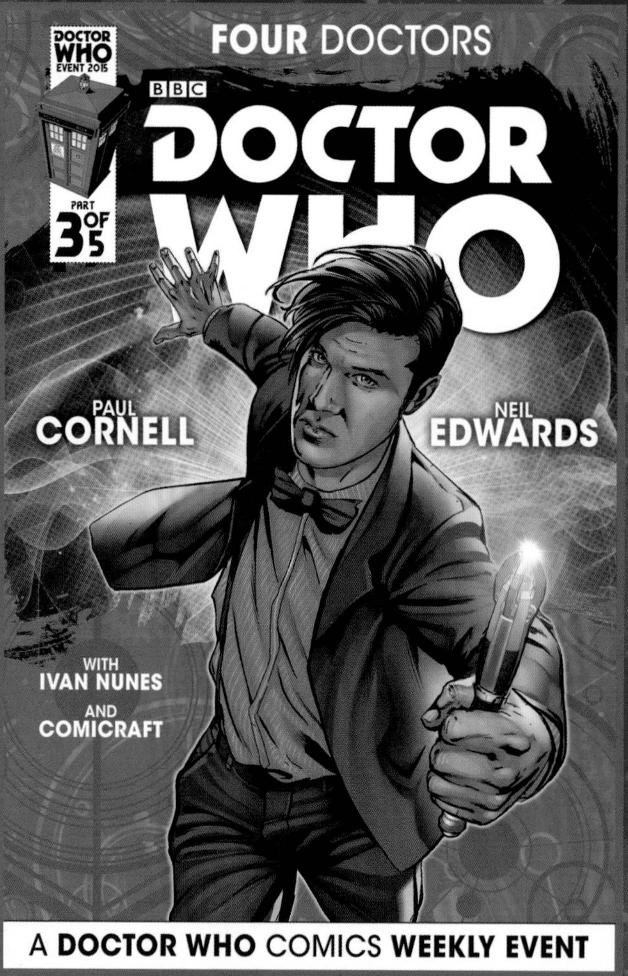
FOUR DOCTORS
DOCTOR WHO EVENT 2015
PART 3 OF 5
BBC
DOCTOR WHO
PAUL CORNELL
NEIL EDWARDS
WITH IVAN NUNES AND COMICRAFT
A DOCTOR WHO COMICS WEEKLY EVENT

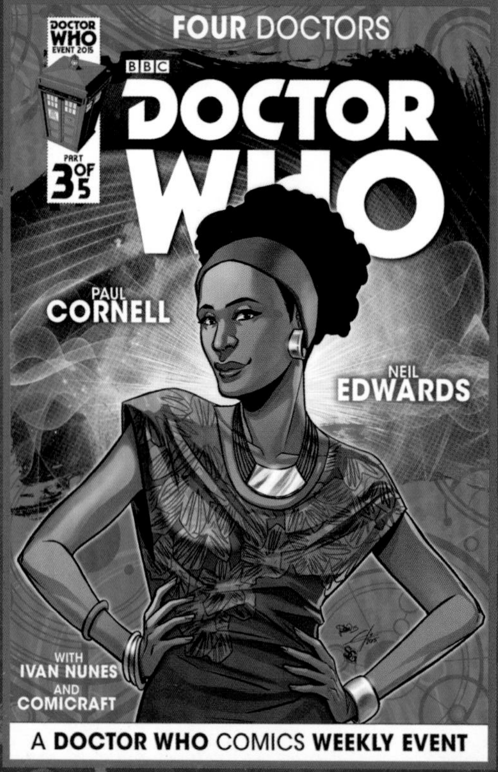
FOUR DOCTORS
DOCTOR WHO EVENT 2015
PART 3 OF 5
BBC
DOCTOR WHO
PAUL CORNELL
NEIL EDWARDS
WITH IVAN NUNES AND COMICRAFT
A DOCTOR WHO COMICS WEEKLY EVENT

COMPANION Cover by Elena Casagrande, Eleonora Carlini & Claudia SG Iannicello

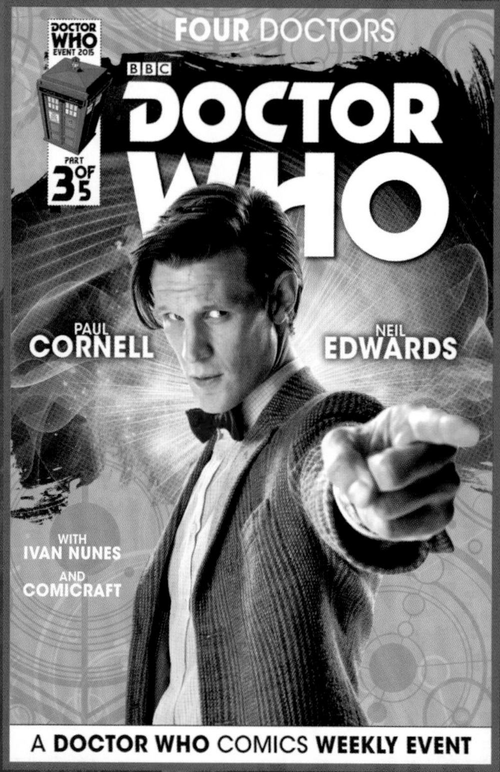
FOUR DOCTORS
DOCTOR WHO EVENT 2015
PART 3 OF 5
BBC
DOCTOR WHO
PAUL CORNELL
NEIL EDWARDS
WITH IVAN NUNES AND COMICRAFT
A DOCTOR WHO COMICS WEEKLY EVENT

SUBSCRIPTION Cover by AJ & Rob Farmer

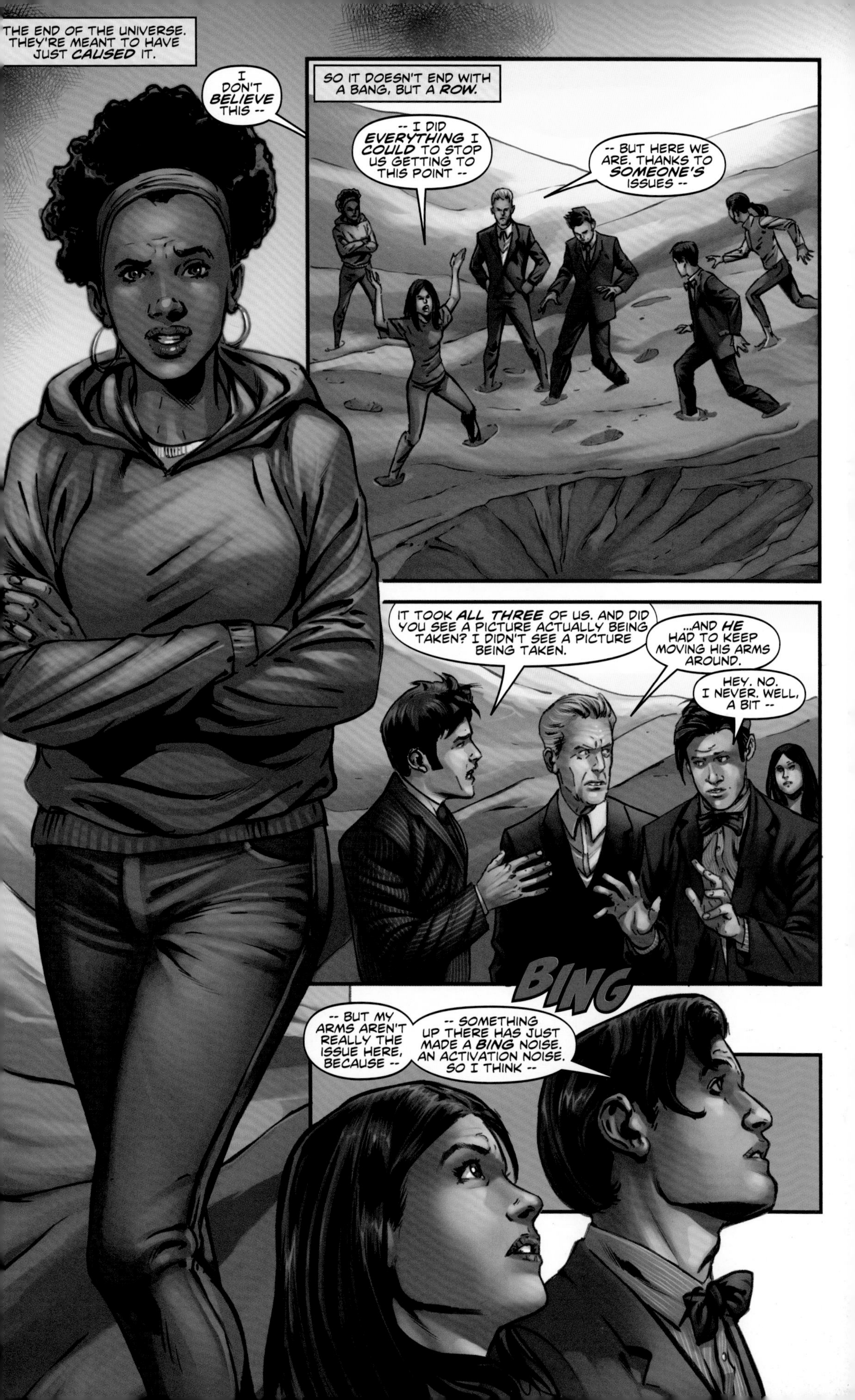

THE END OF THE UNIVERSE. THEY'RE MEANT TO HAVE JUST *CAUSED* IT.
I DON'T *BELIEVE* THIS --
SO IT DOESN'T END WITH A BANG, BUT A *ROW*.
-- I DID *EVERYTHING* I *COULD* TO STOP US GETTING TO THIS POINT --
-- BUT HERE WE ARE. THANKS TO *SOMEONE'S* ISSUES --
IT TOOK *ALL THREE* OF US. AND DID YOU SEE A PICTURE ACTUALLY BEING TAKEN? I DIDN'T SEE A PICTURE BEING TAKEN.
...AND *HE* HAD TO KEEP MOVING HIS ARMS AROUND.
HEY. NO. I NEVER. WELL, A BIT --
BING
-- BUT MY ARMS AREN'T REALLY THE ISSUE HERE, BECAUSE --
-- SOMETHING UP THERE HAS JUST MADE A *BING* NOISE. AN ACTIVATION NOISE. SO I THINK --

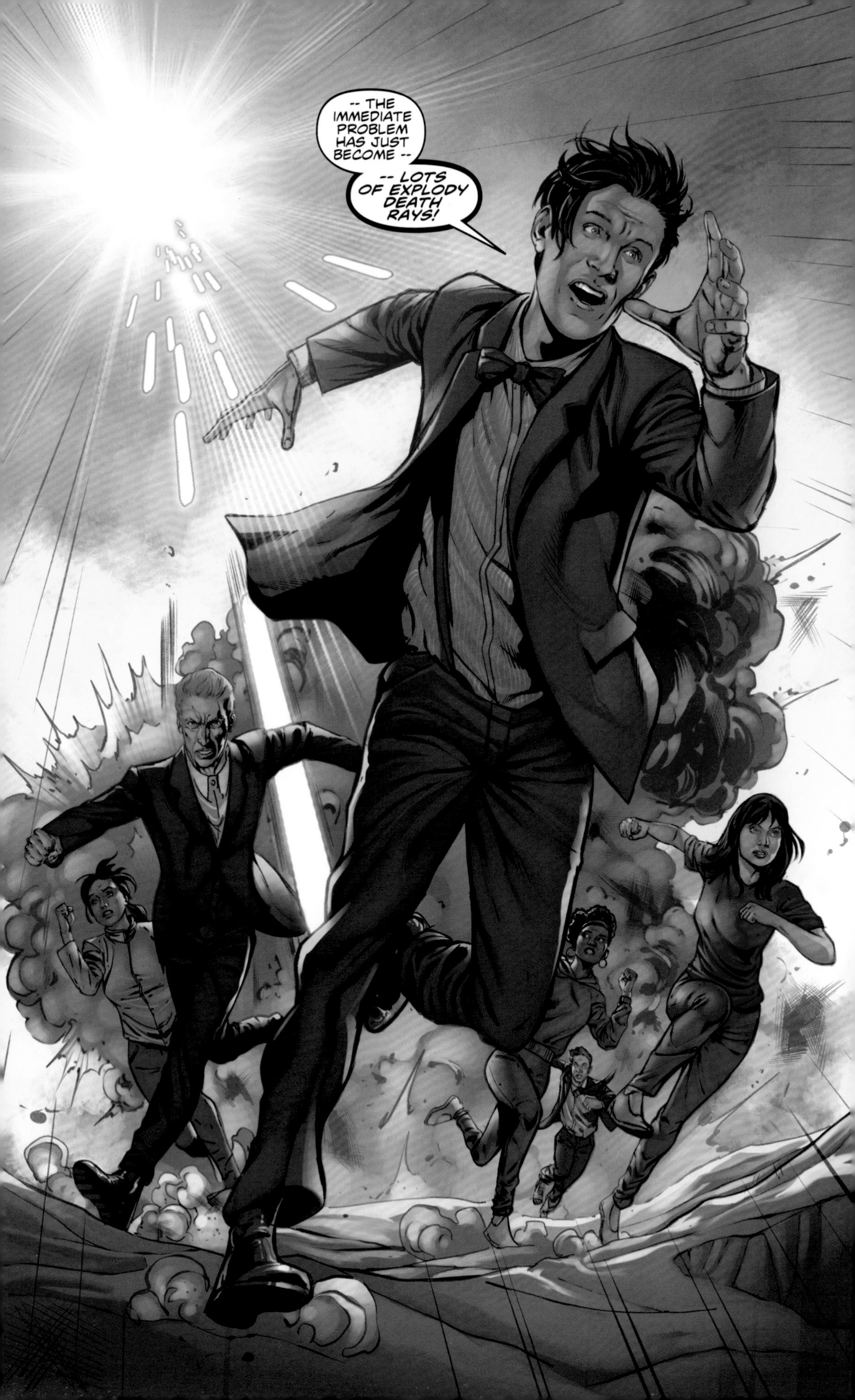
-- THE IMMEDIATE PROBLEM HAS JUST BECOME --
-- LOTS OF EXPLODY DEATH RAYS!

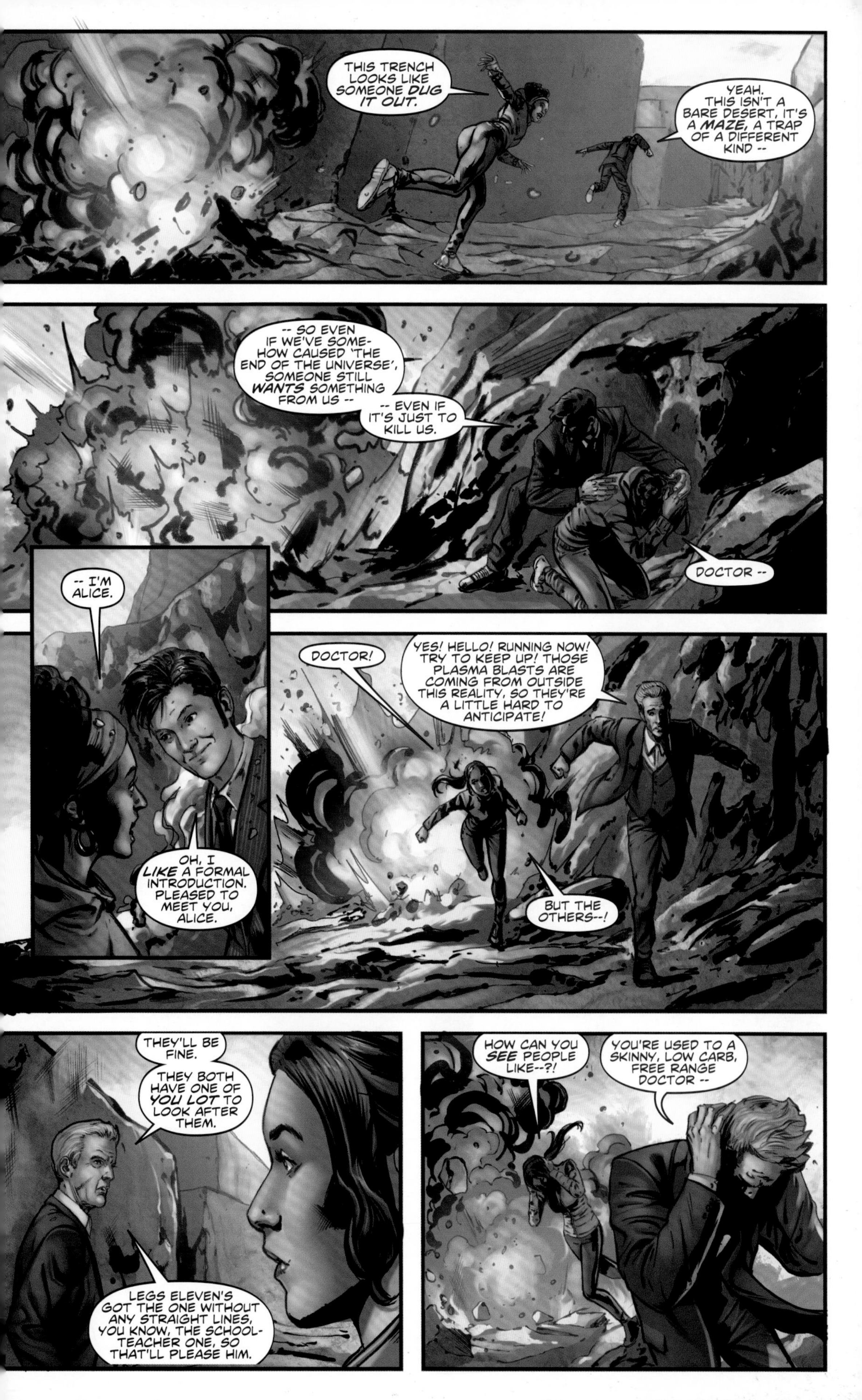
THIS TRENCH LOOKS LIKE SOMEONE DUG IT OUT.
YEAH. THIS ISN'T A BARE DESERT, IT'S A MAZE, A TRAP OF A DIFFERENT KIND --
-- SO EVEN IF WE'VE SOME-HOW CAUSED 'THE END OF THE UNIVERSE', SOMEONE STILL WANTS SOMETHING FROM US --
-- EVEN IF IT'S JUST TO KILL US.
DOCTOR --
-- I'M ALICE.
OH, I LIKE A FORMAL INTRODUCTION. PLEASED TO MEET YOU, ALICE.
DOCTOR!
YES! HELLO! RUNNING NOW! TRY TO KEEP UP! THOSE PLASMA BLASTS ARE COMING FROM OUTSIDE THIS REALITY, SO THEY'RE A LITTLE HARD TO ANTICIPATE!
BUT THE OTHERS--!
THEY'LL BE FINE.
THEY BOTH HAVE ONE OF YOU LOT TO LOOK AFTER THEM.
LEGS ELEVEN'S GOT THE ONE WITHOUT ANY STRAIGHT LINES, YOU KNOW, THE SCHOOL-TEACHER ONE, SO THAT'LL PLEASE HIM.
HOW CAN YOU SEE PEOPLE LIKE--?!
YOU'RE USED TO A SKINNY, LOW CARB, FREE RANGE DOCTOR --

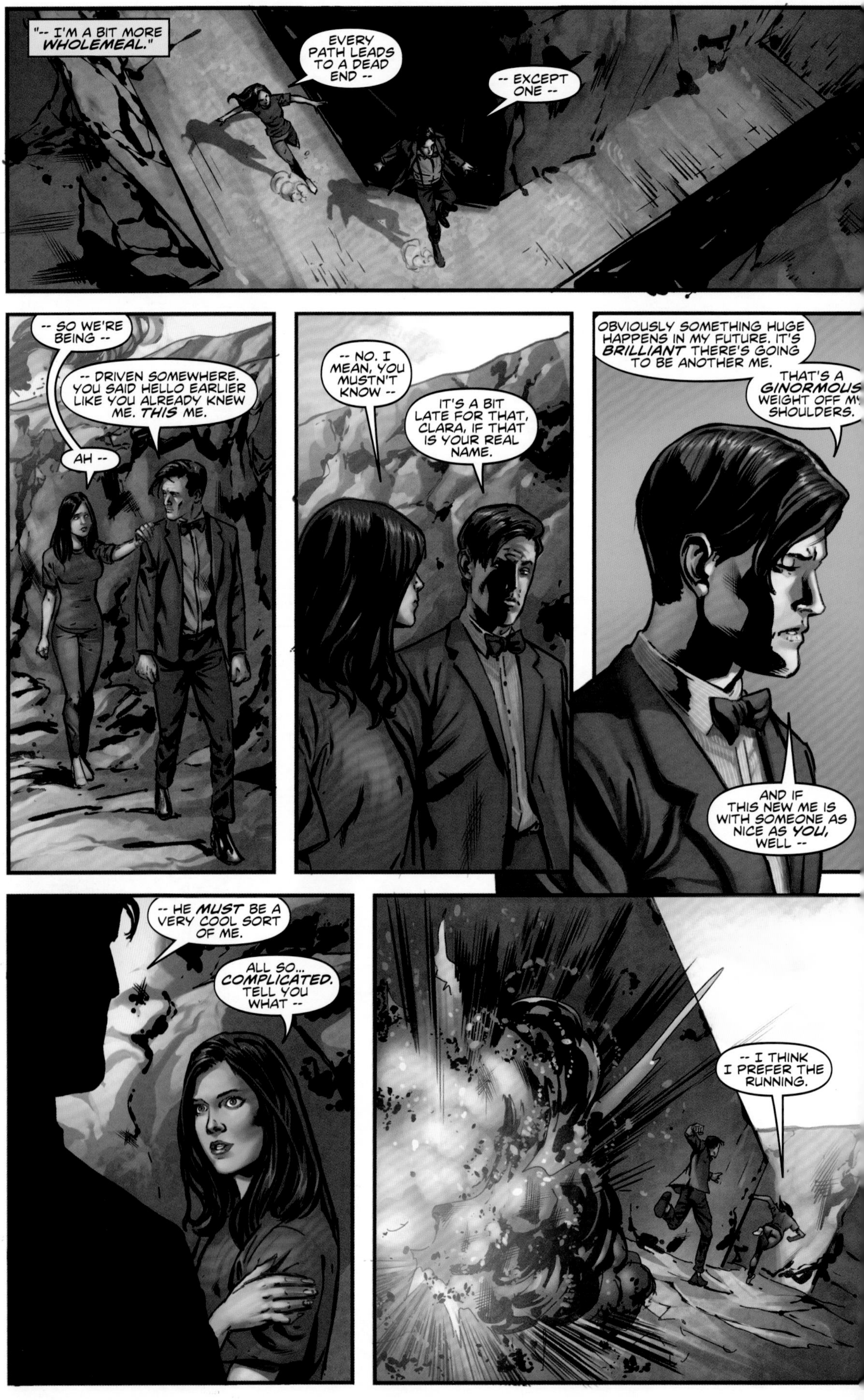
"-- I'M A BIT MORE WHOLEMEAL."
EVERY PATH LEADS TO A DEAD END --
-- EXCEPT ONE --
-- SO WE'RE BEING --
-- DRIVEN SOMEWHERE. YOU SAID HELLO EARLIER LIKE YOU ALREADY KNEW ME. THIS ME.
AH --
-- NO. I MEAN, YOU MUSTN'T KNOW --
IT'S A BIT LATE FOR THAT, CLARA, IF THAT IS YOUR REAL NAME.
OBVIOUSLY SOMETHING HUGE HAPPENS IN MY FUTURE. IT'S BRILLIANT THERE'S GOING TO BE ANOTHER ME.
THAT'S A GINORMOUS WEIGHT OFF MY SHOULDERS.
AND IF THIS NEW ME IS WITH SOMEONE AS NICE AS YOU, WELL --
-- HE MUST BE A VERY COOL SORT OF ME.
ALL SO... COMPLICATED. TELL YOU WHAT --
-- I THINK I PREFER THE RUNNING.

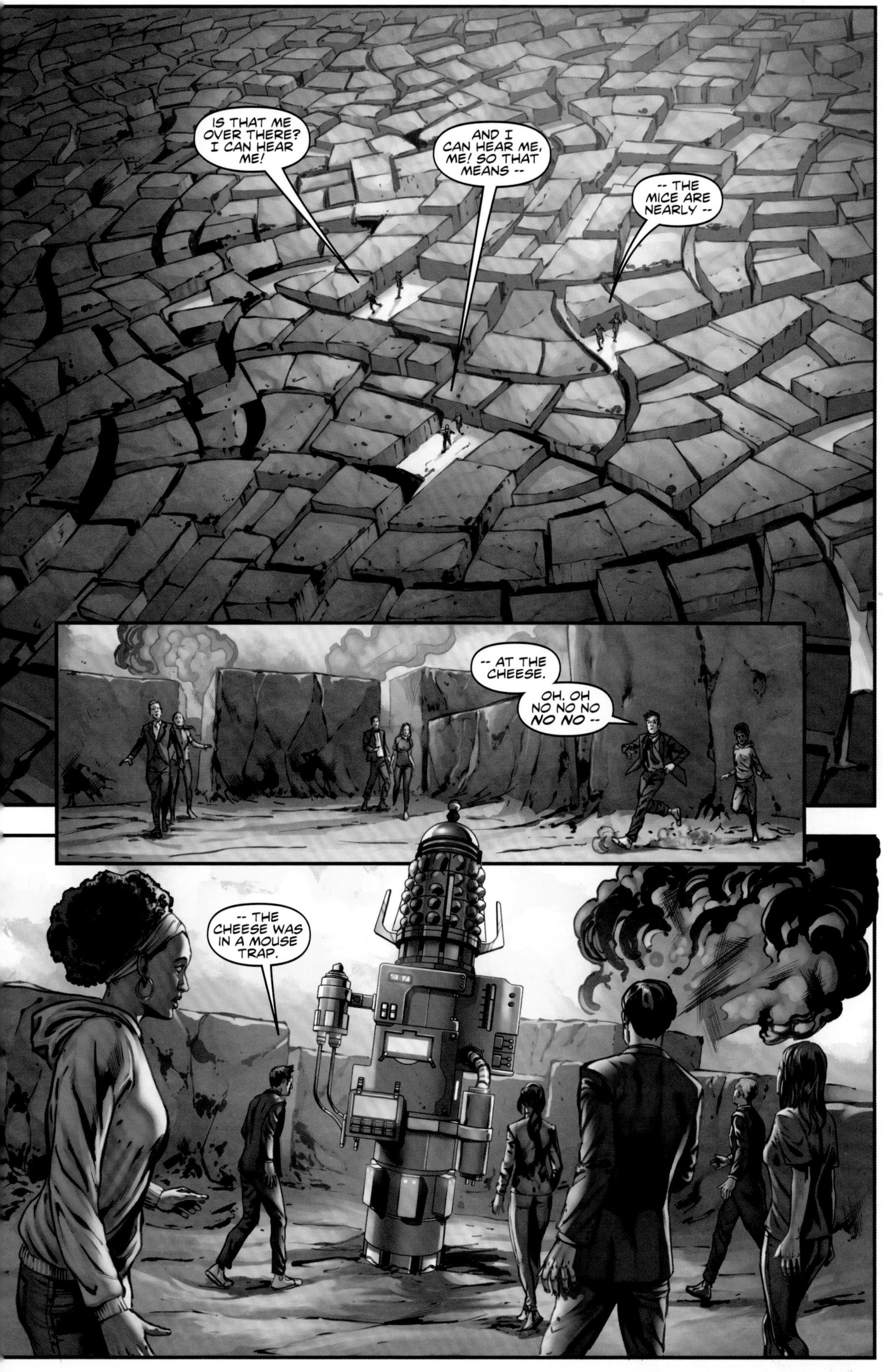
IS THAT ME OVER THERE? I CAN HEAR ME!
AND I CAN HEAR ME, ME! SO THAT MEANS --
-- THE MICE ARE NEARLY --
-- AT THE CHEESE.
OH. OH NO NO NO NO NO --
-- THE CHEESE WAS IN A MOUSE TRAP.

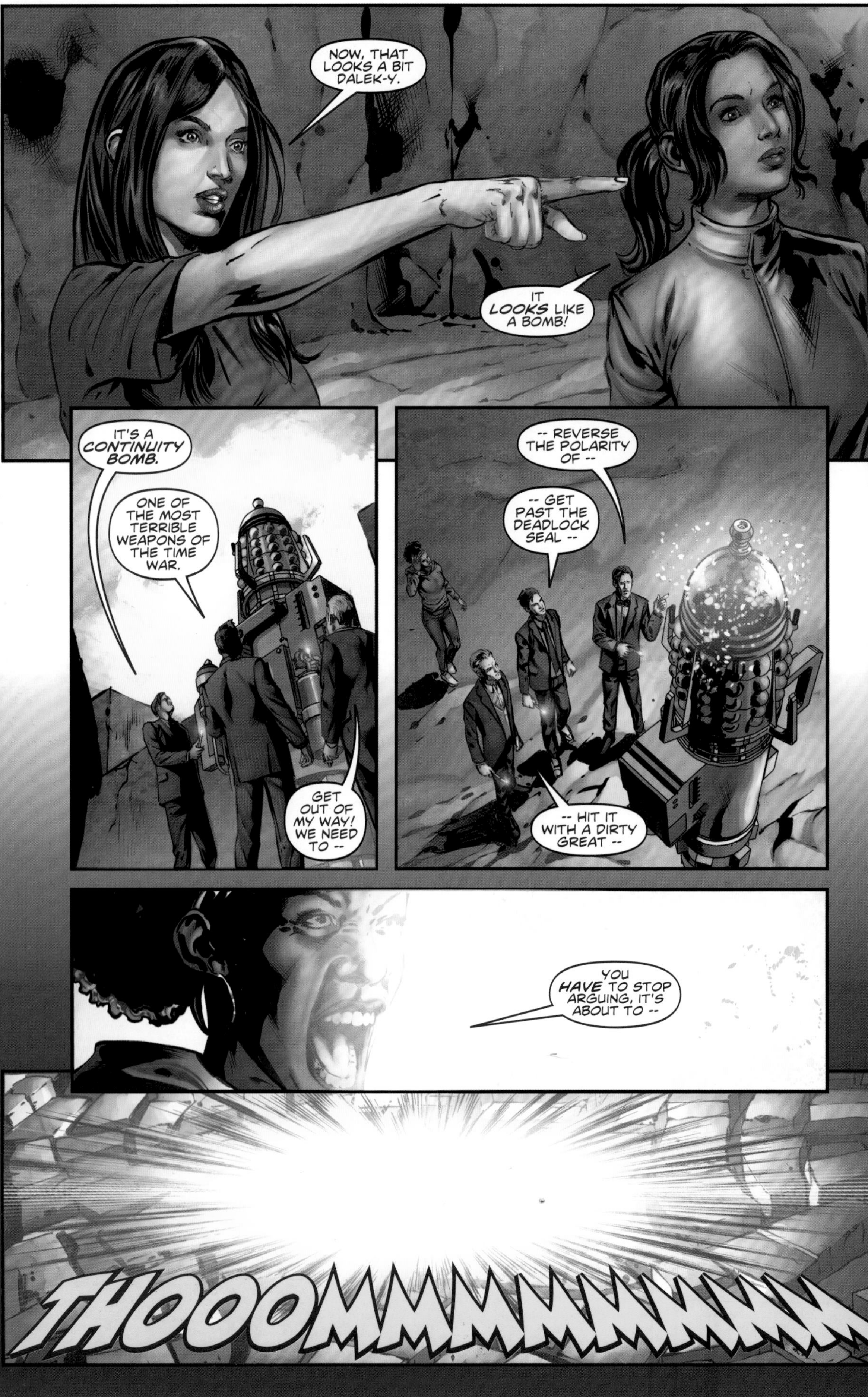
NOW, THAT LOOKS A BIT DALEK-Y.
IT LOOKS LIKE A BOMB!
IT'S A CONTINUITY BOMB.
ONE OF THE MOST TERRIBLE WEAPONS OF THE TIME WAR.
GET OUT OF MY WAY! WE NEED TO --
-- REVERSE THE POLARITY OF --
-- GET PAST THE DEADLOCK SEAL --
-- HIT IT WITH A DIRTY GREAT --
YOU HAVE TO STOP ARGUING, IT'S ABOUT TO --
THOOOMMMMMMMM

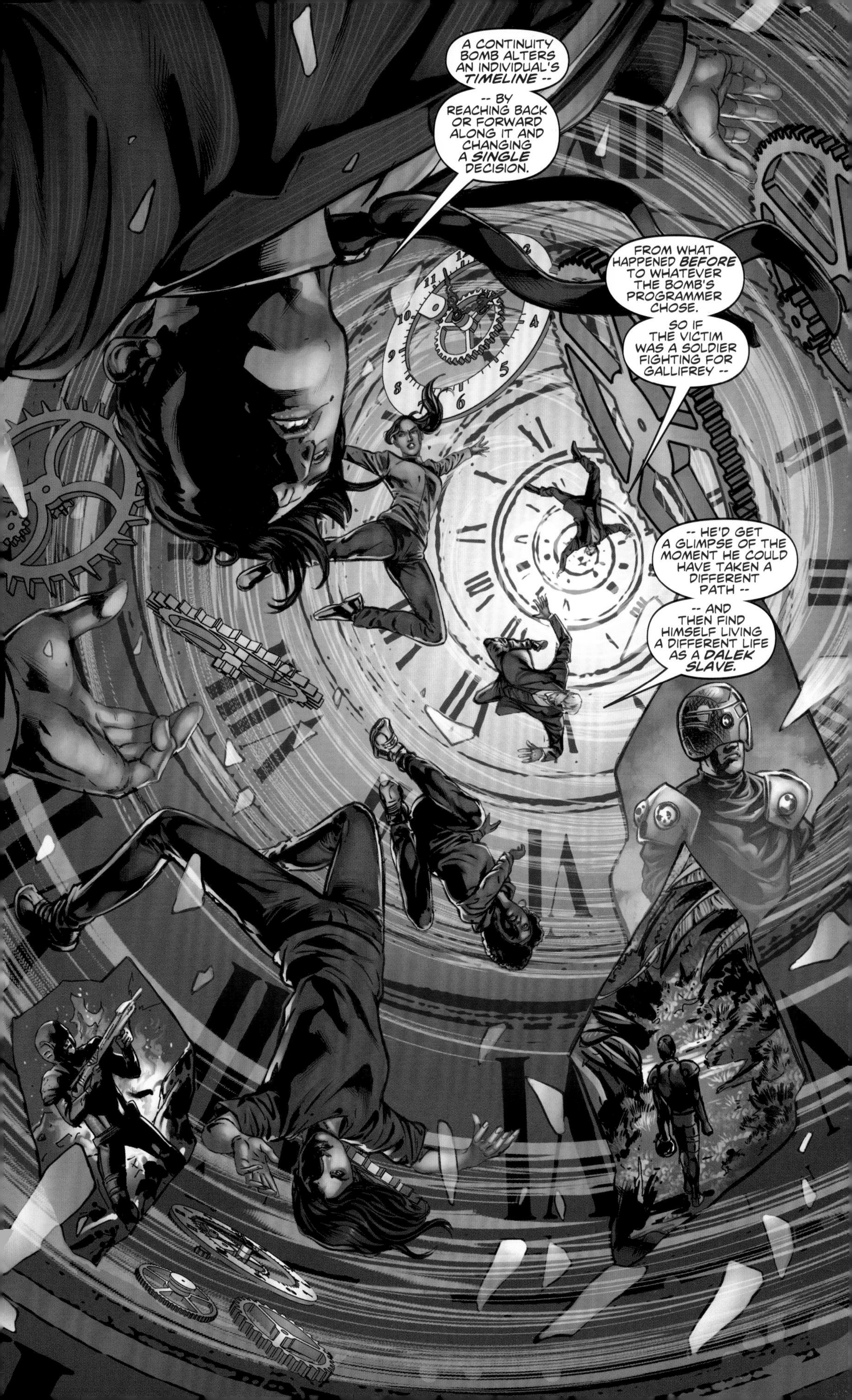
A CONTINUITY BOMB ALTERS AN INDIVIDUAL'S *TIMELINE* --
-- BY REACHING BACK OR FORWARD ALONG IT AND CHANGING A *SINGLE* DECISION.
FROM WHAT HAPPENED *BEFORE* TO WHATEVER THE BOMB'S PROGRAMMER CHOSE.
SO IF THE VICTIM WAS A SOLDIER FIGHTING FOR GALLIFREY --
-- HE'D GET A GLIMPSE OF THE MOMENT HE COULD HAVE TAKEN A DIFFERENT PATH --
-- AND THEN FIND HIMSELF LIVING A DIFFERENT LIFE AS A *DALEK SLAVE.*

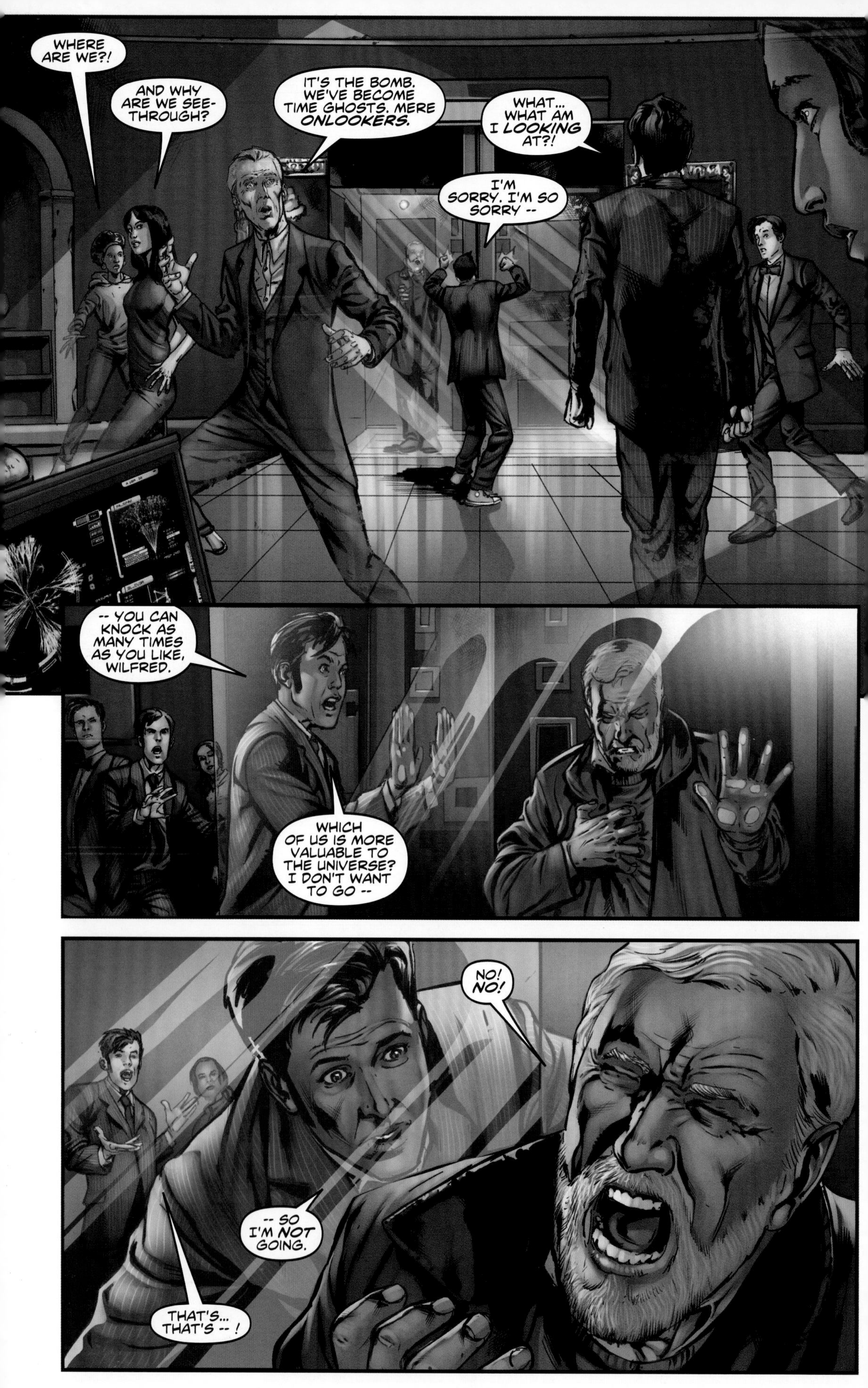
WHERE ARE WE?!
AND WHY ARE WE SEE-THROUGH?
IT'S THE BOMB. WE'VE BECOME TIME GHOSTS. MERE ONLOOKERS.
WHAT... WHAT AM I LOOKING AT?!
I'M SORRY. I'M SO SORRY --
-- YOU CAN KNOCK AS MANY TIMES AS YOU LIKE, WILFRED.
WHICH OF US IS MORE VALUABLE TO THE UNIVERSE? I DON'T WANT TO GO --
NO! NO!
-- SO I'M NOT GOING.
THAT'S... THAT'S -- !

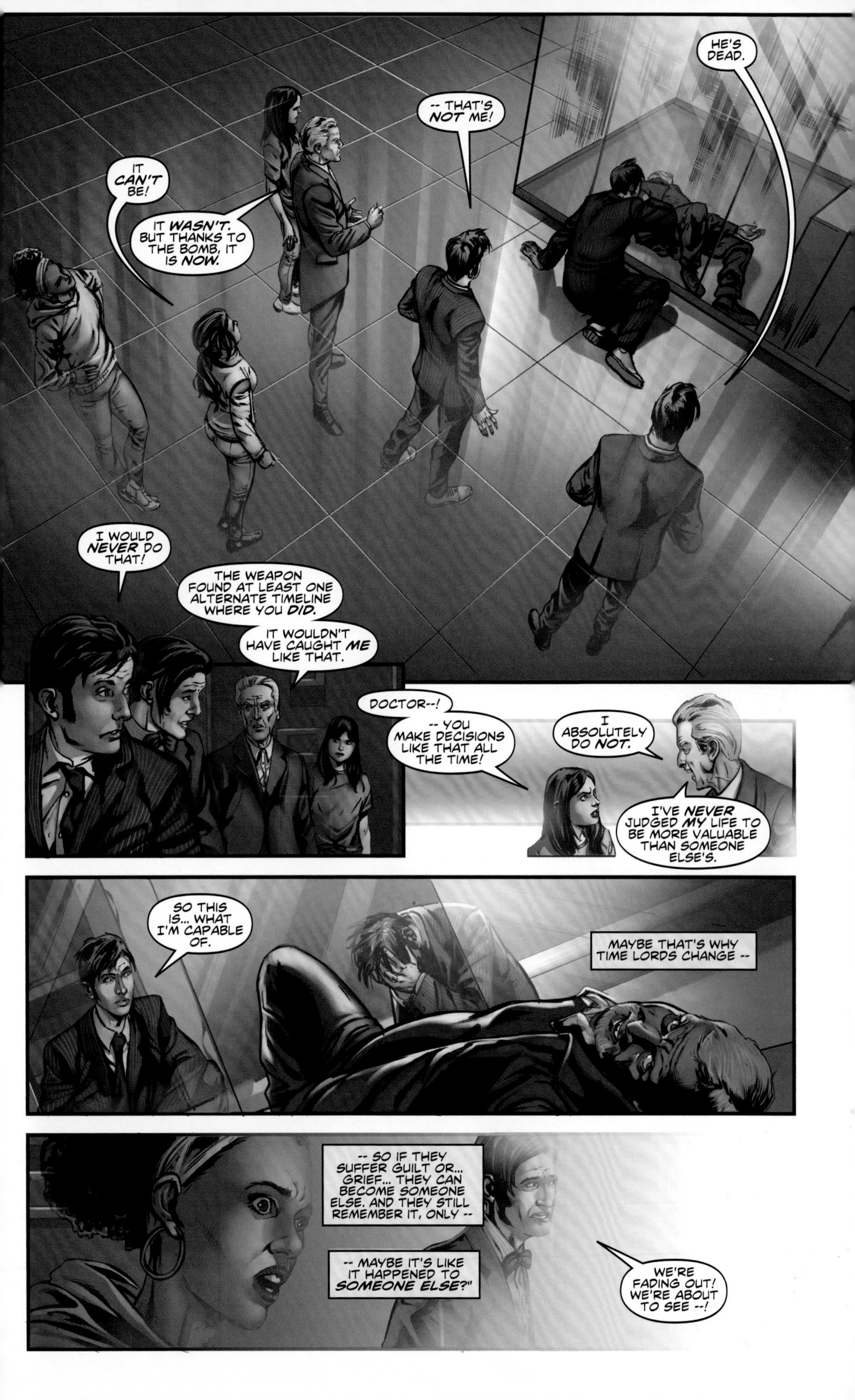
HE'S DEAD.
-- THAT'S NOT ME!
IT CAN'T BE!
IT WASN'T. BUT THANKS TO THE BOMB, IT IS NOW.
I WOULD NEVER DO THAT!
THE WEAPON FOUND AT LEAST ONE ALTERNATE TIMELINE WHERE YOU DID.
IT WOULDN'T HAVE CAUGHT ME LIKE THAT.
DOCTOR--!
-- YOU MAKE DECISIONS LIKE THAT ALL THE TIME!
I ABSOLUTELY DO NOT.
I'VE NEVER JUDGED MY LIFE TO BE MORE VALUABLE THAN SOMEONE ELSE'S.
SO THIS IS... WHAT I'M CAPABLE OF.
MAYBE THAT'S WHY TIME LORDS CHANGE --
-- SO IF THEY SUFFER GUILT OR... GRIEF... THEY CAN BECOME SOMEONE ELSE. AND THEY STILL REMEMBER IT, ONLY --
-- MAYBE IT'S LIKE IT HAPPENED TO SOMEONE ELSE?"
WE'RE FADING OUT! WE'RE ABOUT TO SEE --!

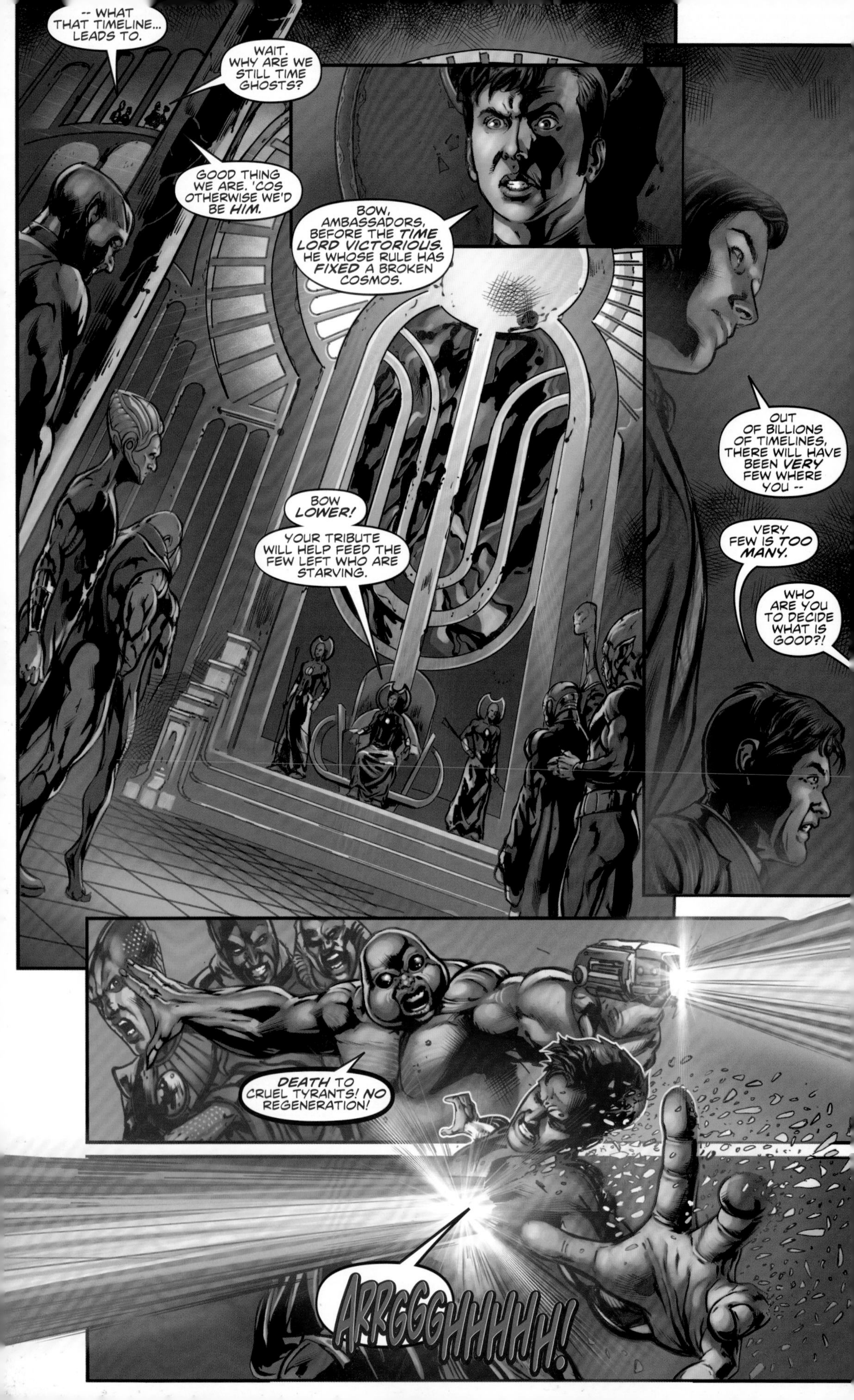

-- WHAT THAT TIMELINE... LEADS TO.
WAIT. WHY ARE WE STILL TIME GHOSTS?
GOOD THING WE ARE. 'COS OTHERWISE WE'D BE *HIM*.
BOW, AMBASSADORS, BEFORE THE *TIME LORD VICTORIOUS*. HE WHOSE RULE HAS *FIXED* A BROKEN COSMOS.
BOW *LOWER!*
YOUR TRIBUTE WILL HELP FEED THE FEW LEFT WHO ARE STARVING.
OUT OF BILLIONS OF TIMELINES, THERE WILL HAVE BEEN *VERY* FEW WHERE YOU --
VERY FEW IS *TOO MANY*.
WHO ARE YOU TO DECIDE WHAT IS GOOD?!
DEATH TO CRUEL TYRANTS! *NO* REGENERATION!
ARRGGGHHHHHH!

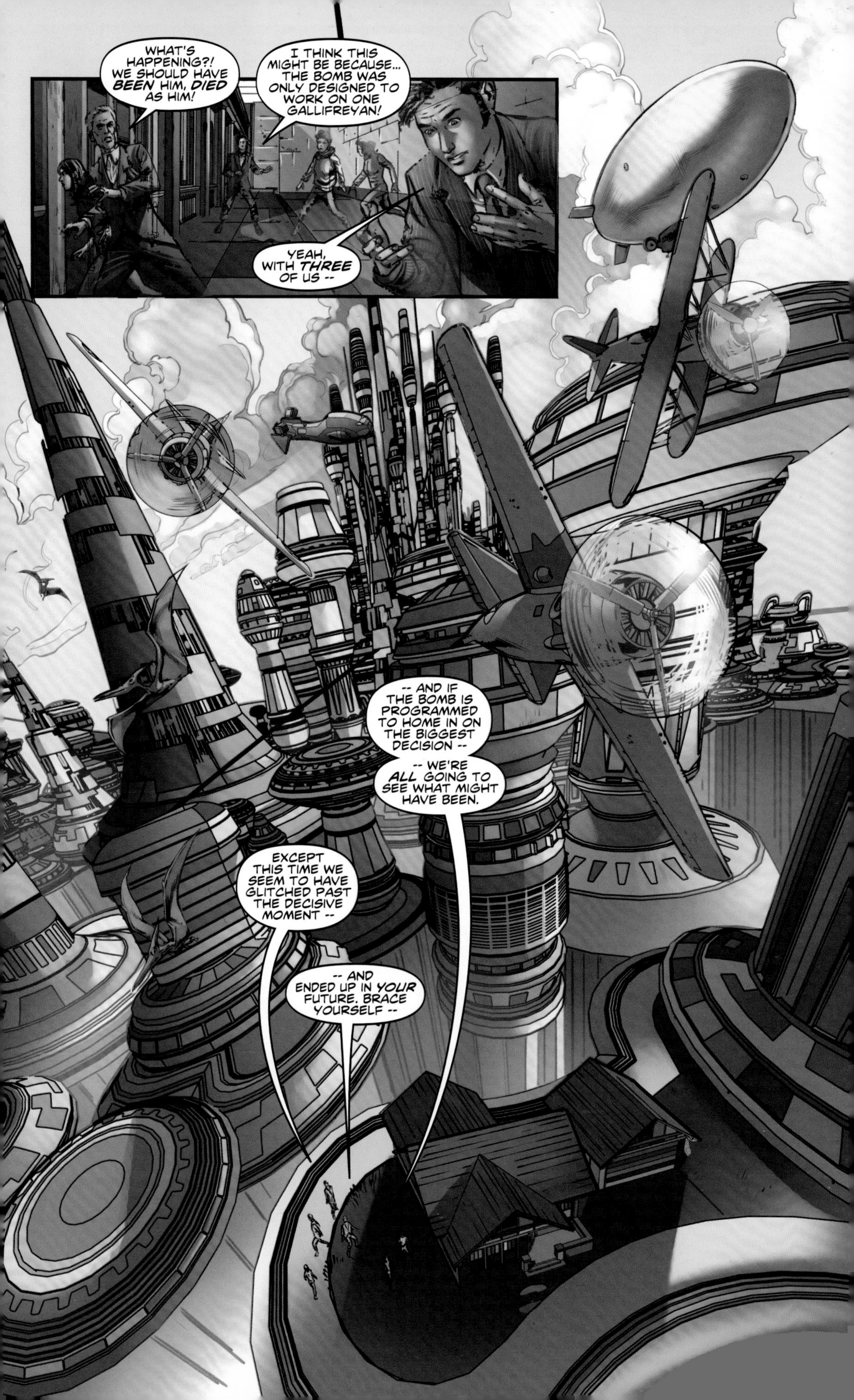
WHAT'S HAPPENING?! WE SHOULD HAVE BEEN HIM, DIED AS HIM!
I THINK THIS MIGHT BE BECAUSE... THE BOMB WAS ONLY DESIGNED TO WORK ON ONE GALLIFREYAN!
YEAH, WITH THREE OF US --
-- AND IF THE BOMB IS PROGRAMMED TO HOME IN ON THE BIGGEST DECISION --
-- WE'RE ALL GOING TO SEE WHAT MIGHT HAVE BEEN.
EXCEPT THIS TIME WE SEEM TO HAVE GLITCHED PAST THE DECISIVE MOMENT --
-- AND ENDED UP IN YOUR FUTURE. BRACE YOURSELF --

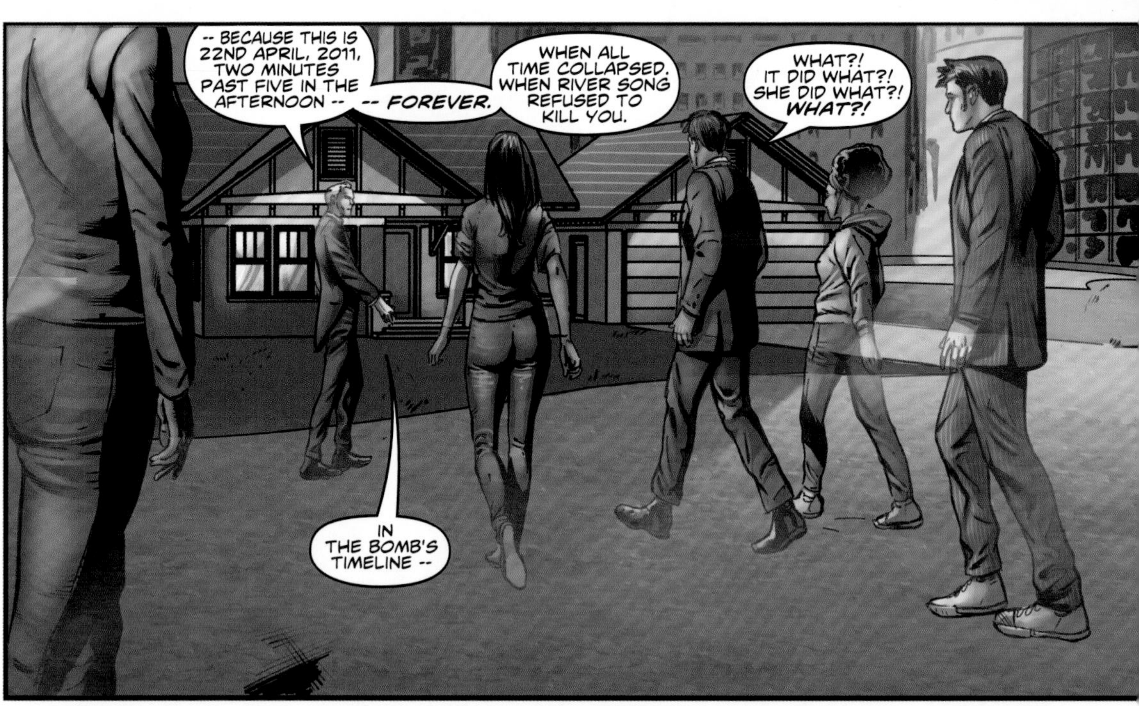
-- BECAUSE THIS IS 22ND APRIL, 2011, TWO MINUTES PAST FIVE IN THE AFTERNOON --
-- FOREVER.
WHEN ALL TIME COLLAPSED. WHEN RIVER SONG REFUSED TO KILL YOU.
WHAT?! IT DID WHAT?! SHE DID WHAT?! WHAT?!
IN THE BOMB'S TIMELINE --

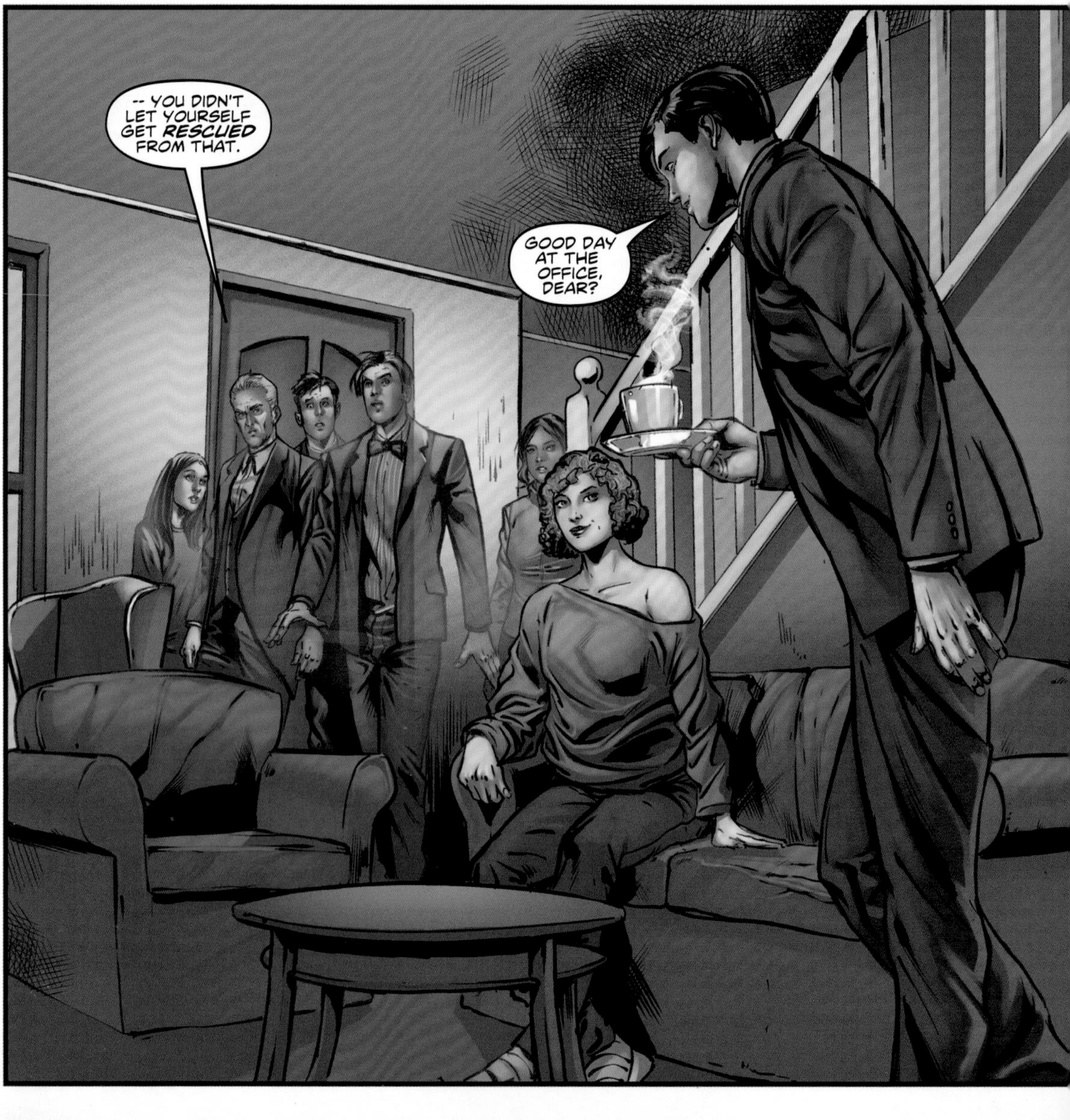
-- YOU DIDN'T LET YOURSELF GET RESCUED FROM THAT.
GOOD DAY AT THE OFFICE, DEAR?

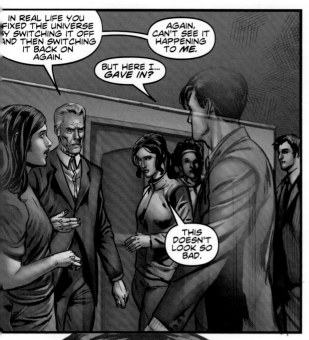

IN REAL LIFE YOU FIXED THE UNIVERSE BY SWITCHING IT OFF AND THEN SWITCHING IT BACK ON AGAIN.

AGAIN, CAN'T SEE IT HAPPENING TO *ME*.

BUT HERE I... GAVE IN?

THIS DOESN'T LOOK SO BAD.

IT DOESN'T.

BUT OUTSIDE, ALL OF HISTORY IS HAPPENING AT ONCE. I CAN *FEEL* IT. THE UNIVERSE IS DYING. AND I'M *LETTING* IT.

SO IF WE'RE TRAPPED IN *THIS* TIMELINE, THE PROPHECY CLARA FOUND WILL BE FULFILLED. GAME OVER.

WE'RE SWITCHING BETWEEN POSSIBLE FUTURES. IT'S NOT EVEN A PARADOX.

BUT DOESN'T THIS TIMELINE CONTRADICT THE LAST ONE? IF THE PREVIOUS YOU DIED --

PLEASE, NOBODY SAY 'TIMEY' ANYTHING.

WAIT A MOMENT, I CAN FEEL...

AH YES, HERE WE GO AGAIN. WHICH IS BOTH A RELIEF AND --

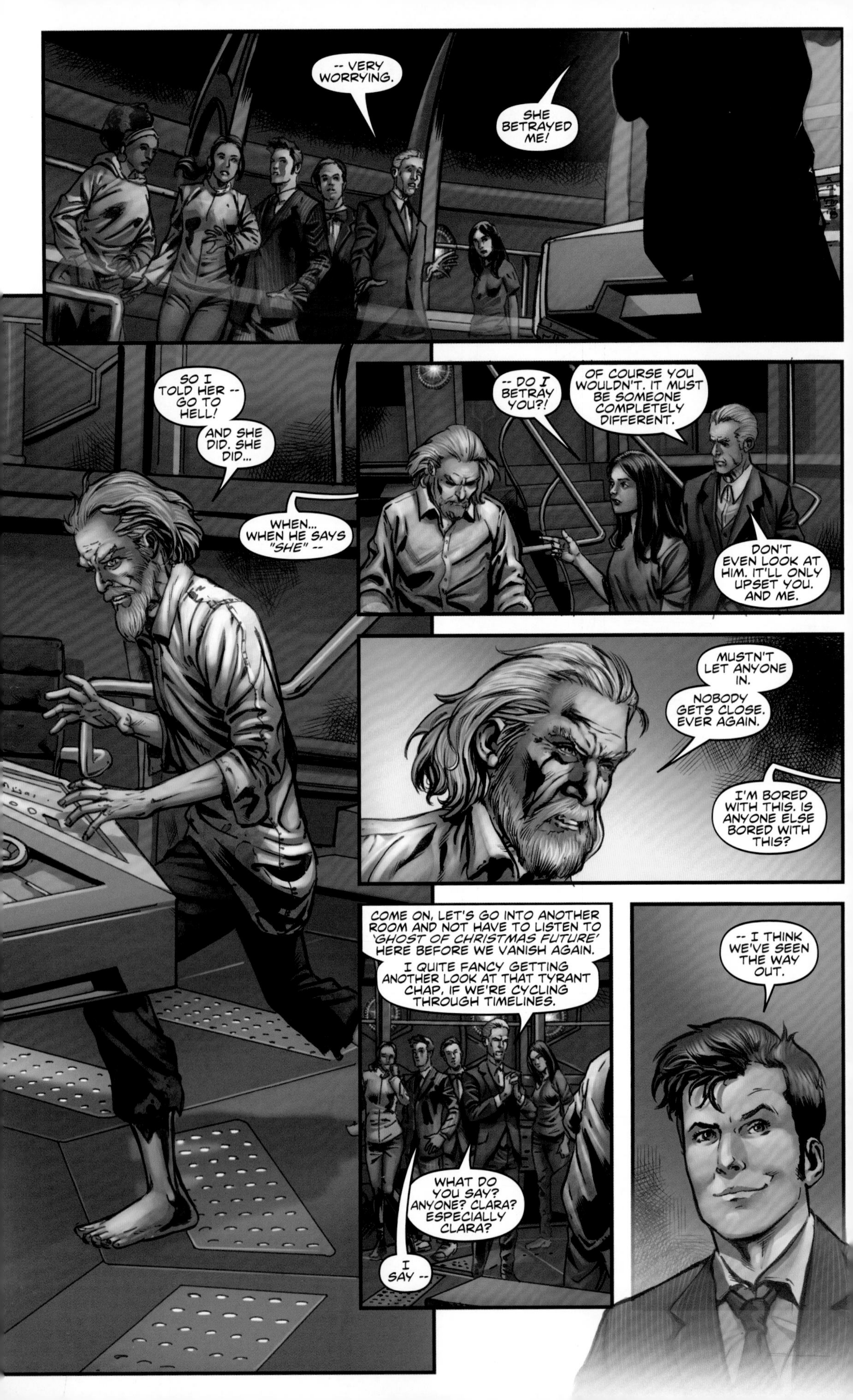
-- VERY WORRYING.
SHE BETRAYED ME!
SO I TOLD HER -- GO TO HELL!
AND SHE DID. SHE DID...
WHEN... WHEN HE SAYS "SHE" --
-- DO I BETRAY YOU?!
OF COURSE YOU WOULDN'T. IT MUST BE SOMEONE COMPLETELY DIFFERENT.
DON'T EVEN LOOK AT HIM. IT'LL ONLY UPSET YOU. AND ME.
MUSTN'T LET ANYONE IN.
NOBODY GETS CLOSE. EVER AGAIN.
I'M BORED WITH THIS. IS ANYONE ELSE BORED WITH THIS?
COME ON, LET'S GO INTO ANOTHER ROOM AND NOT HAVE TO LISTEN TO 'GHOST OF CHRISTMAS FUTURE' HERE BEFORE WE VANISH AGAIN.
I QUITE FANCY GETTING ANOTHER LOOK AT THAT TYRANT CHAP, IF WE'RE CYCLING THROUGH TIMELINES.
WHAT DO YOU SAY? ANYONE? CLARA? ESPECIALLY CLARA?
I SAY --
-- I THINK WE'VE SEEN THE WAY OUT.

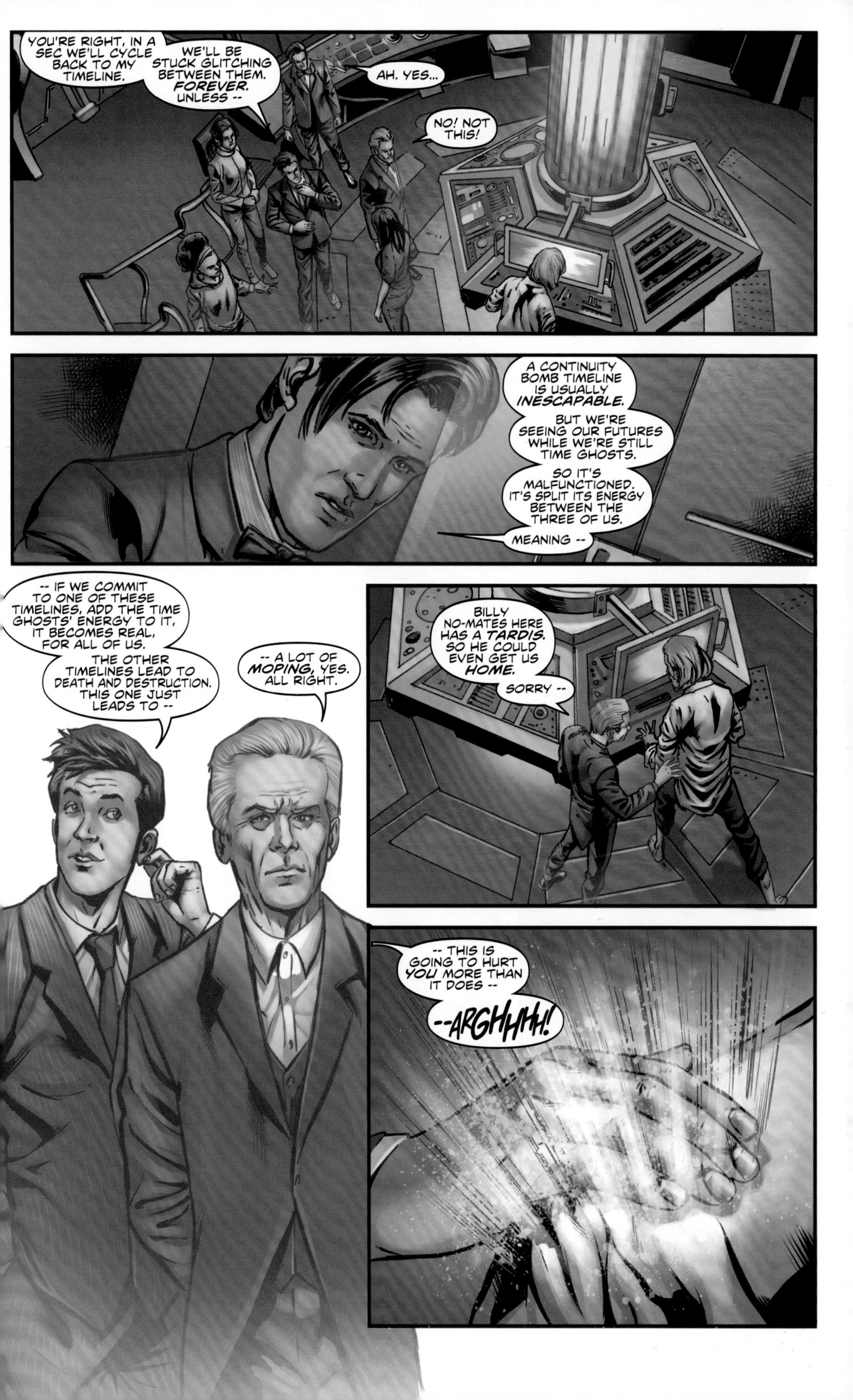
YOU'RE RIGHT, IN A SEC WE'LL CYCLE BACK TO MY TIMELINE.
WE'LL BE STUCK GLITCHING BETWEEN THEM. FOREVER. UNLESS --
AH. YES...
NO! NOT THIS!
A CONTINUITY BOMB TIMELINE IS USUALLY INESCAPABLE.
BUT WE'RE SEEING OUR FUTURES WHILE WE'RE STILL TIME GHOSTS.
SO IT'S MALFUNCTIONED. IT'S SPLIT ITS ENERGY BETWEEN THE THREE OF US.
MEANING --
-- IF WE COMMIT TO ONE OF THESE TIMELINES, ADD THE TIME GHOSTS' ENERGY TO IT, IT BECOMES REAL, FOR ALL OF US.
THE OTHER TIMELINES LEAD TO DEATH AND DESTRUCTION. THIS ONE JUST LEADS TO --
-- A LOT OF MOPING, YES. ALL RIGHT.
BILLY NO-MATES HERE HAS A TARDIS. SO HE COULD EVEN GET US HOME.
SORRY --
-- THIS IS GOING TO HURT YOU MORE THAN IT DOES --
--ARGHHHH!

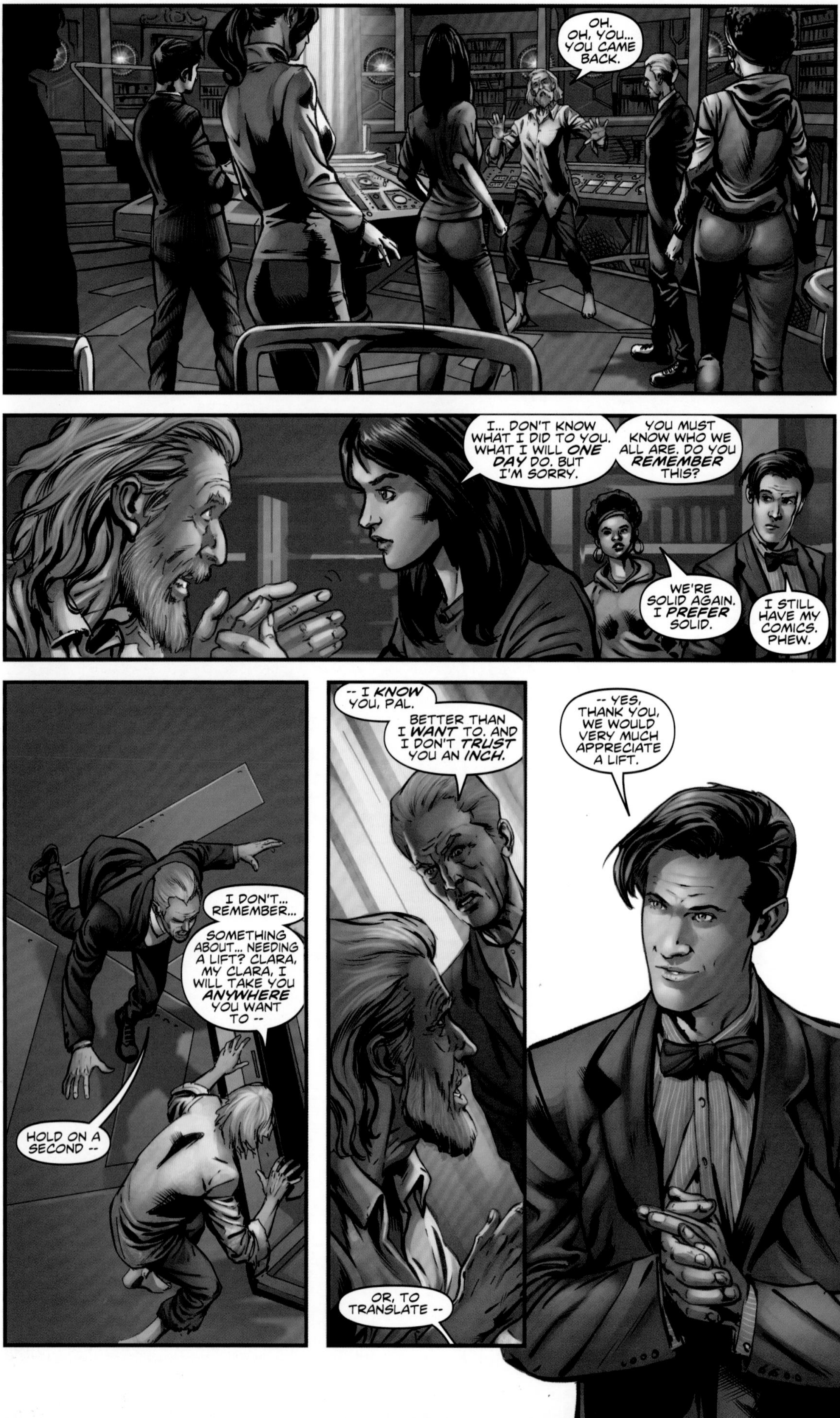
OH. OH, YOU... YOU CAME BACK.
I... DON'T KNOW WHAT I DID TO YOU. WHAT I WILL ONE DAY DO. BUT I'M SORRY.
YOU MUST KNOW WHO WE ALL ARE. DO YOU REMEMBER THIS?
WE'RE SOLID AGAIN. I PREFER SOLID.
I STILL HAVE MY COMICS. PHEW.
I DON'T... REMEMBER...
SOMETHING ABOUT... NEEDING A LIFT? CLARA, MY CLARA, I WILL TAKE YOU ANYWHERE YOU WANT TO --
HOLD ON A SECOND --
-- I KNOW YOU, PAL.
BETTER THAN I WANT TO. AND I DON'T TRUST YOU AN INCH.
OR, TO TRANSLATE --
-- YES, THANK YOU, WE WOULD VERY MUCH APPRECIATE A LIFT.

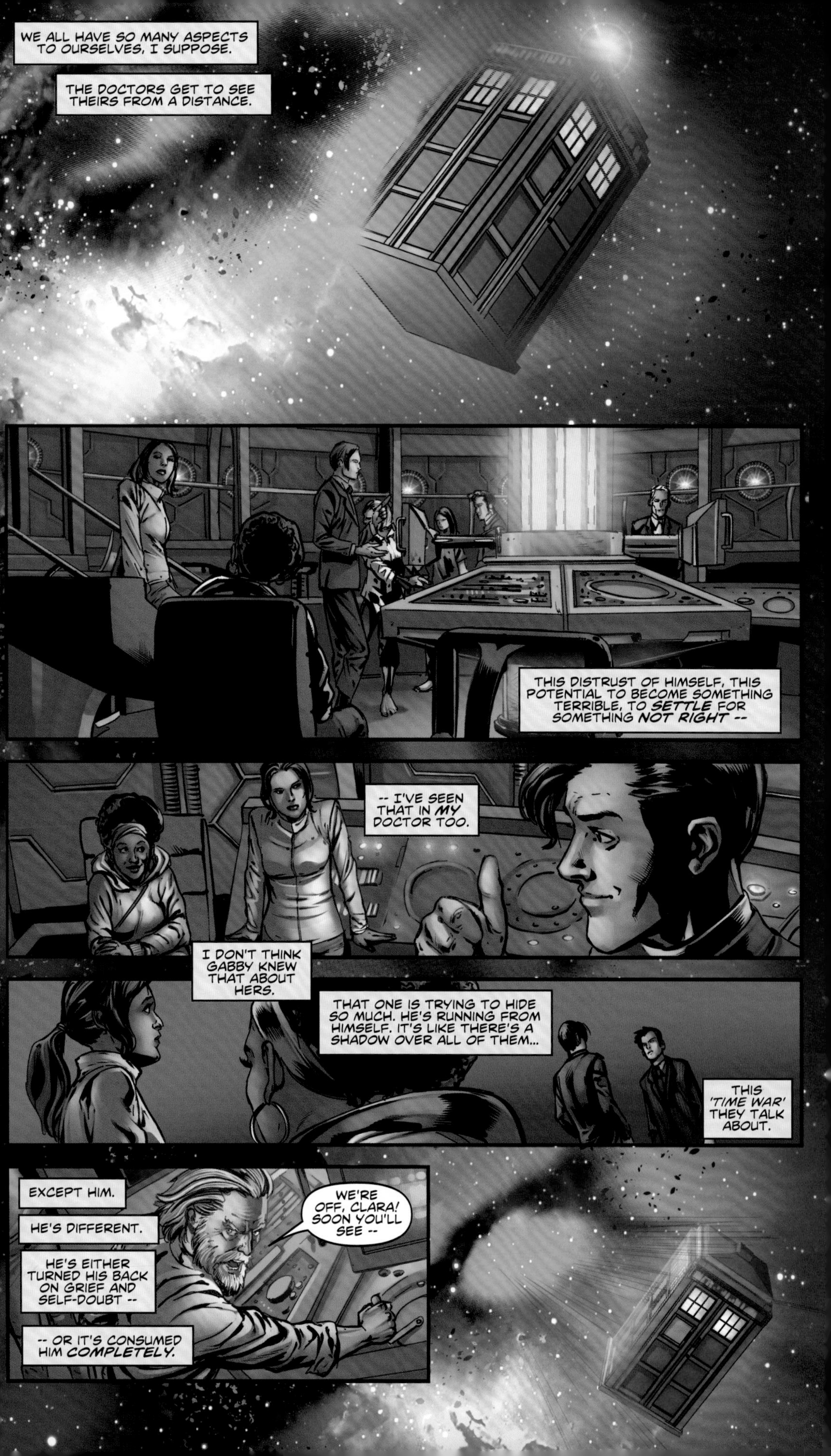
WE ALL HAVE SO MANY ASPECTS TO OURSELVES, I SUPPOSE.
THE DOCTORS GET TO SEE THEIRS FROM A DISTANCE.
THIS DISTRUST OF HIMSELF, THIS POTENTIAL TO BECOME SOMETHING TERRIBLE, TO SETTLE FOR SOMETHING NOT RIGHT --
-- I'VE SEEN THAT IN MY DOCTOR TOO.
I DON'T THINK GABBY KNEW THAT ABOUT HERS.
THAT ONE IS TRYING TO HIDE SO MUCH. HE'S RUNNING FROM HIMSELF. IT'S LIKE THERE'S A SHADOW OVER ALL OF THEM...
THIS 'TIME WAR' THEY TALK ABOUT.
EXCEPT HIM.
HE'S DIFFERENT.
HE'S EITHER TURNED HIS BACK ON GRIEF AND SELF-DOUBT --
-- OR IT'S CONSUMED HIM COMPLETELY.
WE'RE OFF, CLARA! SOON YOU'LL SEE --

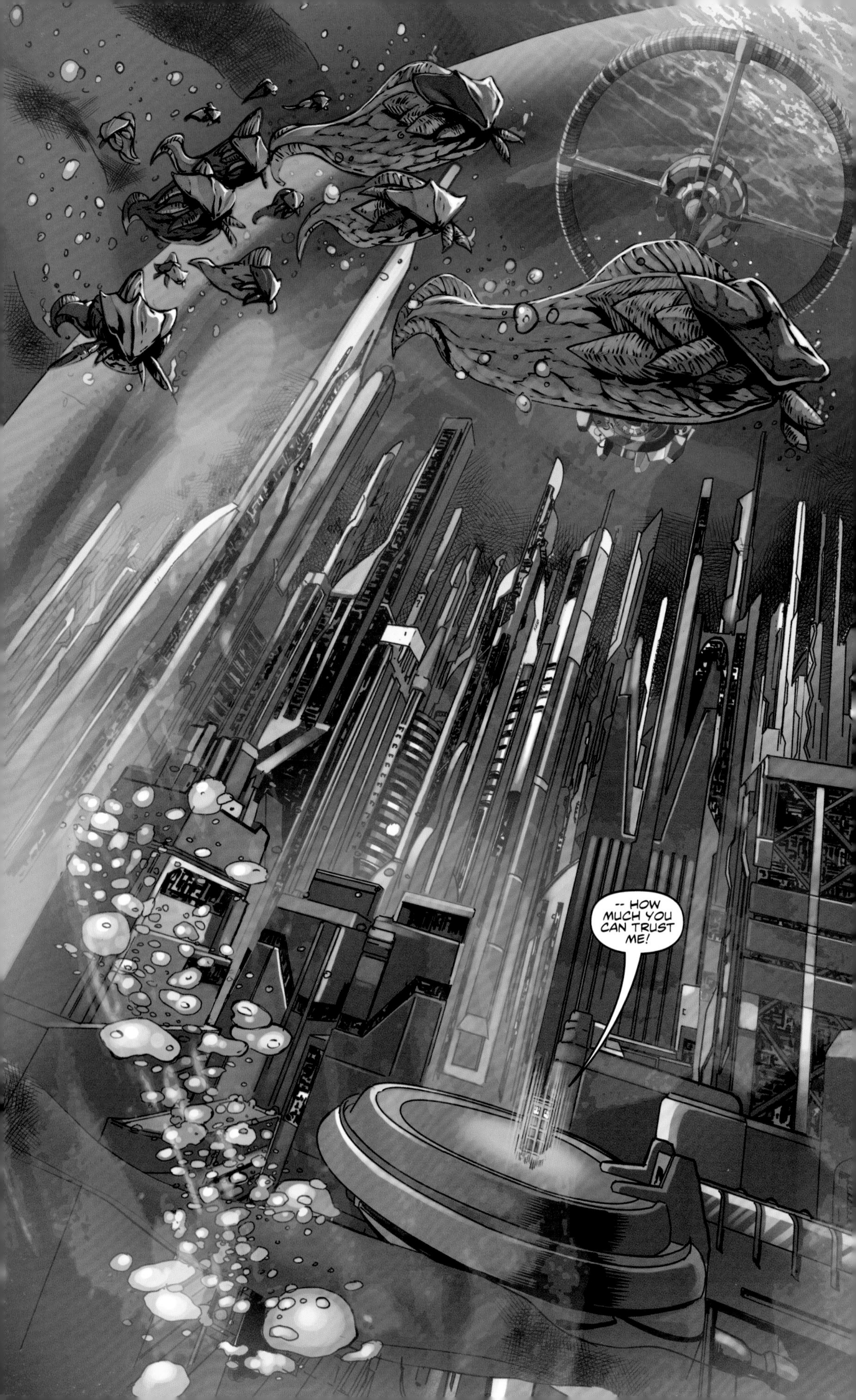
-- HOW MUCH YOU CAN TRUST ME!

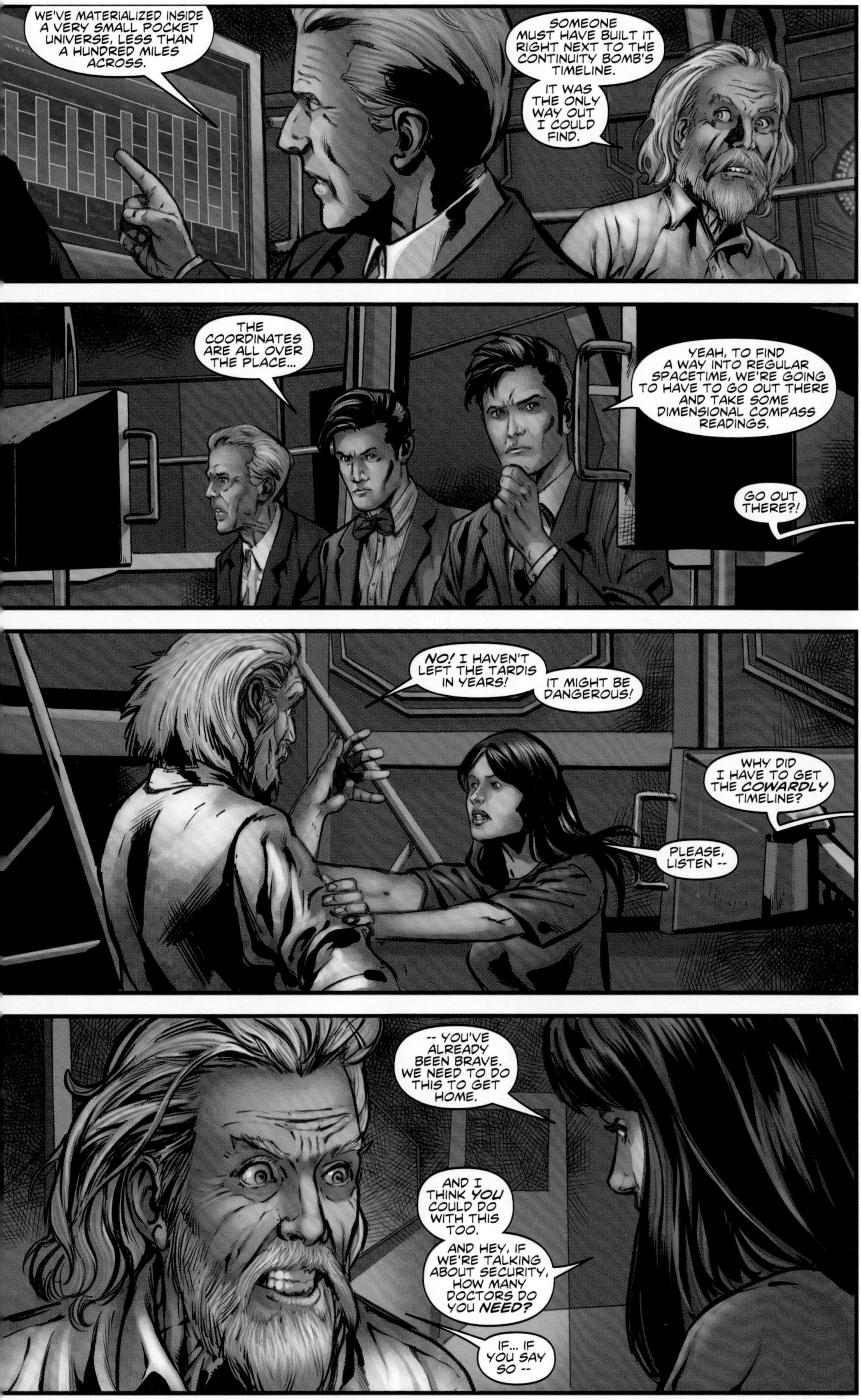
WE'VE MATERIALIZED INSIDE A VERY SMALL POCKET UNIVERSE, LESS THAN A HUNDRED MILES ACROSS.
SOMEONE MUST HAVE BUILT IT RIGHT NEXT TO THE CONTINUITY BOMB'S TIMELINE.
IT WAS THE ONLY WAY OUT I COULD FIND.
THE COORDINATES ARE ALL OVER THE PLACE...
YEAH, TO FIND A WAY INTO REGULAR SPACETIME, WE'RE GOING TO HAVE TO GO OUT THERE AND TAKE SOME DIMENSIONAL COMPASS READINGS.
GO OUT THERE?!
NO! I HAVEN'T LEFT THE TARDIS IN YEARS!
IT MIGHT BE DANGEROUS!
WHY DID I HAVE TO GET THE COWARDLY TIMELINE?
PLEASE, LISTEN --
-- YOU'VE ALREADY BEEN BRAVE. WE NEED TO DO THIS TO GET HOME.
AND I THINK YOU COULD DO WITH THIS TOO.
AND HEY, IF WE'RE TALKING ABOUT SECURITY, HOW MANY DOCTORS DO YOU NEED?
IF... IF YOU SAY SO --

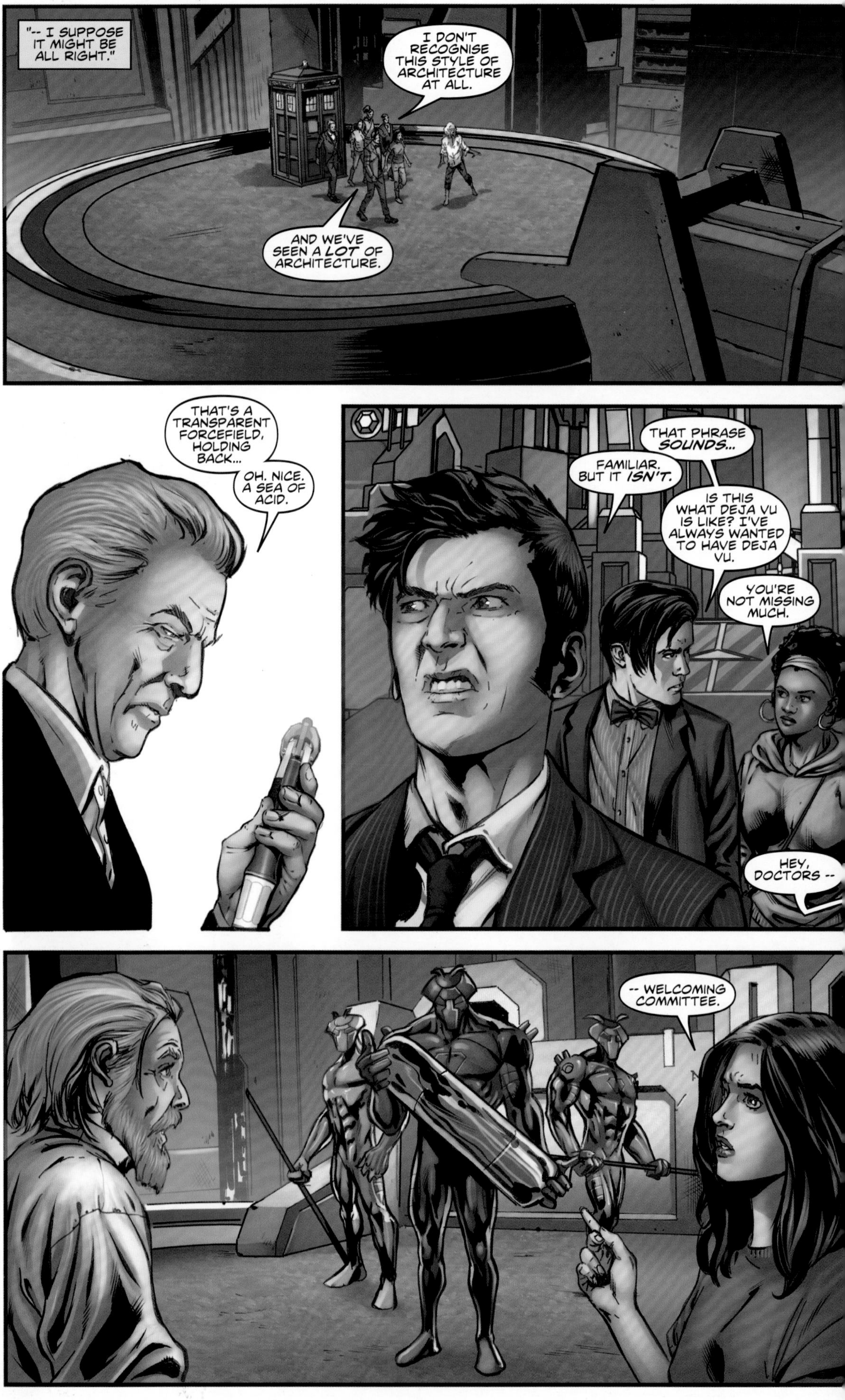
"-- I SUPPOSE IT MIGHT BE ALL RIGHT."
I DON'T RECOGNISE THIS STYLE OF ARCHITECTURE AT ALL.
AND WE'VE SEEN A *LOT* OF ARCHITECTURE.
THAT'S A TRANSPARENT FORCEFIELD, HOLDING BACK...
OH. NICE. A SEA OF ACID.
THAT PHRASE *SOUNDS*...
FAMILIAR. BUT IT *ISN'T.*
IS THIS WHAT DEJA VU IS LIKE? I'VE ALWAYS WANTED TO HAVE DEJA VU.
YOU'RE NOT MISSING MUCH.
HEY, DOCTORS --
-- WELCOMING COMMITTEE.

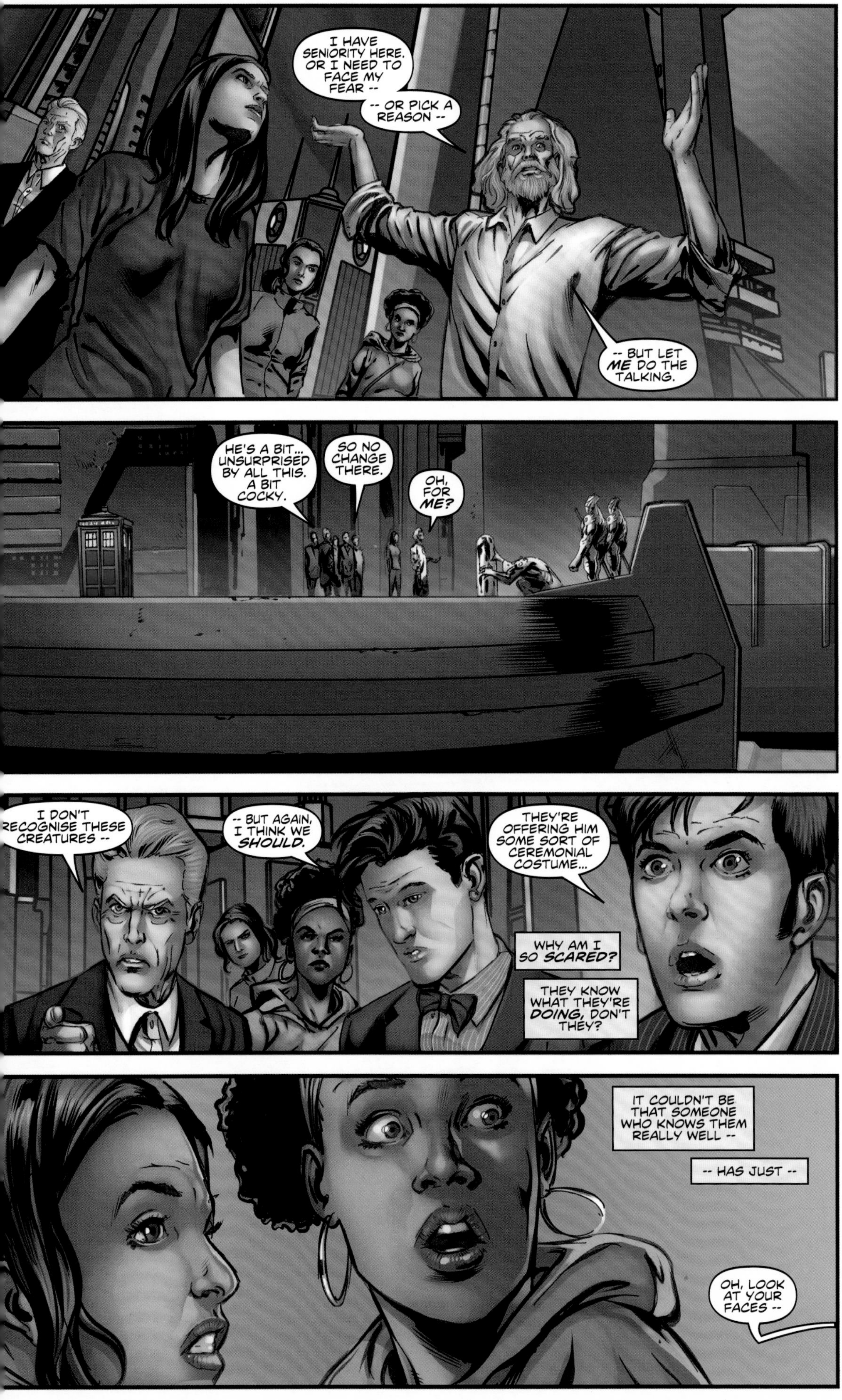
I HAVE SENIORITY HERE. OR I NEED TO FACE MY FEAR --
-- OR PICK A REASON --
-- BUT LET ME DO THE TALKING.
HE'S A BIT... UNSURPRISED BY ALL THIS. A BIT COCKY.
SO NO CHANGE THERE.
OH, FOR ME?
I DON'T RECOGNISE THESE CREATURES --
-- BUT AGAIN, I THINK WE SHOULD.
THEY'RE OFFERING HIM SOME SORT OF CEREMONIAL COSTUME...
WHY AM I SO SCARED?
THEY KNOW WHAT THEY'RE DOING, DON'T THEY?
IT COULDN'T BE THAT SOMEONE WHO KNOWS THEM REALLY WELL --
-- HAS JUST --
OH, LOOK AT YOUR FACES --

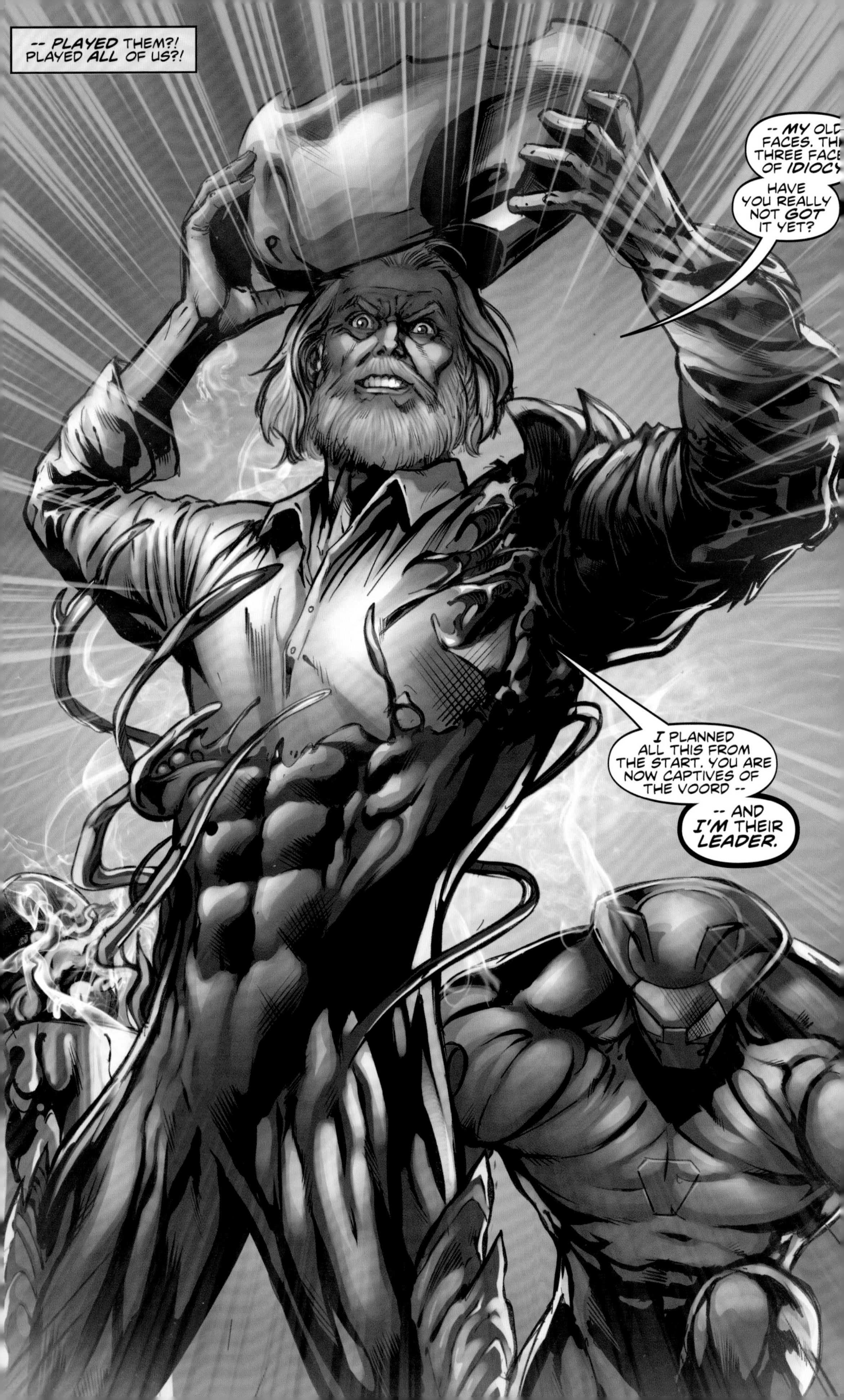
-- PLAYED THEM?! PLAYED ALL OF US?!
-- MY OLD FACES. TH THREE FACE OF IDIOCY
HAVE YOU REALLY NOT GOT IT YET?
I PLANNED ALL THIS FROM THE START. YOU ARE NOW CAPTIVES OF THE VOORD --
-- AND I'M THEIR LEADER.

BBC DOCTOR WHO

'THE MEETING'

BY PAUL CORNELL & RACHAEL SMITH

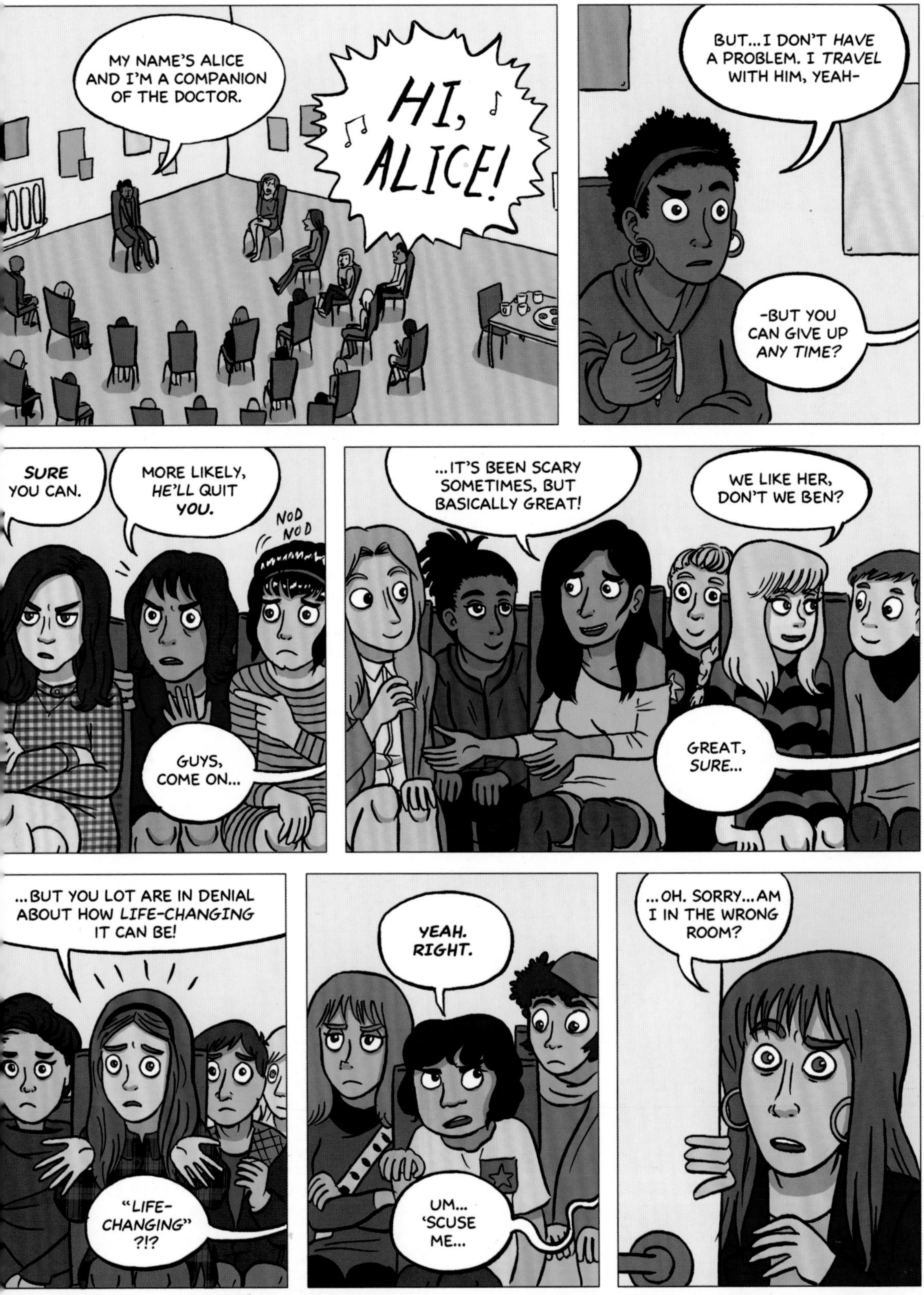
MY NAME'S ALICE AND I'M A COMPANION OF THE DOCTOR.
HI, ALICE!
BUT...I DON'T *HAVE* A PROBLEM. I *TRAVEL* WITH HIM, YEAH-
-BUT YOU CAN GIVE UP ANY TIME?
SURE YOU CAN.
MORE LIKELY, HE'LL QUIT *YOU.*
NOD NOD
GUYS, COME ON...
...IT'S BEEN SCARY SOMETIMES, BUT BASICALLY GREAT!
WE LIKE HER, DON'T WE BEN?
GREAT, *SURE*...
...BUT YOU LOT ARE IN DENIAL ABOUT HOW *LIFE-CHANGING* IT CAN BE!
"LIFE-CHANGING" ?!?
YEAH. RIGHT.
UM... 'SCUSE ME...
...OH. SORRY...AM I IN THE WRONG ROOM?

COVER 4

REGULAR Cover by Neil Edwards & Ivan Nunes

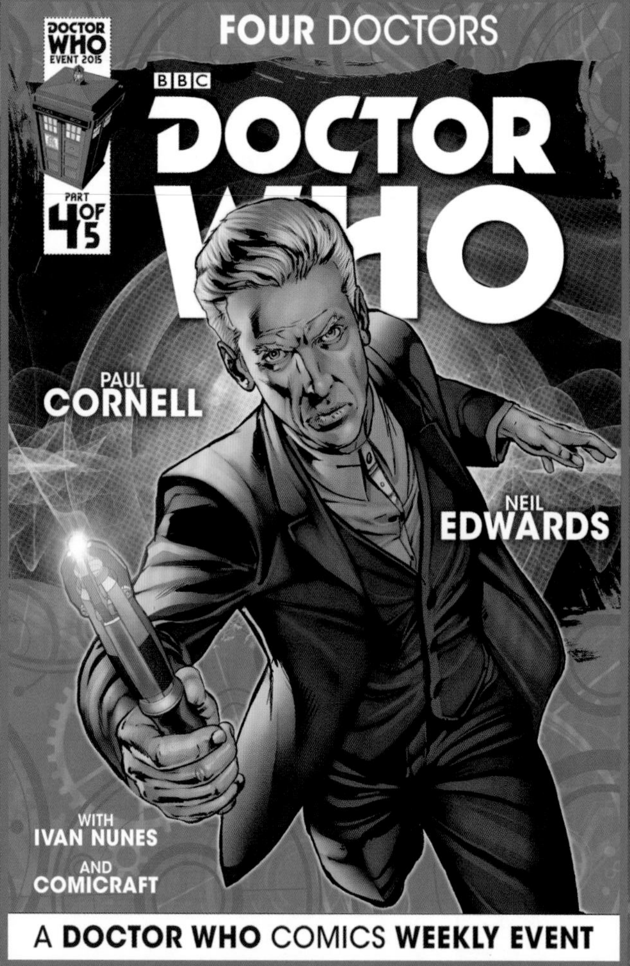
FOUR DOCTORS
DOCTOR WHO EVENT 2015
BBC
DOCTOR WHO
PART 4 OF 5
PAUL CORNELL
NEIL EDWARDS
WITH IVAN NUNES
AND COMICRAFT
A DOCTOR WHO COMICS WEEKLY EVENT

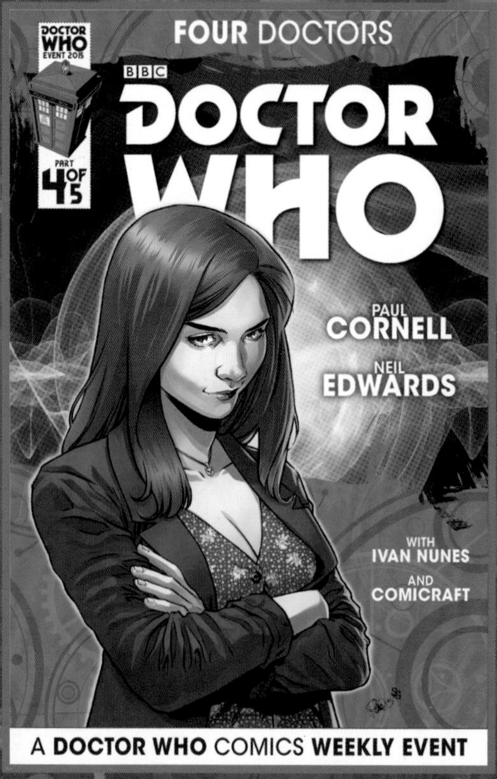
FOUR DOCTORS
DOCTOR WHO EVENT 2015
BBC
DOCTOR WHO
PART 4 OF 5
PAUL CORNELL
NEIL EDWARDS
WITH IVAN NUNES
AND COMICRAFT
A DOCTOR WHO COMICS WEEKLY EVENT

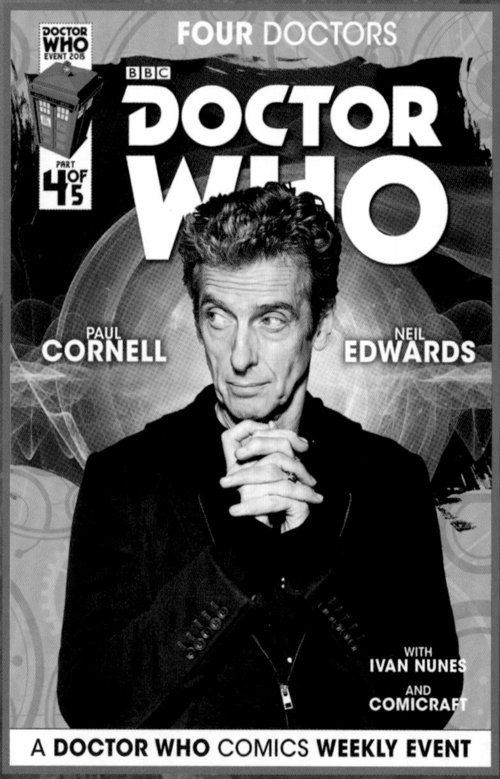
FOUR DOCTORS
DOCTOR WHO EVENT 2015
BBC
DOCTOR WHO
PART 4 OF 5
PAUL CORNELL
NEIL EDWARDS
WITH IVAN NUNES
AND COMICRAFT
A DOCTOR WHO COMICS WEEKLY EVENT

COMPANION Cover by Elena Casagrande, Eleonora Carlini & Claudia SG Iannicello

SUBSCRIPTION Cover by AJ & Rob Farmer

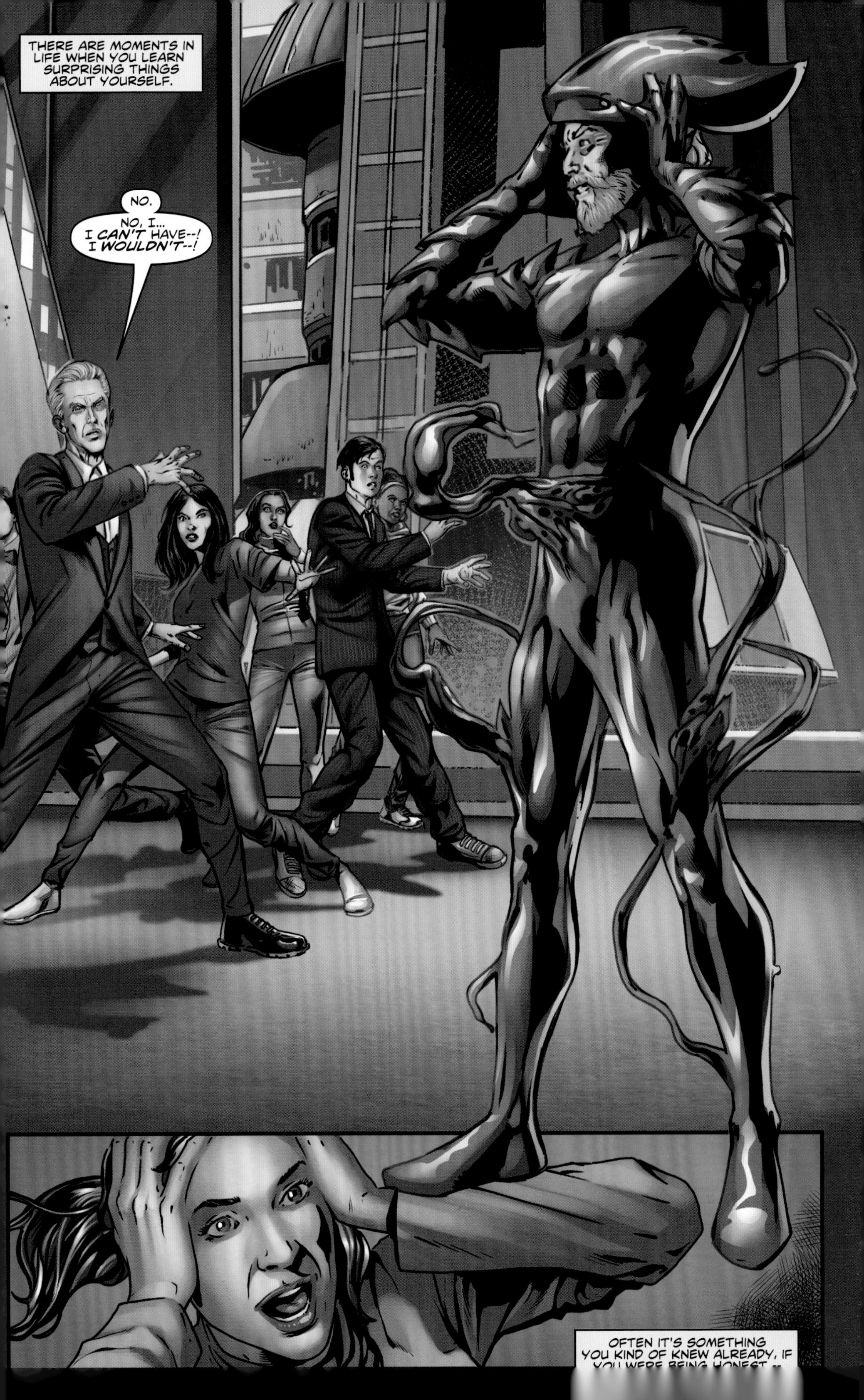

THERE ARE MOMENTS IN LIFE WHEN YOU LEARN SURPRISING THINGS ABOUT YOURSELF.
NO.
NO, I... I *CAN'T* HAVE--! I *WOULDN'T*--!
OFTEN IT'S SOMETHING YOU KIND OF KNEW ALREADY, IF

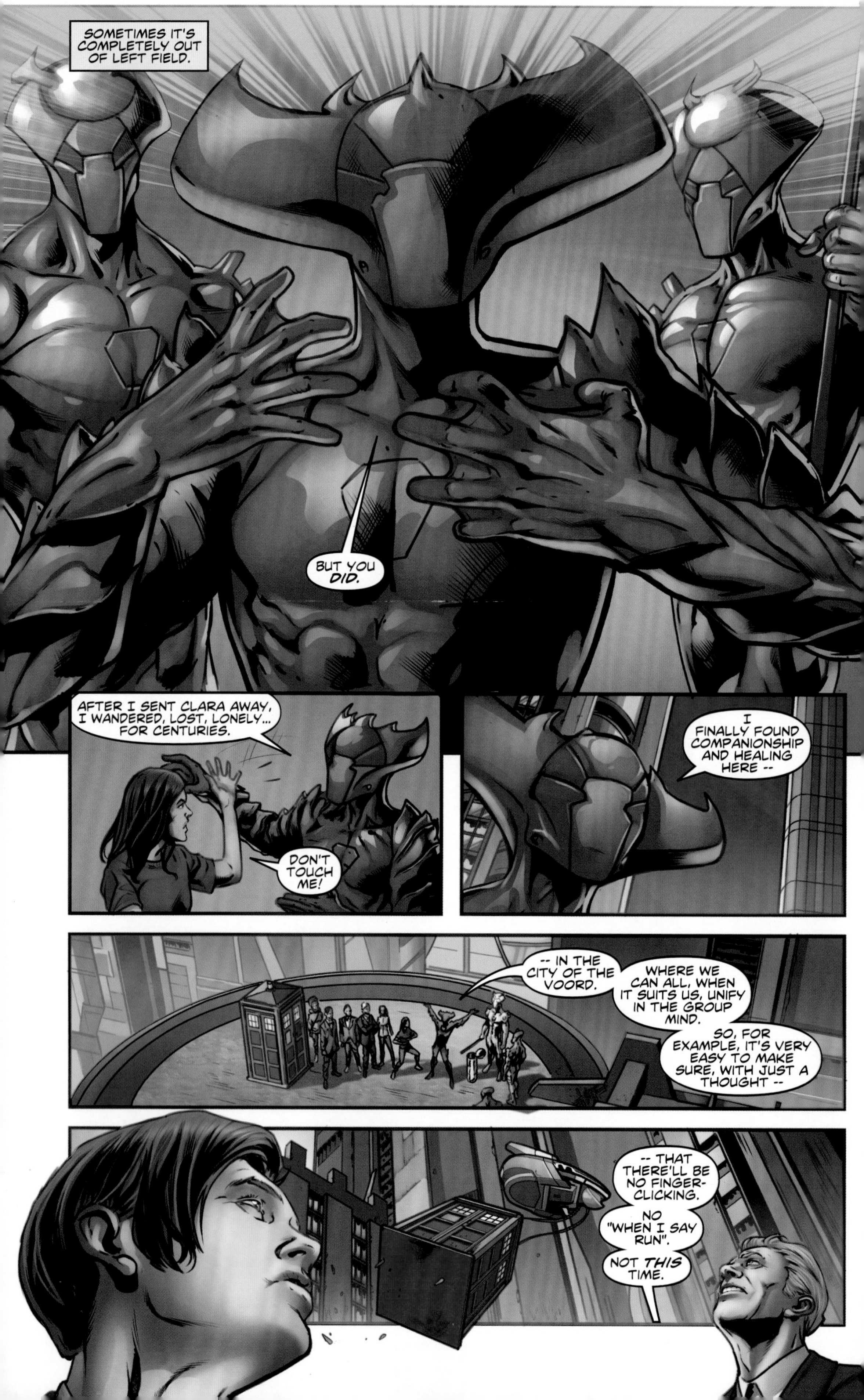

SOMETIMES IT'S COMPLETELY OUT OF LEFT FIELD.
BUT YOU DID.
AFTER I SENT CLARA AWAY, I WANDERED, LOST, LONELY... FOR CENTURIES.
DON'T TOUCH ME!
I FINALLY FOUND COMPANIONSHIP AND HEALING HERE --
-- IN THE CITY OF THE VOORD.
WHERE WE CAN ALL, WHEN IT SUITS US, UNIFY IN THE GROUP MIND.
SO, FOR EXAMPLE, IT'S VERY EASY TO MAKE SURE, WITH JUST A THOUGHT --
-- THAT THERE'LL BE NO FINGER-CLICKING.
NO "WHEN I SAY RUN".
NOT THIS TIME.

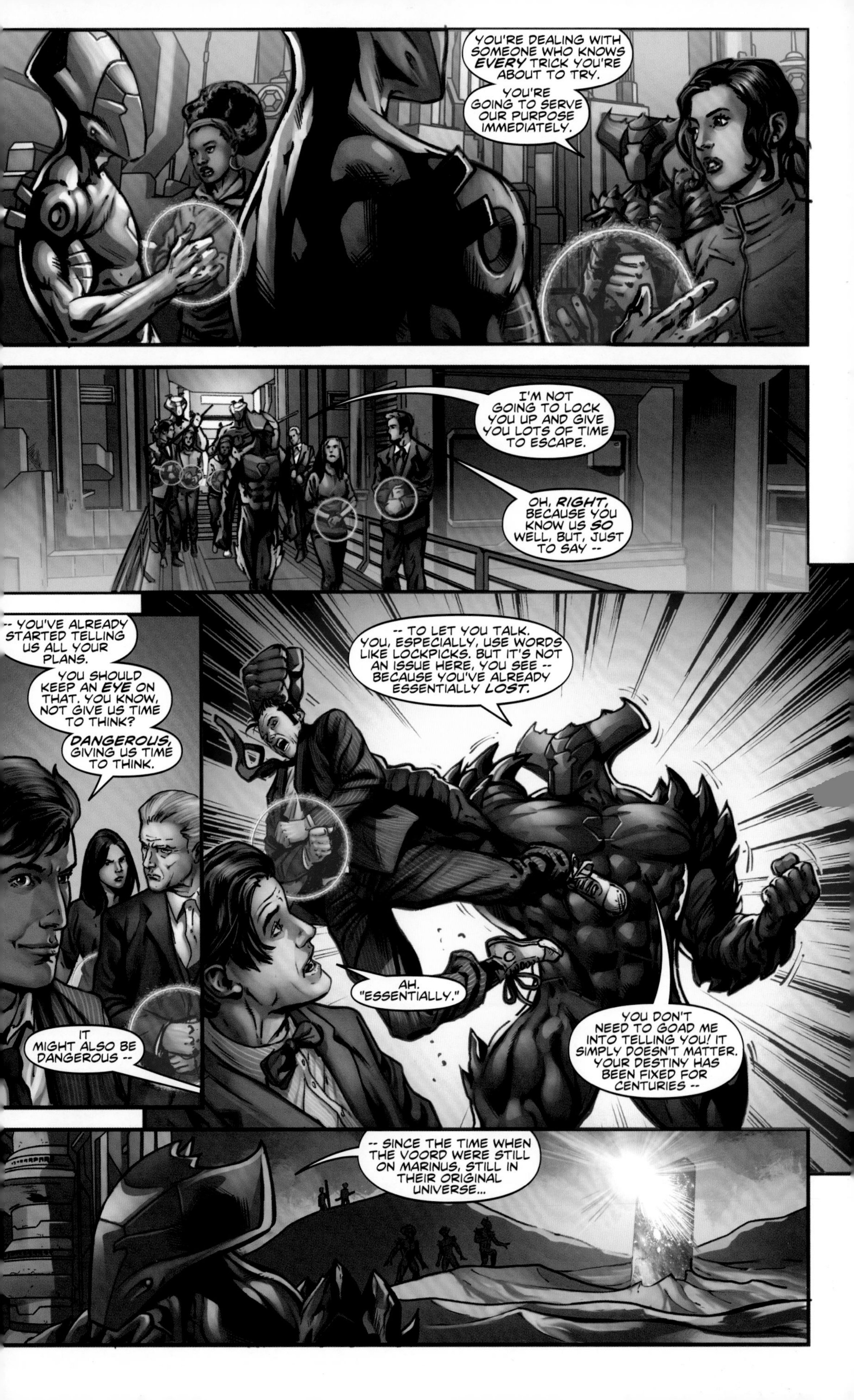
YOU'RE DEALING WITH SOMEONE WHO KNOWS EVERY TRICK YOU'RE ABOUT TO TRY.
YOU'RE GOING TO SERVE OUR PURPOSE IMMEDIATELY.
I'M NOT GOING TO LOCK YOU UP AND GIVE YOU LOTS OF TIME TO ESCAPE.
OH, RIGHT, BECAUSE YOU KNOW US SO WELL, BUT, JUST TO SAY --
-- YOU'VE ALREADY STARTED TELLING US ALL YOUR PLANS.
YOU SHOULD KEEP AN EYE ON THAT. YOU KNOW, NOT GIVE US TIME TO THINK?
DANGEROUS, GIVING US TIME TO THINK.
IT MIGHT ALSO BE DANGEROUS --
-- TO LET YOU TALK. YOU, ESPECIALLY, USE WORDS LIKE LOCKPICKS. BUT IT'S NOT AN ISSUE HERE, YOU SEE -- BECAUSE YOU'VE ALREADY ESSENTIALLY LOST.
AH. "ESSENTIALLY."
YOU DON'T NEED TO GOAD ME INTO TELLING YOU! IT SIMPLY DOESN'T MATTER. YOUR DESTINY HAS BEEN FIXED FOR CENTURIES --
-- SINCE THE TIME WHEN THE VOORD WERE STILL ON MARINUS, STILL IN THEIR ORIGINAL UNIVERSE...

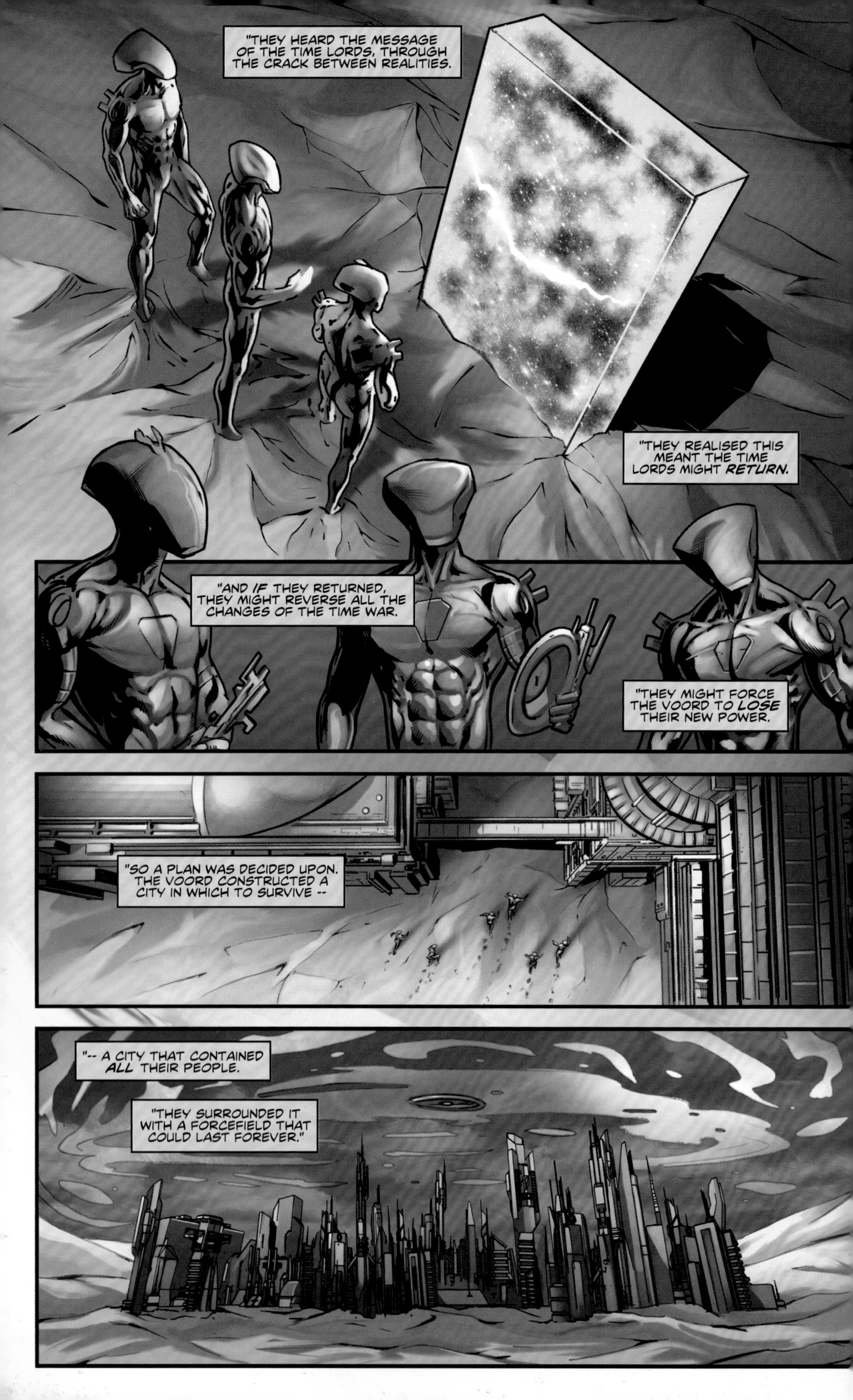
"THEY HEARD THE MESSAGE OF THE TIME LORDS, THROUGH THE CRACK BETWEEN REALITIES.
"THEY REALISED THIS MEANT THE TIME LORDS MIGHT RETURN.
"AND IF THEY RETURNED, THEY MIGHT REVERSE ALL THE CHANGES OF THE TIME WAR.
"THEY MIGHT FORCE THE VOORD TO LOSE THEIR NEW POWER.
"SO A PLAN WAS DECIDED UPON. THE VOORD CONSTRUCTED A CITY IN WHICH TO SURVIVE --
"-- A CITY THAT CONTAINED ALL THEIR PEOPLE.
"THEY SURROUNDED IT WITH A FORCEFIELD THAT COULD LAST FOREVER."

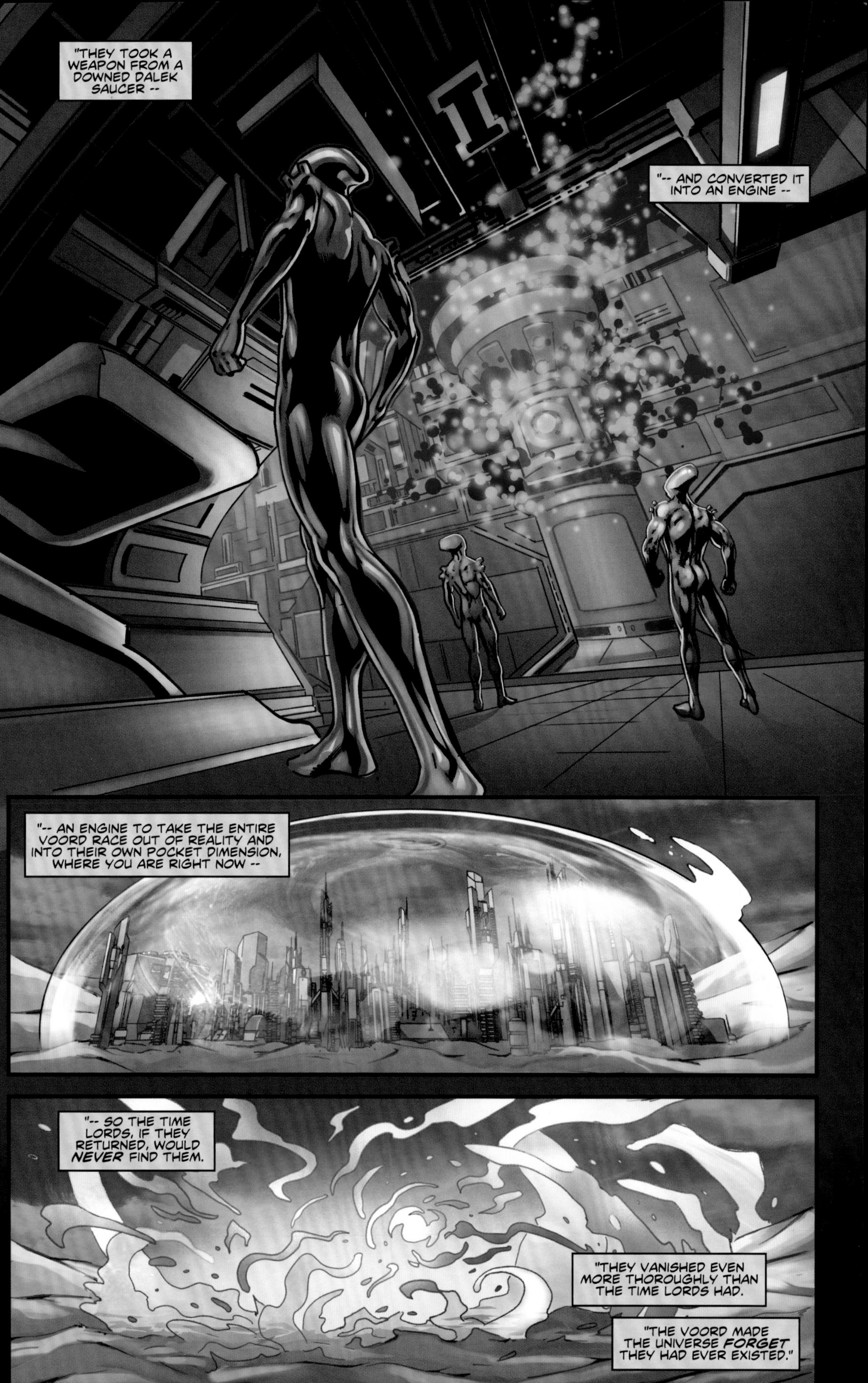
"THEY TOOK A WEAPON FROM A DOWNED DALEK SAUCER --
"-- AND CONVERTED IT INTO AN ENGINE --
"-- AN ENGINE TO TAKE THE ENTIRE VOORD RACE OUT OF REALITY AND INTO THEIR OWN POCKET DIMENSION, WHERE YOU ARE RIGHT NOW --
"-- SO THE TIME LORDS, IF THEY RETURNED, WOULD *NEVER* FIND THEM.
"THEY VANISHED EVEN MORE THOROUGHLY THAN THE TIME LORDS HAD.
"THE VOORD MADE THE UNIVERSE *FORGET* THEY HAD EVER EXISTED."

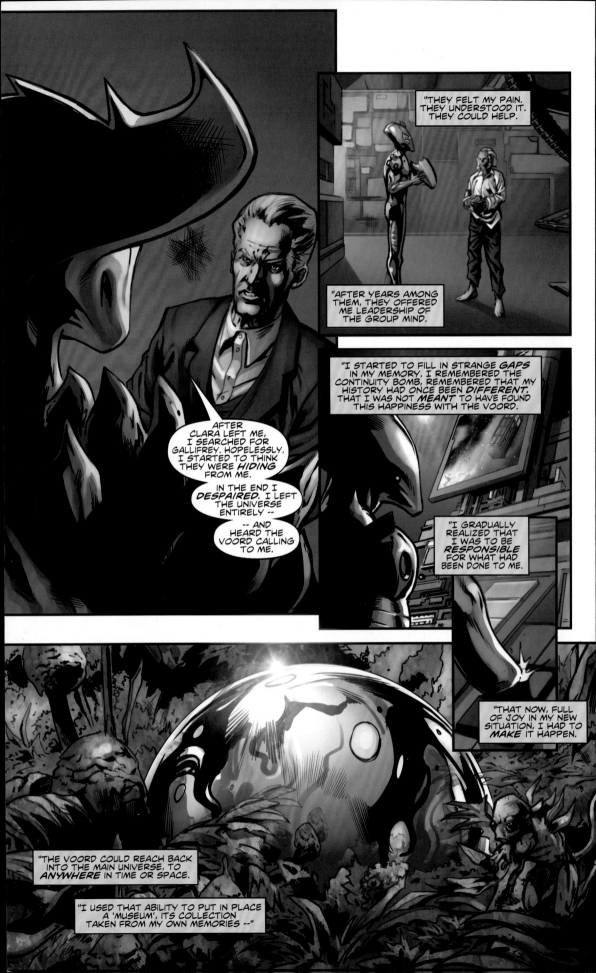

"THEY FELT MY PAIN. THEY UNDERSTOOD IT. THEY COULD HELP.

"AFTER YEARS AMONG THEM, THEY OFFERED ME LEADERSHIP OF THE GROUP MIND.

"I STARTED TO FILL IN STRANGE *GAPS* IN MY MEMORY. I REMEMBERED THE CONTINUITY BOMB, REMEMBERED THAT MY HISTORY HAD ONCE BEEN *DIFFERENT*. THAT I WAS NOT *MEANT* TO HAVE FOUND THIS HAPPINESS WITH THE VOORD.

"I GRADUALLY REALIZED THAT I WAS TO BE *RESPONSIBLE* FOR WHAT HAD BEEN DONE TO ME.

AFTER CLARA LEFT ME, I SEARCHED FOR GALLIFREY. HOPELESSLY. I STARTED TO THINK THEY WERE *HIDING* FROM ME.

IN THE END I *DESPAIRED*. I LEFT THE UNIVERSE ENTIRELY --

-- AND HEARD THE VOORD CALLING TO ME.

"THAT NOW, FULL OF JOY IN MY NEW SITUATION, I HAD TO *MAKE* IT HAPPEN.

"THE VOORD COULD REACH BACK INTO THE MAIN UNIVERSE, TO *ANYWHERE* IN TIME OR SPACE.

"I USED THAT ABILITY TO PUT IN PLACE A 'MUSEUM', ITS COLLECTION TAKEN FROM MY OWN MEMORIES --"

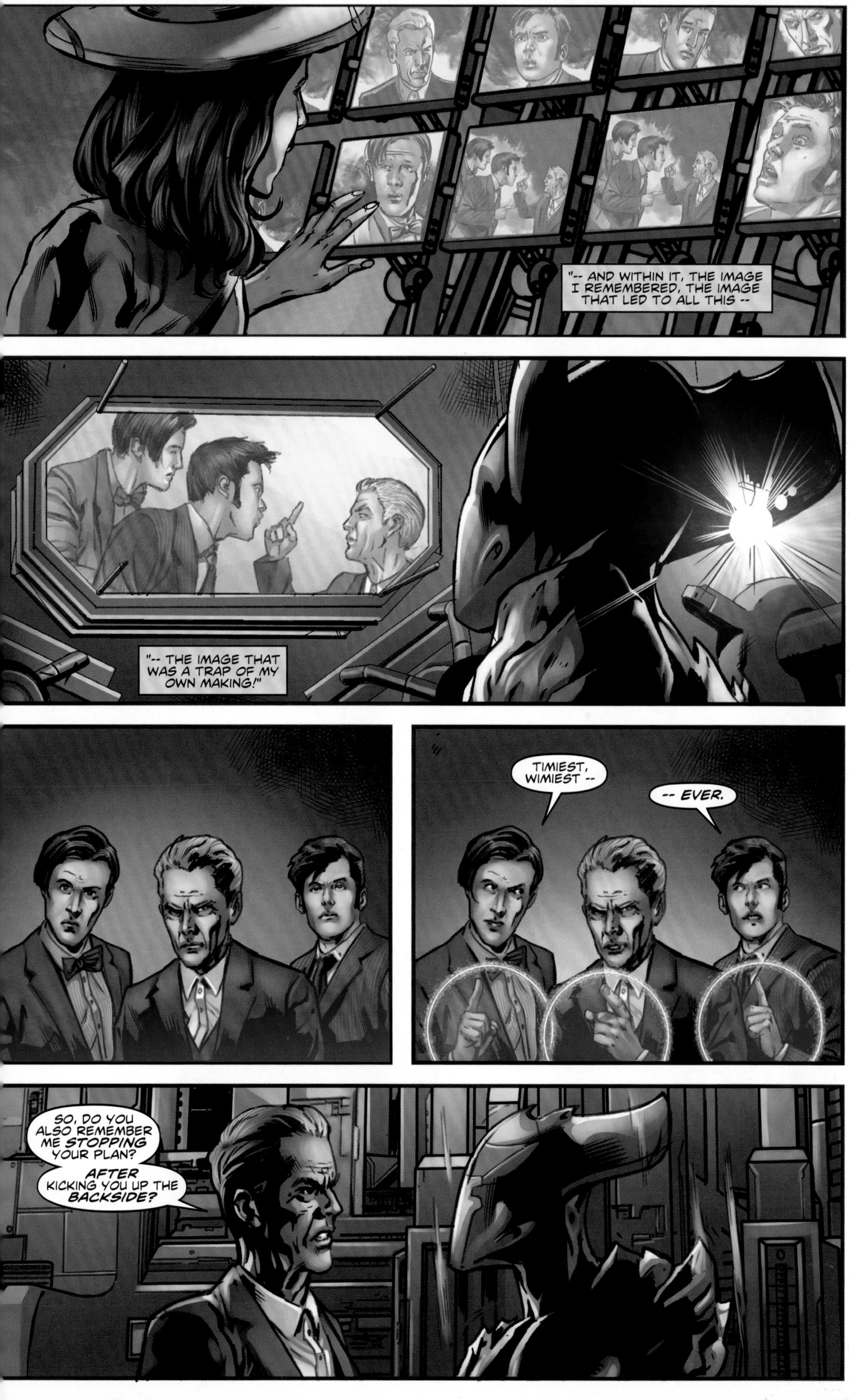
"-- AND WITHIN IT, THE IMAGE I REMEMBERED, THE IMAGE THAT LED TO ALL THIS --
"-- THE IMAGE THAT WAS A TRAP OF MY OWN MAKING!"
TIMIEST, WIMIEST --
-- EVER.
SO, DO YOU ALSO REMEMBER ME STOPPING YOUR PLAN?
AFTER KICKING YOU UP THE BACKSIDE?

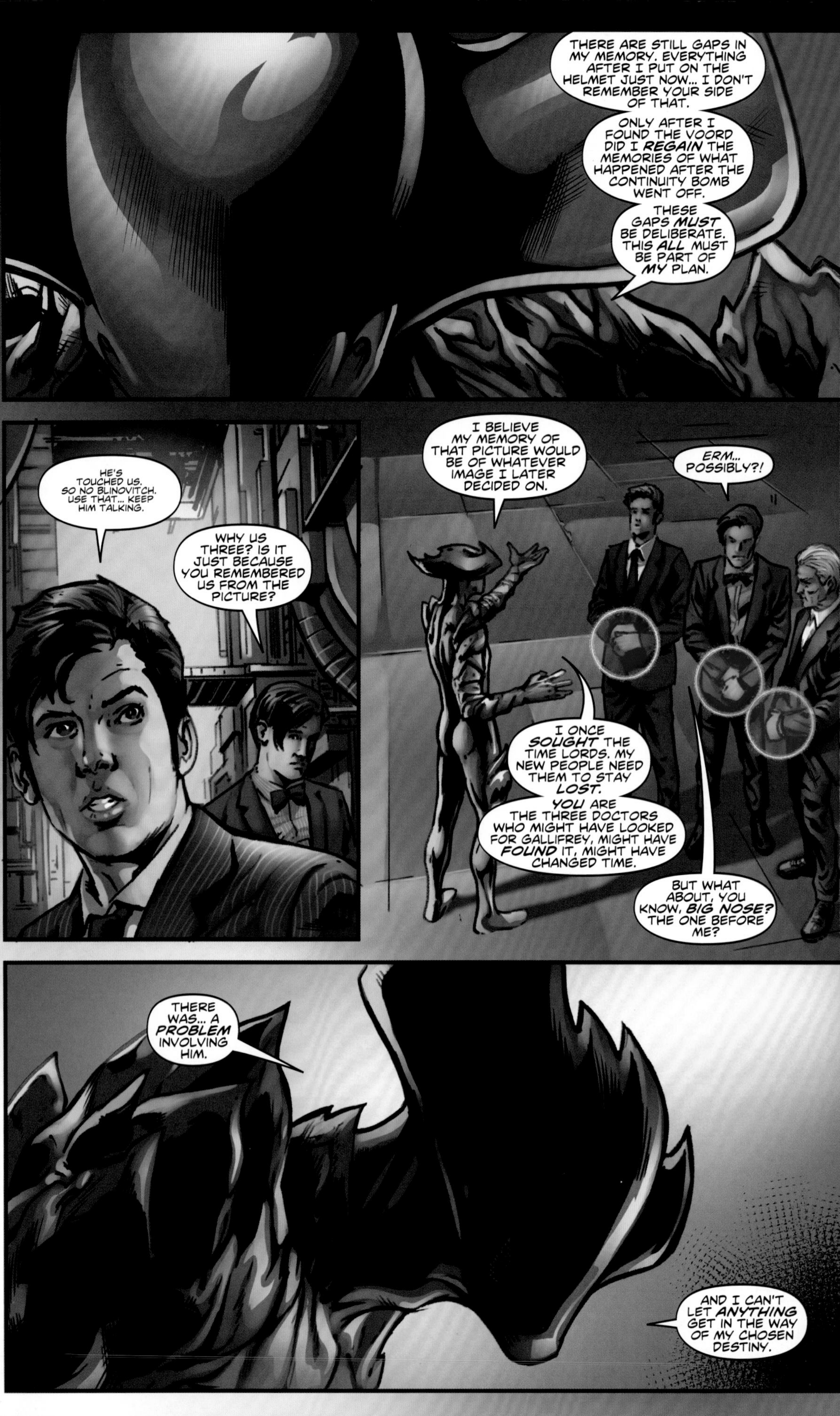
THERE ARE STILL GAPS IN MY MEMORY. EVERYTHING AFTER I PUT ON THE HELMET JUST NOW... I DON'T REMEMBER YOUR SIDE OF THAT.
ONLY AFTER I FOUND THE VOORD DID I REGAIN THE MEMORIES OF WHAT HAPPENED AFTER THE CONTINUITY BOMB WENT OFF.
THESE GAPS MUST BE DELIBERATE. THIS ALL MUST BE PART OF MY PLAN.
HE'S TOUCHED US. SO NO BLINOVITCH. USE THAT... KEEP HIM TALKING.
WHY US THREE? IS IT JUST BECAUSE YOU REMEMBERED US FROM THE PICTURE?
I BELIEVE MY MEMORY OF THAT PICTURE WOULD BE OF WHATEVER IMAGE I LATER DECIDED ON.
ERM... POSSIBLY?!
I ONCE SOUGHT THE TIME LORDS. MY NEW PEOPLE NEED THEM TO STAY LOST.
YOU ARE THE THREE DOCTORS WHO MIGHT HAVE LOOKED FOR GALLIFREY, MIGHT HAVE FOUND IT, MIGHT HAVE CHANGED TIME.
BUT WHAT ABOUT, YOU KNOW, BIG NOSE? THE ONE BEFORE ME?
THERE WAS... A PROBLEM INVOLVING HIM.
AND I CAN'T LET ANYTHING GET IN THE WAY OF MY CHOSEN DESTINY.

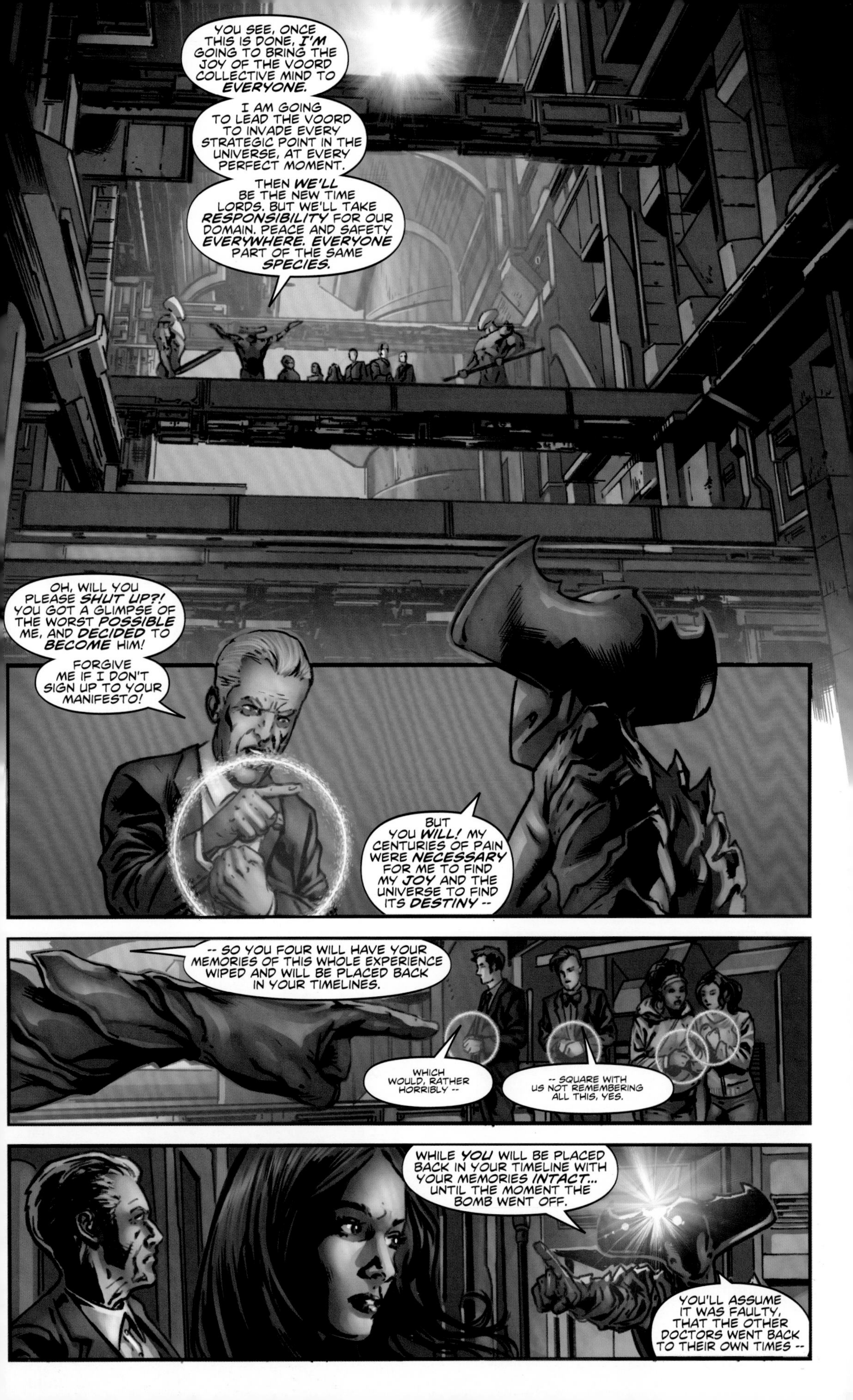

YOU SEE, ONCE THIS IS DONE, I'M GOING TO BRING THE JOY OF THE VOORD COLLECTIVE MIND TO EVERYONE.
I AM GOING TO LEAD THE VOORD TO INVADE EVERY STRATEGIC POINT IN THE UNIVERSE, AT EVERY PERFECT MOMENT.
THEN WE'LL BE THE NEW TIME LORDS. BUT WE'LL TAKE RESPONSIBILITY FOR OUR DOMAIN. PEACE AND SAFETY EVERYWHERE. EVERYONE PART OF THE SAME SPECIES.
OH, WILL YOU PLEASE SHUT UP?! YOU GOT A GLIMPSE OF THE WORST POSSIBLE ME, AND DECIDED TO BECOME HIM!
FORGIVE ME IF I DON'T SIGN UP TO YOUR MANIFESTO!
BUT YOU WILL! MY CENTURIES OF PAIN WERE NECESSARY FOR ME TO FIND MY JOY AND THE UNIVERSE TO FIND ITS DESTINY --
-- SO YOU FOUR WILL HAVE YOUR MEMORIES OF THIS WHOLE EXPERIENCE WIPED AND WILL BE PLACED BACK IN YOUR TIMELINES.
WHICH WOULD, RATHER HORRIBLY --
-- SQUARE WITH US NOT REMEMBERING ALL THIS, YES.
WHILE YOU WILL BE PLACED BACK IN YOUR TIMELINE WITH YOUR MEMORIES INTACT... UNTIL THE MOMENT THE BOMB WENT OFF.
YOU'LL ASSUME IT WAS FAULTY, THAT THE OTHER DOCTORS WENT BACK TO THEIR OWN TIMES --

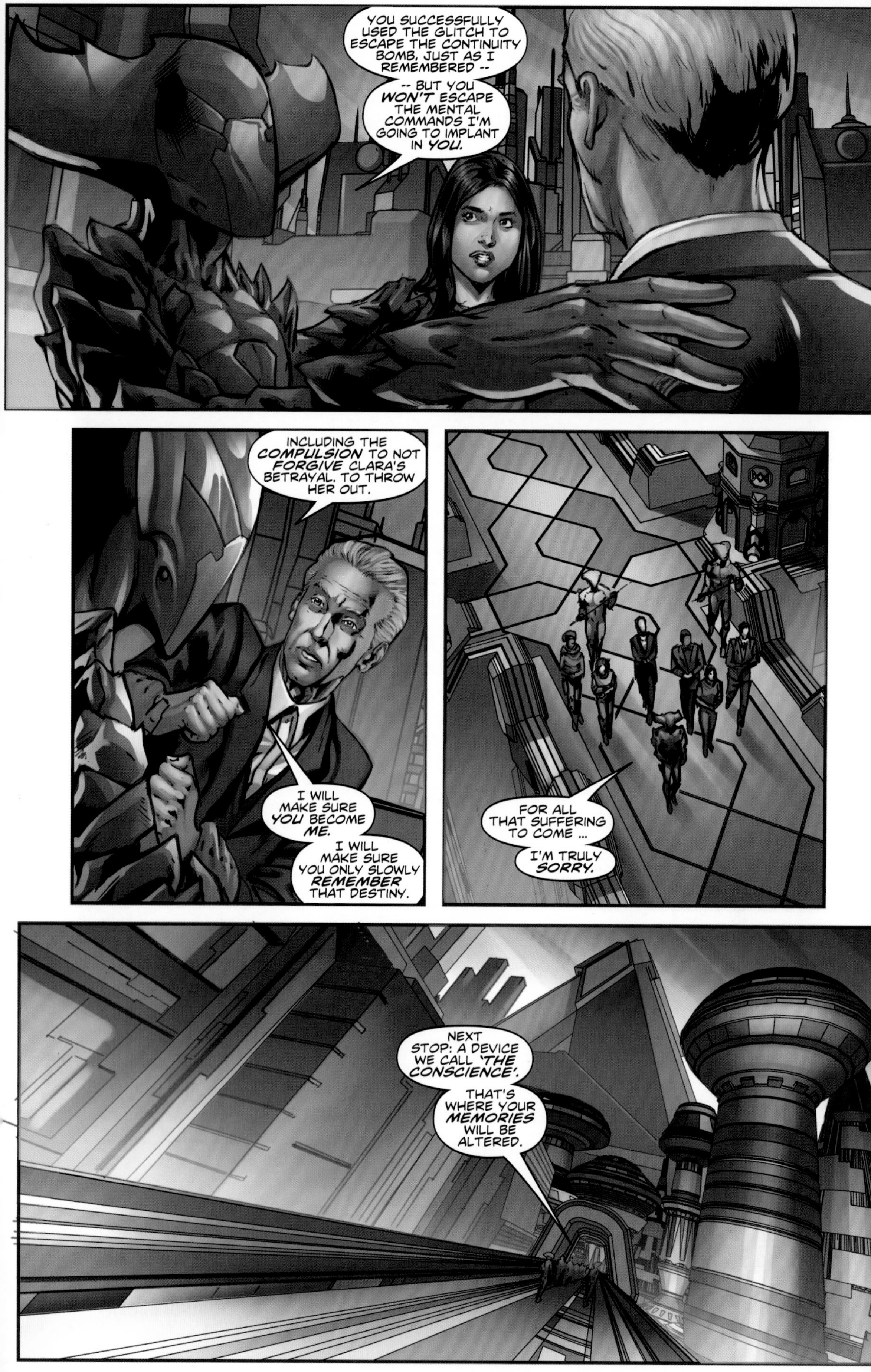
YOU SUCCESSFULLY USED THE GLITCH TO ESCAPE THE CONTINUITY BOMB, JUST AS I REMEMBERED --
-- BUT YOU WON'T ESCAPE THE MENTAL COMMANDS I'M GOING TO IMPLANT IN YOU.
INCLUDING THE COMPULSION TO NOT FORGIVE CLARA'S BETRAYAL. TO THROW HER OUT.
I WILL MAKE SURE YOU BECOME ME.
I WILL MAKE SURE YOU ONLY SLOWLY REMEMBER THAT DESTINY.
FOR ALL THAT SUFFERING TO COME ...
I'M TRULY SORRY.
NEXT STOP: A DEVICE WE CALL 'THE CONSCIENCE'.
THAT'S WHERE YOUR MEMORIES WILL BE ALTERED.

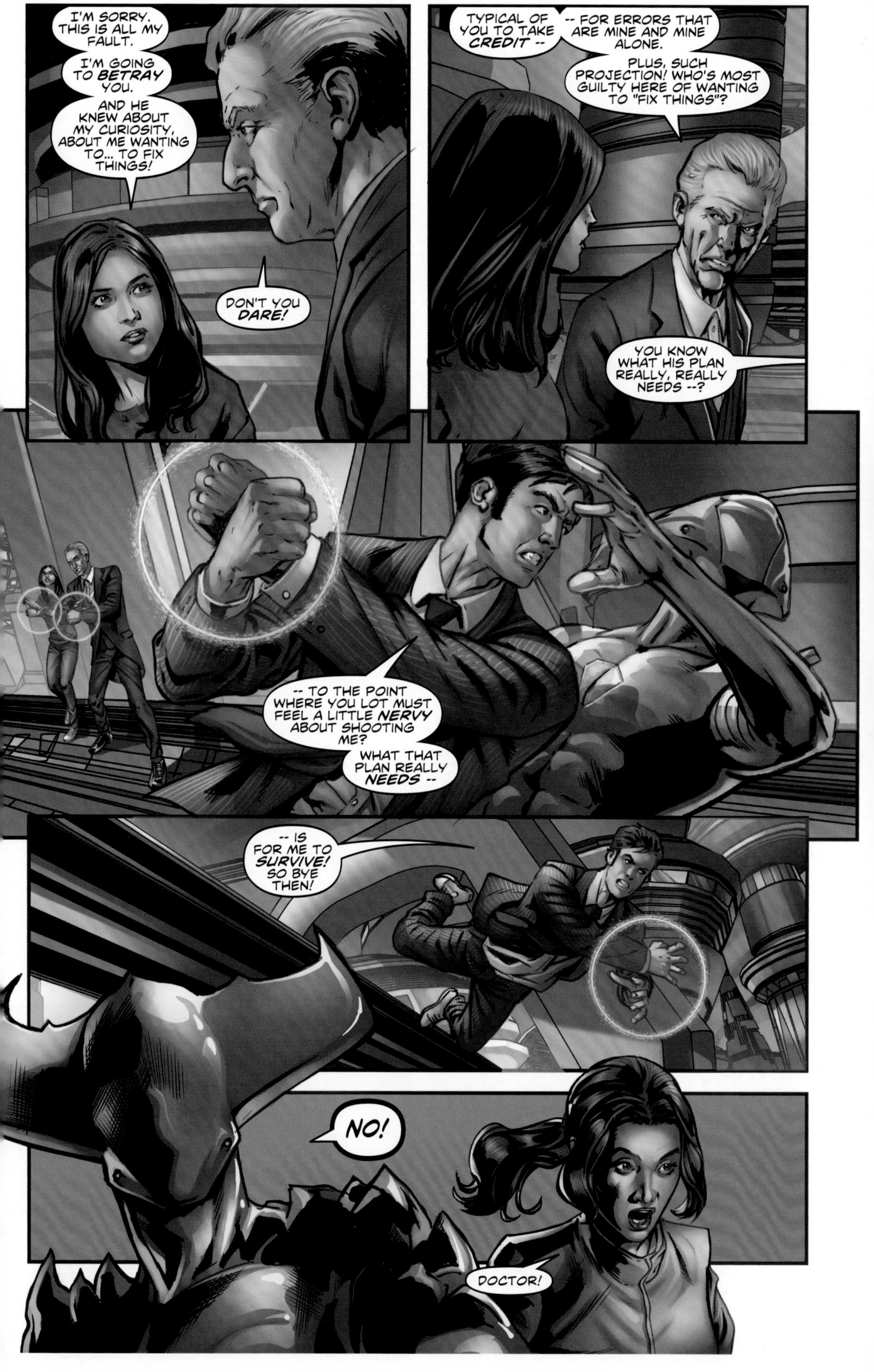

I'M SORRY. THIS IS ALL MY FAULT.
I'M GOING TO BETRAY YOU.
AND HE KNEW ABOUT MY CURIOSITY, ABOUT ME WANTING TO... TO FIX THINGS!
DON'T YOU DARE!
TYPICAL OF YOU TO TAKE CREDIT --
-- FOR ERRORS THAT ARE MINE AND MINE ALONE.
PLUS, SUCH PROJECTION! WHO'S MOST GUILTY HERE OF WANTING TO "FIX THINGS"?
YOU KNOW WHAT HIS PLAN REALLY, REALLY NEEDS --?
-- TO THE POINT WHERE YOU LOT MUST FEEL A LITTLE NERVY ABOUT SHOOTING ME?
WHAT THAT PLAN REALLY NEEDS --
-- IS FOR ME TO SURVIVE! SO BYE THEN!
NO!
DOCTOR!

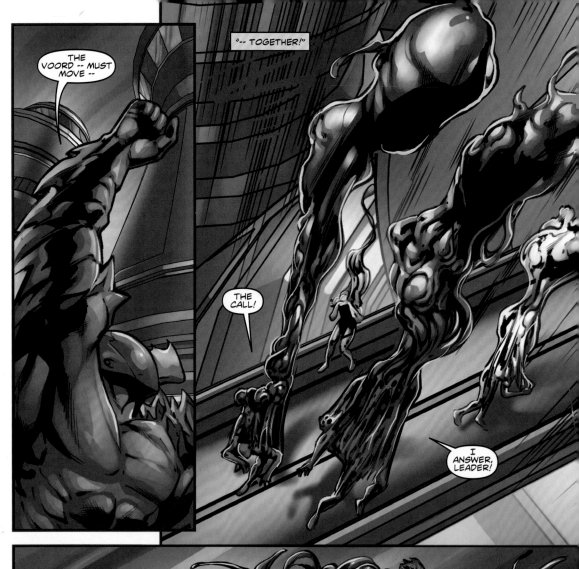

THE VOORD -- MUST MOVE --

"-- TOGETHER!"

THE CALL!

I ANSWER, LEADER!

PHEW! I THANK YOU --

"-- FOR YOUR HELP WITH THAT LITTLE DISTRACTION!"

HE'S FINE! HE KNEW WHAT HE WAS DOING, AS MUCH AS WE EVER DO, AH, YES, TOOK ME A FEW MINUTES TO EXAMINE THE TECH --

-- BUT NOW, WHILE THIS CHAP IS BUSY JOINING IN WITH THE GROUP MIND...

THERE WE GO! WHEN I SAY --

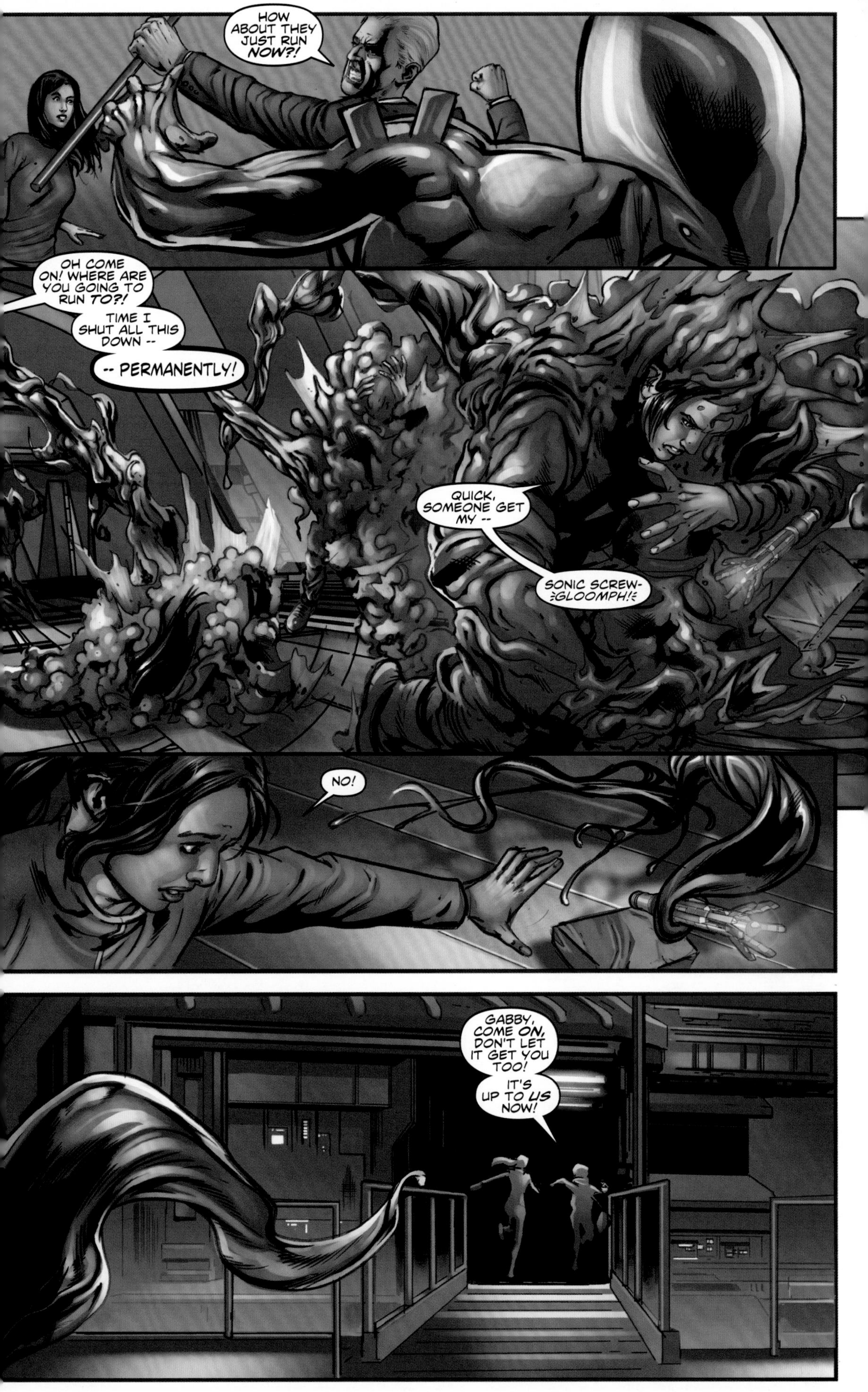
HOW ABOUT THEY JUST RUN NOW?!
OH COME ON! WHERE ARE YOU GOING TO RUN TO?!
TIME I SHUT ALL THIS DOWN --
-- PERMANENTLY!
QUICK, SOMEONE GET MY --
SONIC SCREW- GLOOMPH!
NO!
GABBY, COME ON, DON'T LET IT GET YOU TOO!
IT'S UP TO US NOW!

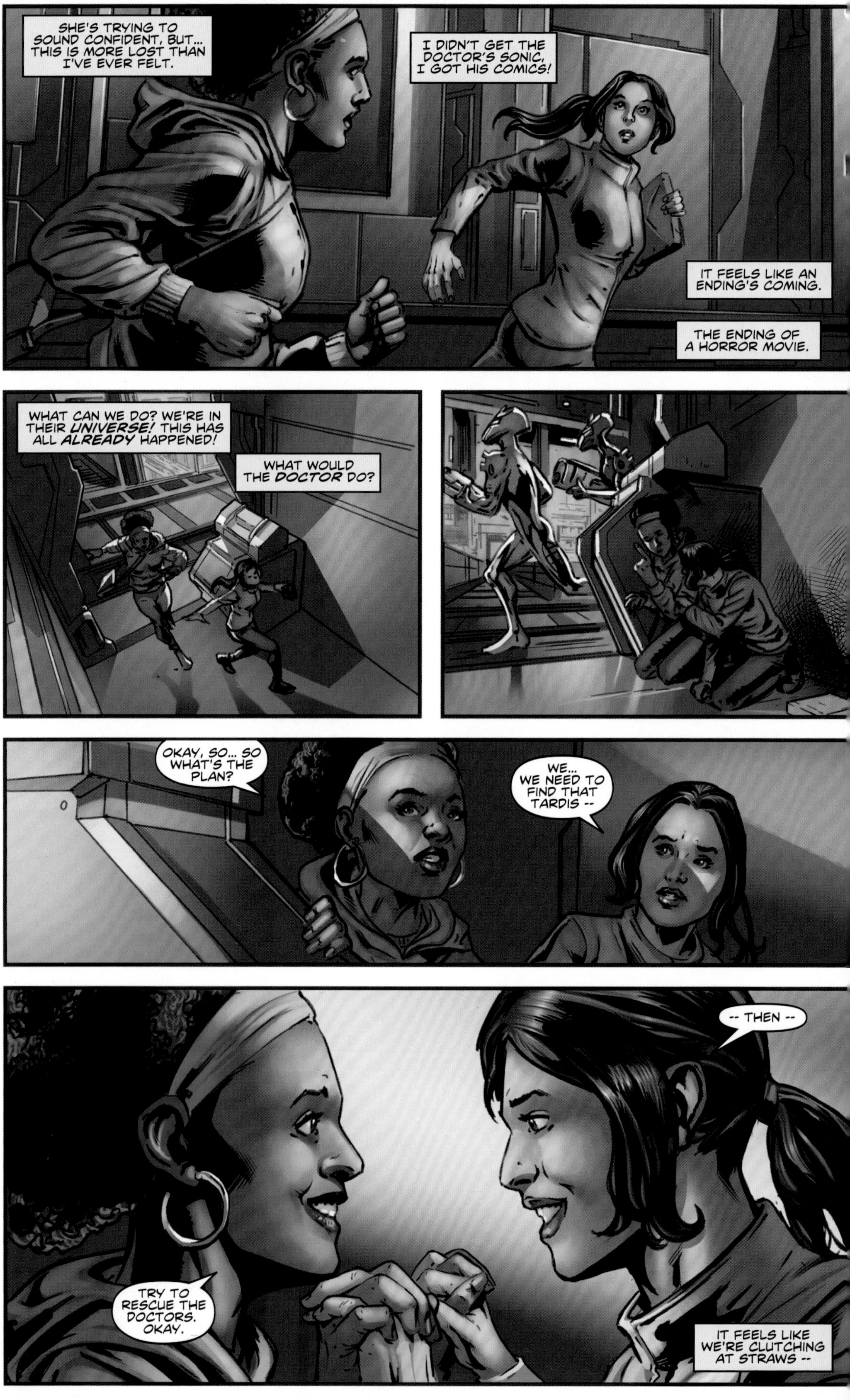
SHE'S TRYING TO SOUND CONFIDENT, BUT... THIS IS MORE LOST THAN I'VE EVER FELT.
I DIDN'T GET THE DOCTOR'S SONIC, I GOT HIS COMICS!
IT FEELS LIKE AN ENDING'S COMING.
THE ENDING OF A HORROR MOVIE.
WHAT CAN WE DO? WE'RE IN THEIR UNIVERSE! THIS HAS ALL ALREADY HAPPENED!
WHAT WOULD THE DOCTOR DO?
OKAY, SO... SO WHAT'S THE PLAN?
WE... WE NEED TO FIND THAT TARDIS --
-- THEN --
TRY TO RESCUE THE DOCTORS. OKAY.
IT FEELS LIKE WE'RE CLUTCHING AT STRAWS --

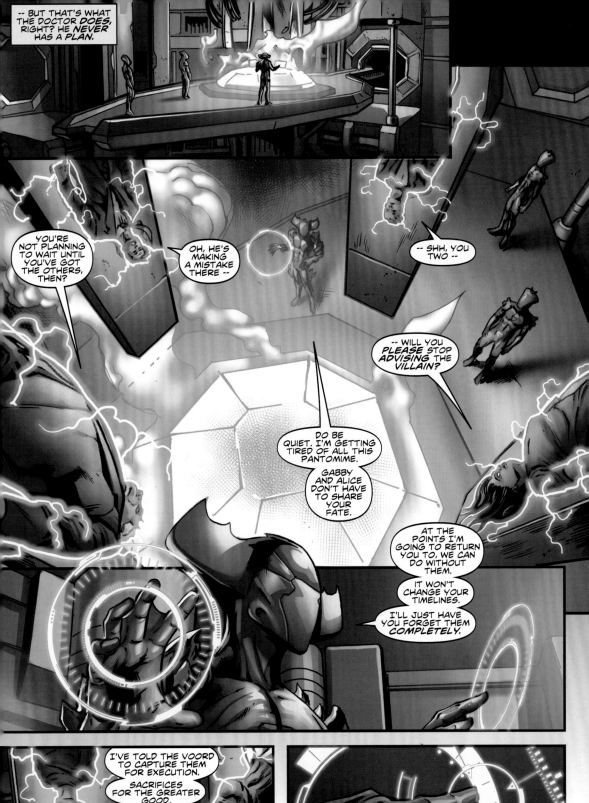

-- BUT THAT'S WHAT THE DOCTOR *DOES*, RIGHT? HE *NEVER* HAS A *PLAN.*

YOU'RE NOT PLANNING TO WAIT UNTIL YOU'VE GOT THE OTHERS, THEN?

OH, HE'S MAKING A MISTAKE THERE --

-- SHH, YOU TWO --

-- WILL YOU *PLEASE* STOP ADVISING THE *VILLAIN?*

DO BE QUIET. I'M GETTING TIRED OF ALL THIS PANTOMIME.

GABBY AND ALICE DON'T HAVE TO SHARE YOUR FATE.

AT THE POINTS I'M GOING TO RETURN YOU TO, WE CAN DO WITHOUT THEM.

IT WON'T CHANGE YOUR TIMELINES.

I'LL JUST HAVE YOU FORGET THEM *COMPLETELY.*

I'VE TOLD THE VOORD TO CAPTURE THEM FOR EXECUTION.

SACRIFICES FOR THE GREATER GOOD.

YOU--!

NO MORE *TALK.*

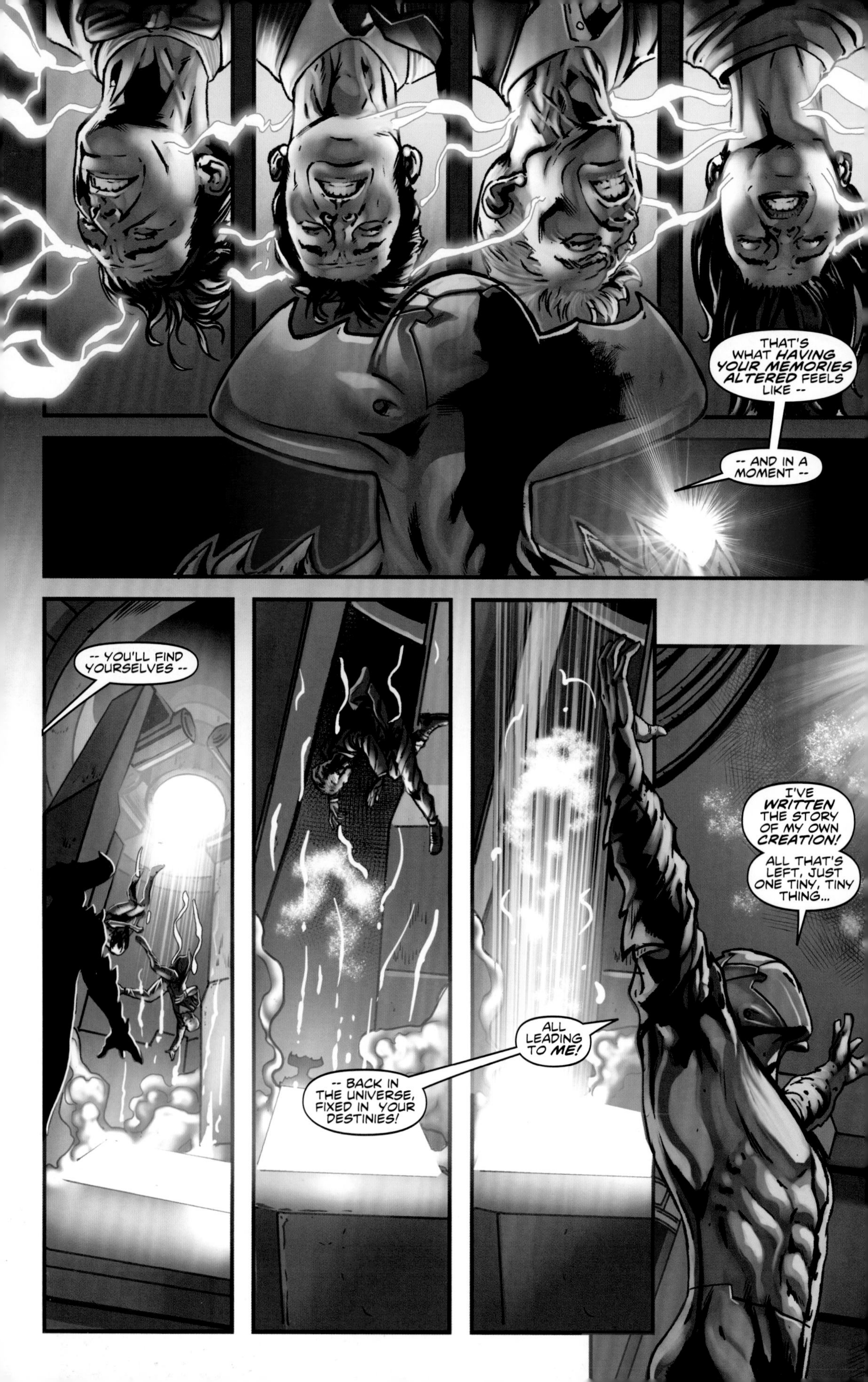
THAT'S WHAT HAVING YOUR MEMORIES ALTERED FEELS LIKE --
-- AND IN A MOMENT --
-- YOU'LL FIND YOURSELVES --
-- BACK IN THE UNIVERSE, FIXED IN YOUR DESTINIES!
ALL LEADING TO ME!
I'VE WRITTEN THE STORY OF MY OWN CREATION!
ALL THAT'S LEFT, JUST ONE TINY, TINY THING...

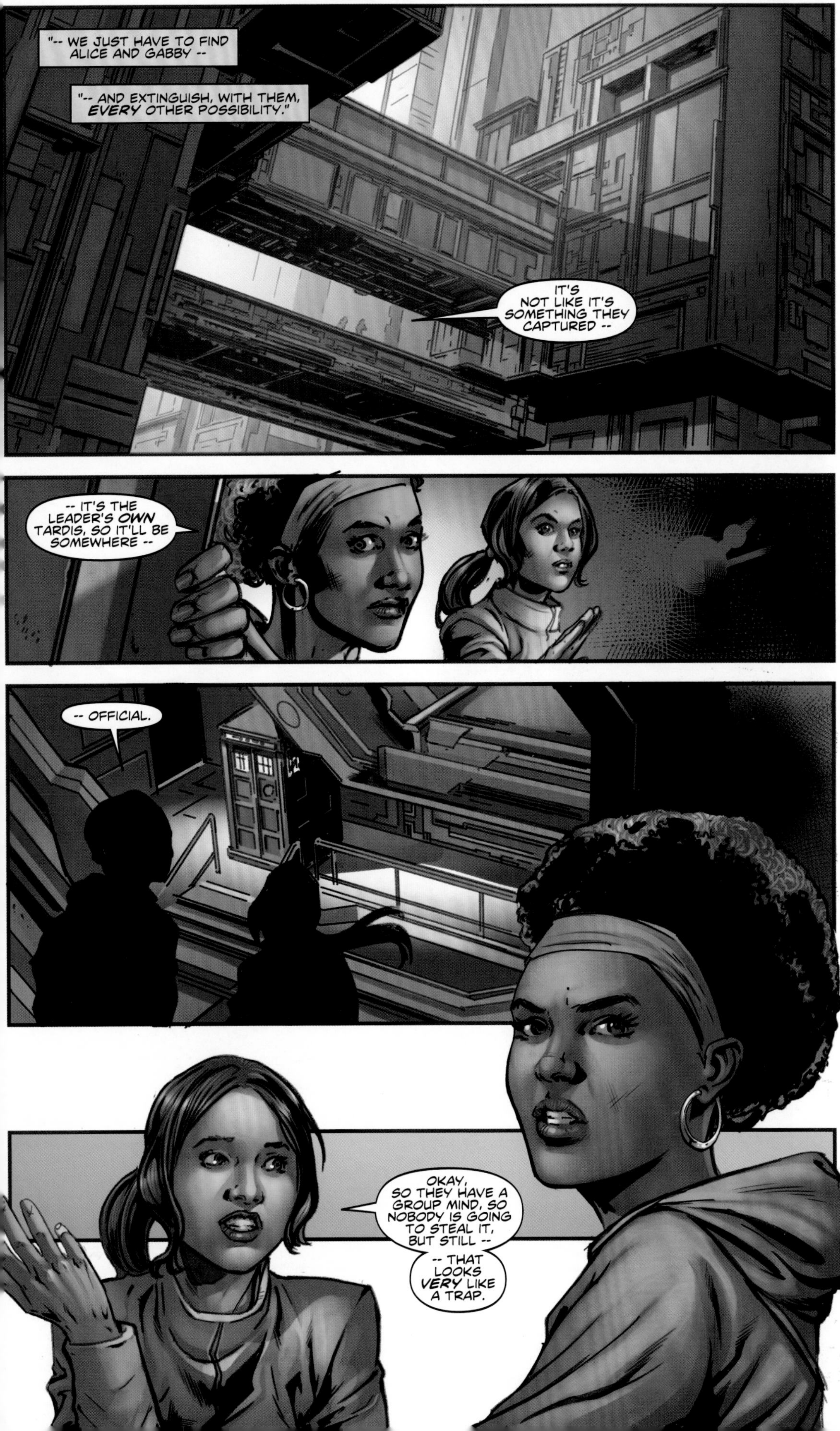
"-- WE JUST HAVE TO FIND ALICE AND GABBY --
"-- AND EXTINGUISH, WITH THEM, EVERY OTHER POSSIBILITY."
IT'S NOT LIKE IT'S SOMETHING THEY CAPTURED --
-- IT'S THE LEADER'S OWN TARDIS, SO IT'LL BE SOMEWHERE --
-- OFFICIAL.
OKAY, SO THEY HAVE A GROUP MIND, SO NOBODY IS GOING TO STEAL IT, BUT STILL --
-- THAT LOOKS VERY LIKE A TRAP.

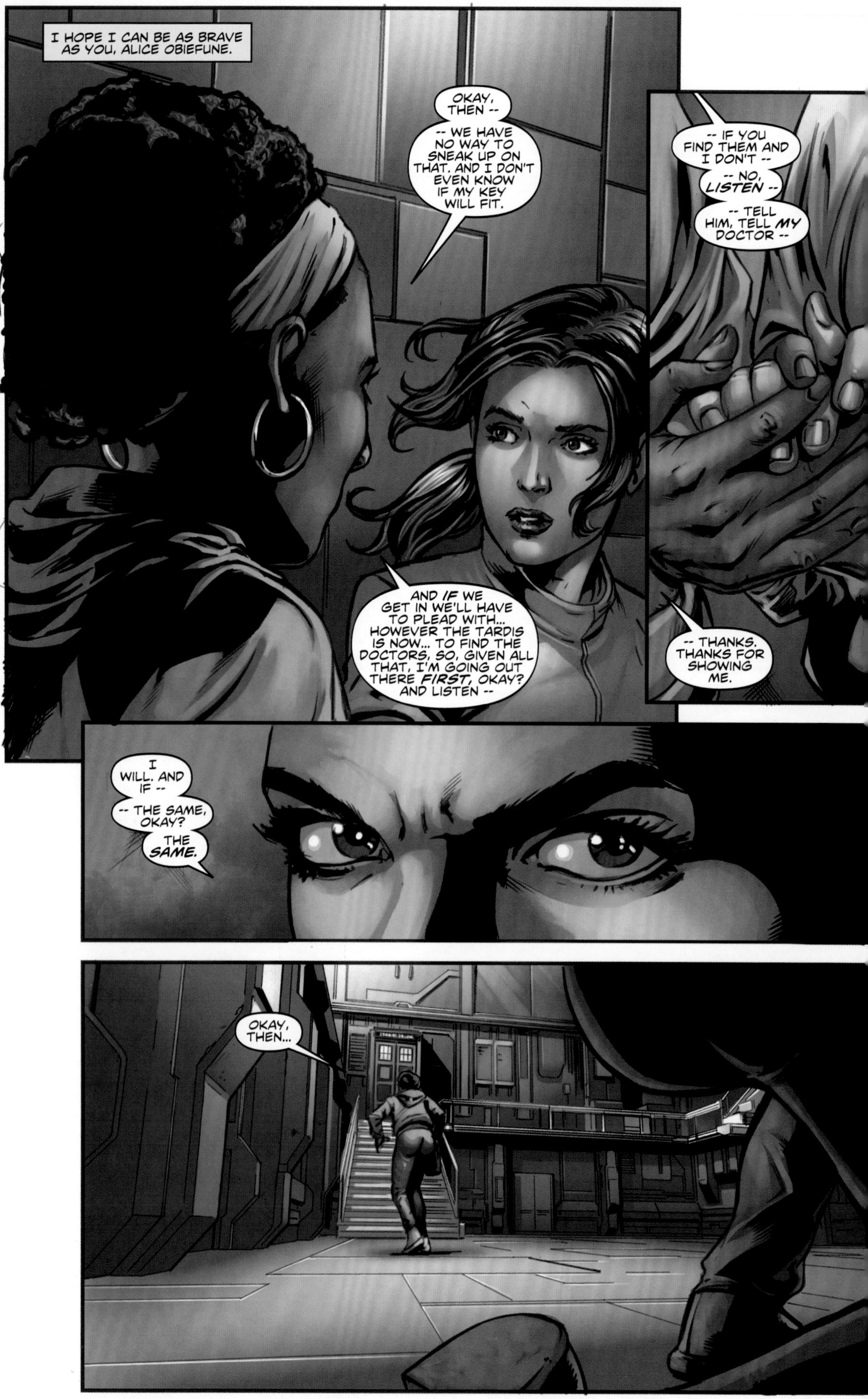
I HOPE I CAN BE AS BRAVE AS YOU, ALICE OBIEFUNE.
OKAY, THEN --
-- WE HAVE NO WAY TO SNEAK UP ON THAT. AND I DON'T EVEN KNOW IF MY KEY WILL FIT.
AND IF WE GET IN WE'LL HAVE TO PLEAD WITH... HOWEVER THE TARDIS IS NOW... TO FIND THE DOCTORS, SO, GIVEN ALL THAT, I'M GOING OUT THERE FIRST, OKAY? AND LISTEN --
-- IF YOU FIND THEM AND I DON'T --
-- NO, LISTEN --
-- TELL HIM, TELL MY DOCTOR --
-- THANKS. THANKS FOR SHOWING ME.
I WILL. AND IF --
-- THE SAME, OKAY?
THE SAME.
OKAY, THEN...

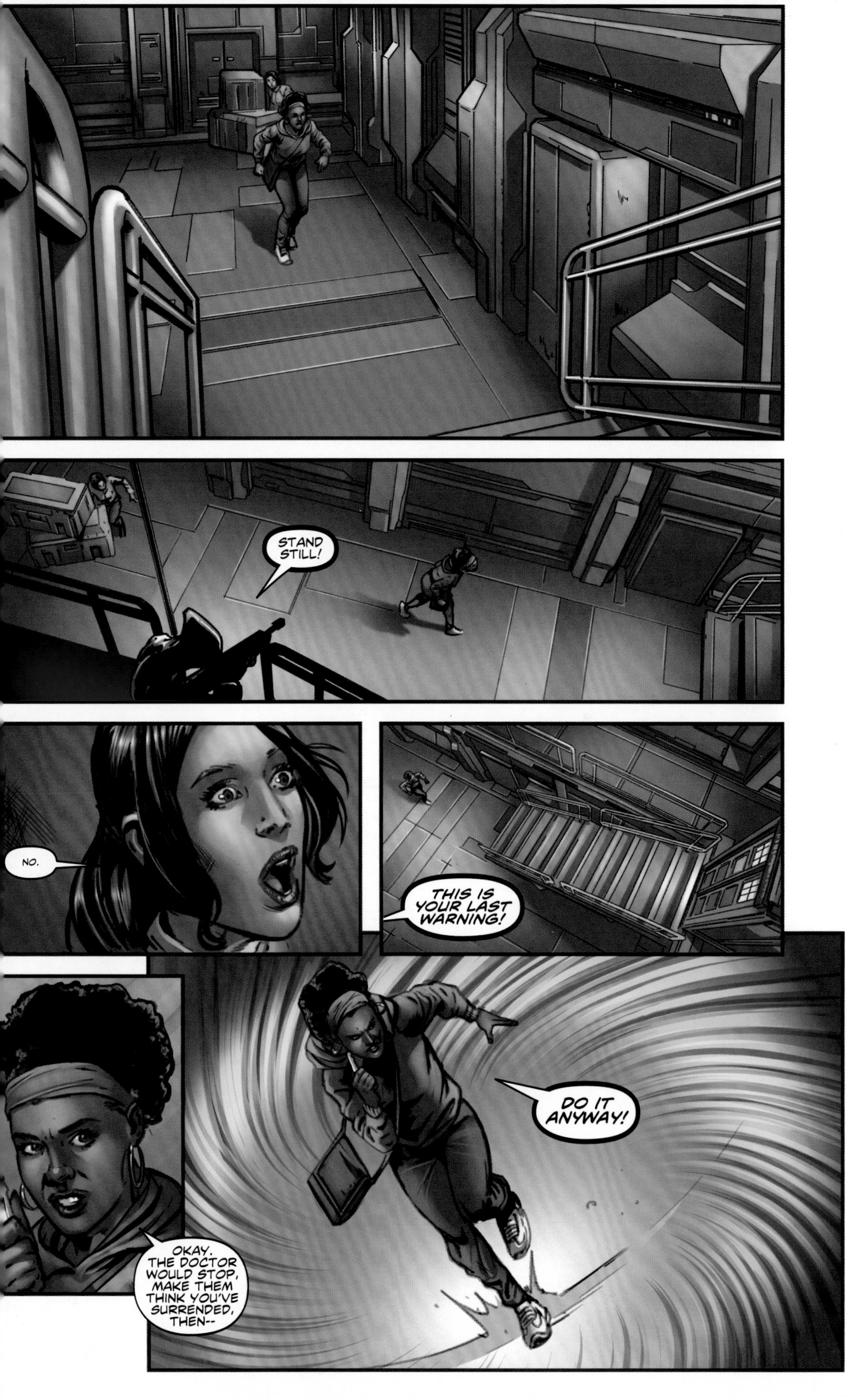
STAND STILL!
NO.
THIS IS YOUR LAST WARNING!
OKAY. THE DOCTOR WOULD STOP, MAKE THEM THINK YOU'VE SURRENDED, THEN--
DO IT ANYWAY!

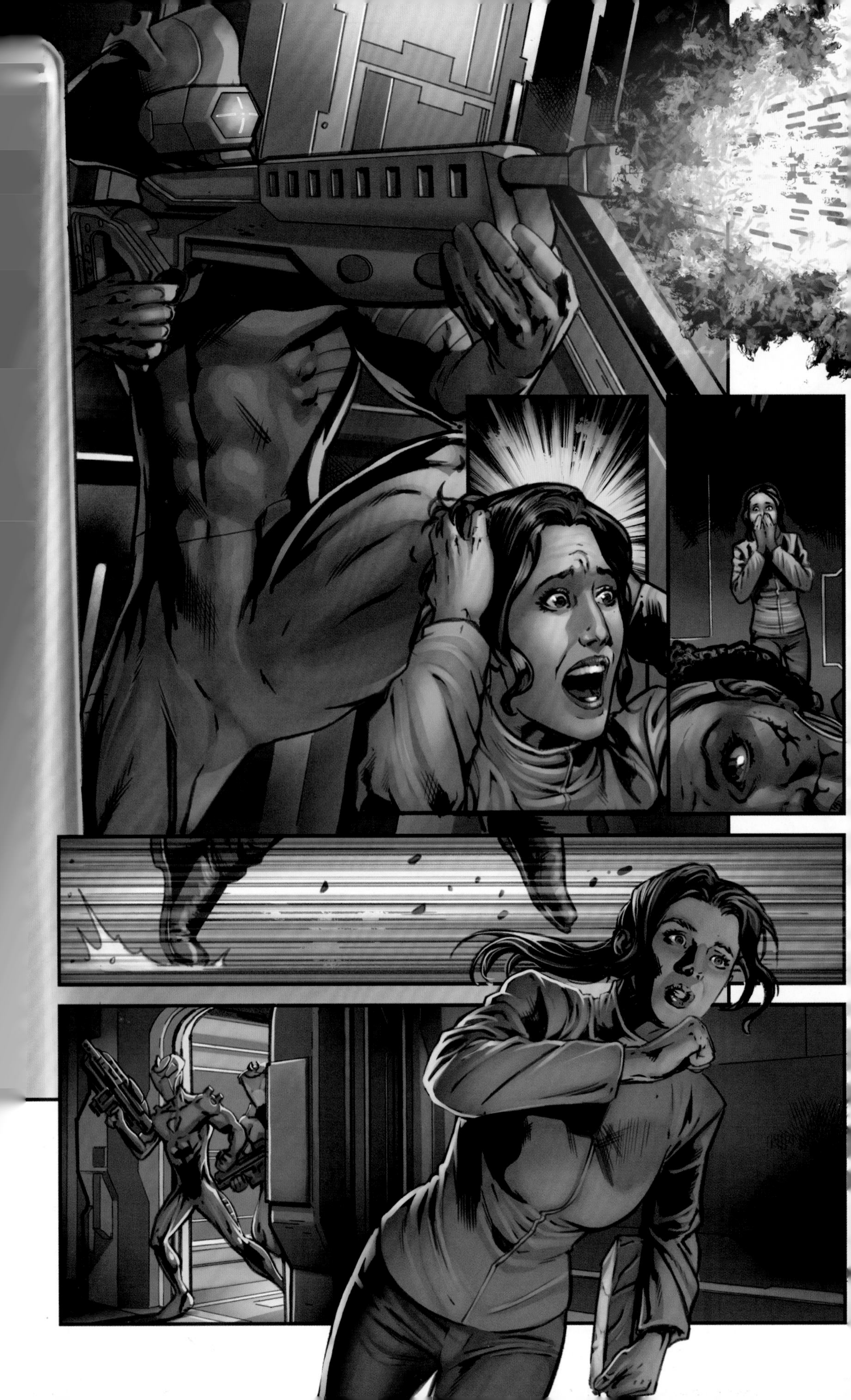

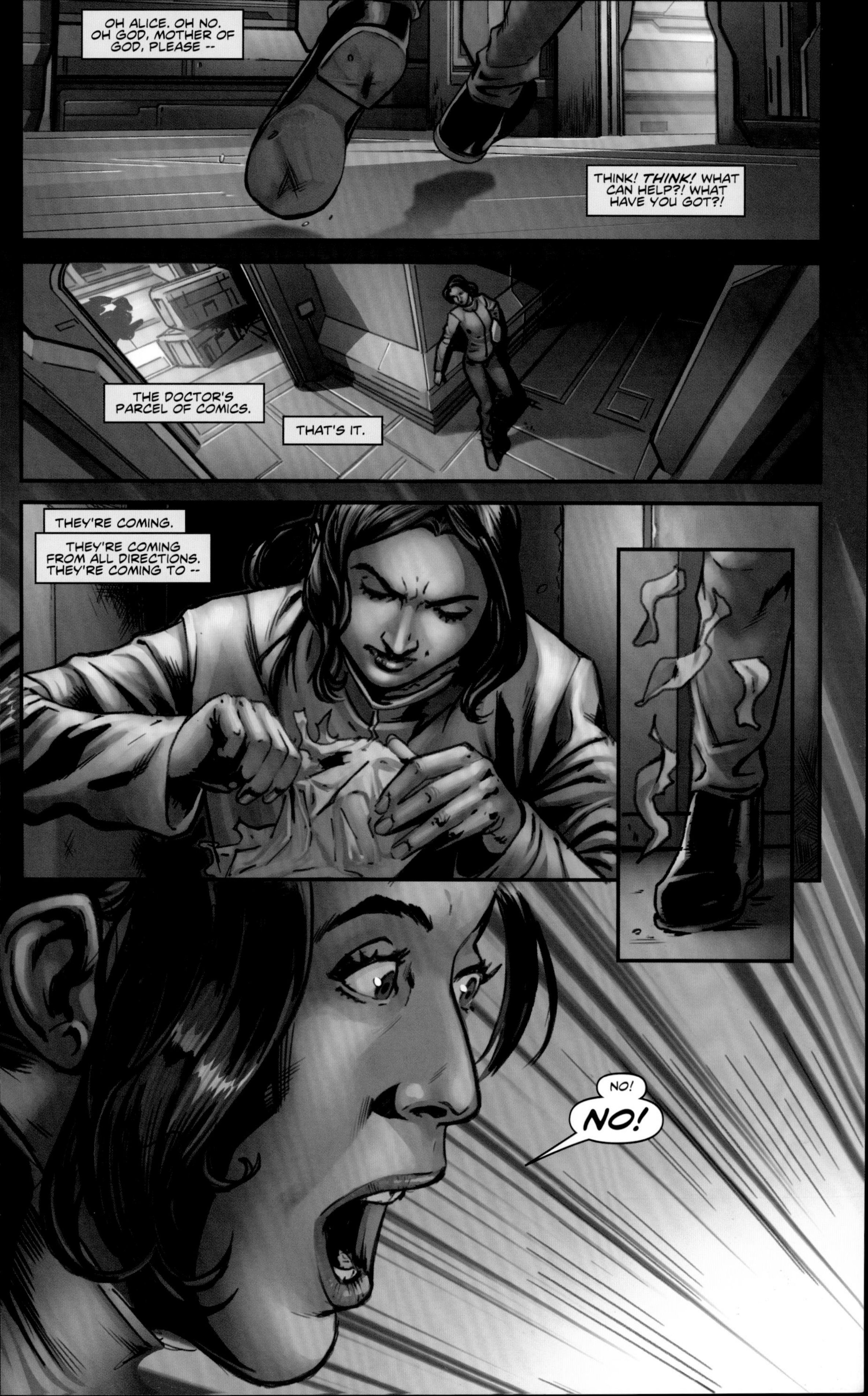
OH ALICE. OH NO. OH GOD, MOTHER OF GOD, PLEASE --
THINK! *THINK!* WHAT CAN HELP?! WHAT HAVE YOU GOT?!
THE DOCTOR'S PARCEL OF COMICS.
THAT'S IT.
THEY'RE COMING.
THEY'RE COMING FROM ALL DIRECTIONS. THEY'RE COMING TO --
NO! **NO!**

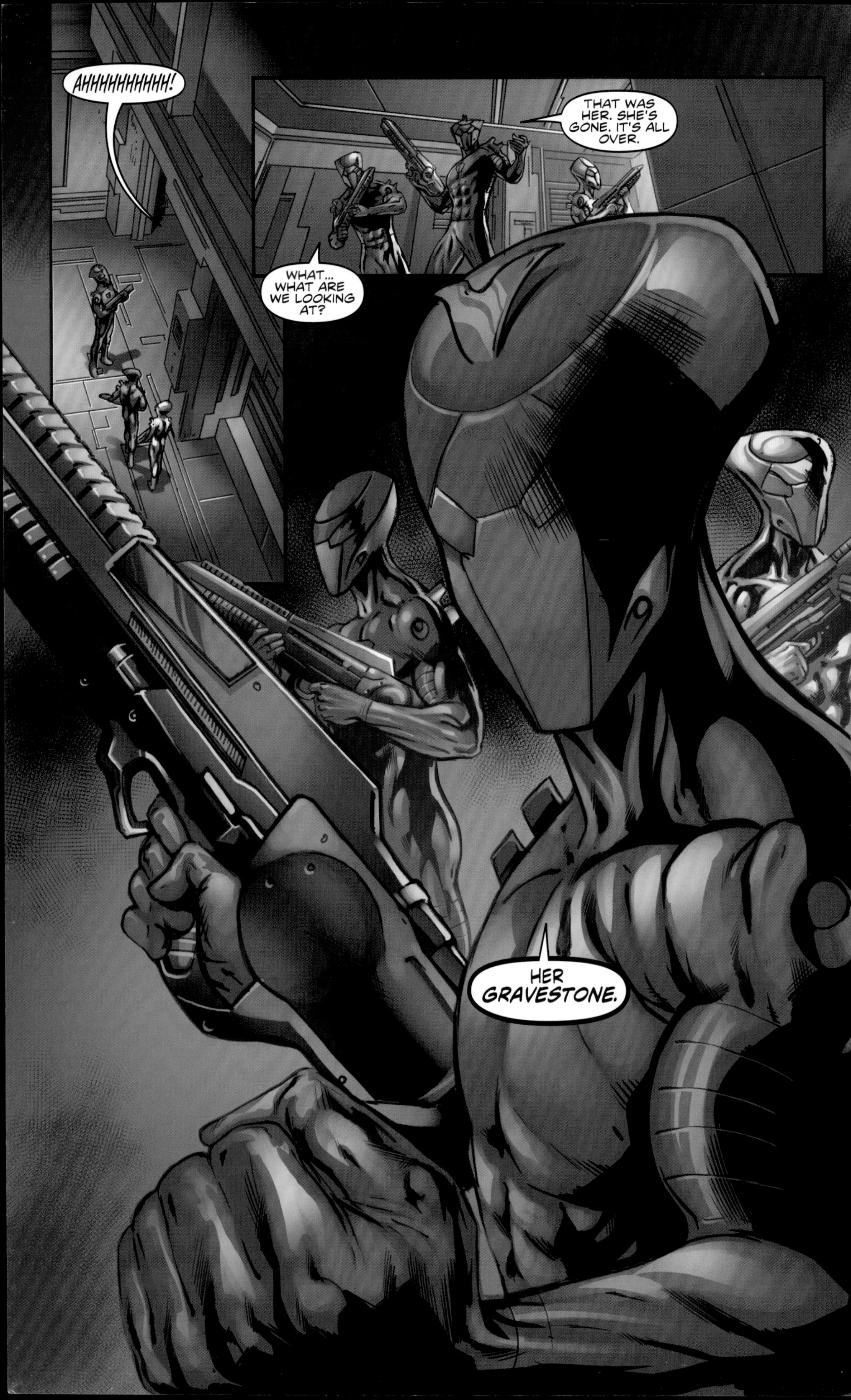
AHHHHHHHHHH!
THAT WAS HER. SHE'S GONE. IT'S ALL OVER.
WHAT... WHAT ARE WE LOOKING AT?
HER GRAVESTONE.

BBC
DOCTOR WHO

"THE DOCTORS DO... CLASSIC COMEDY"

WRITTEN BY PAUL CORNELL • ART BY NEIL SLORANCE • LETTERS BY COLIN BELL

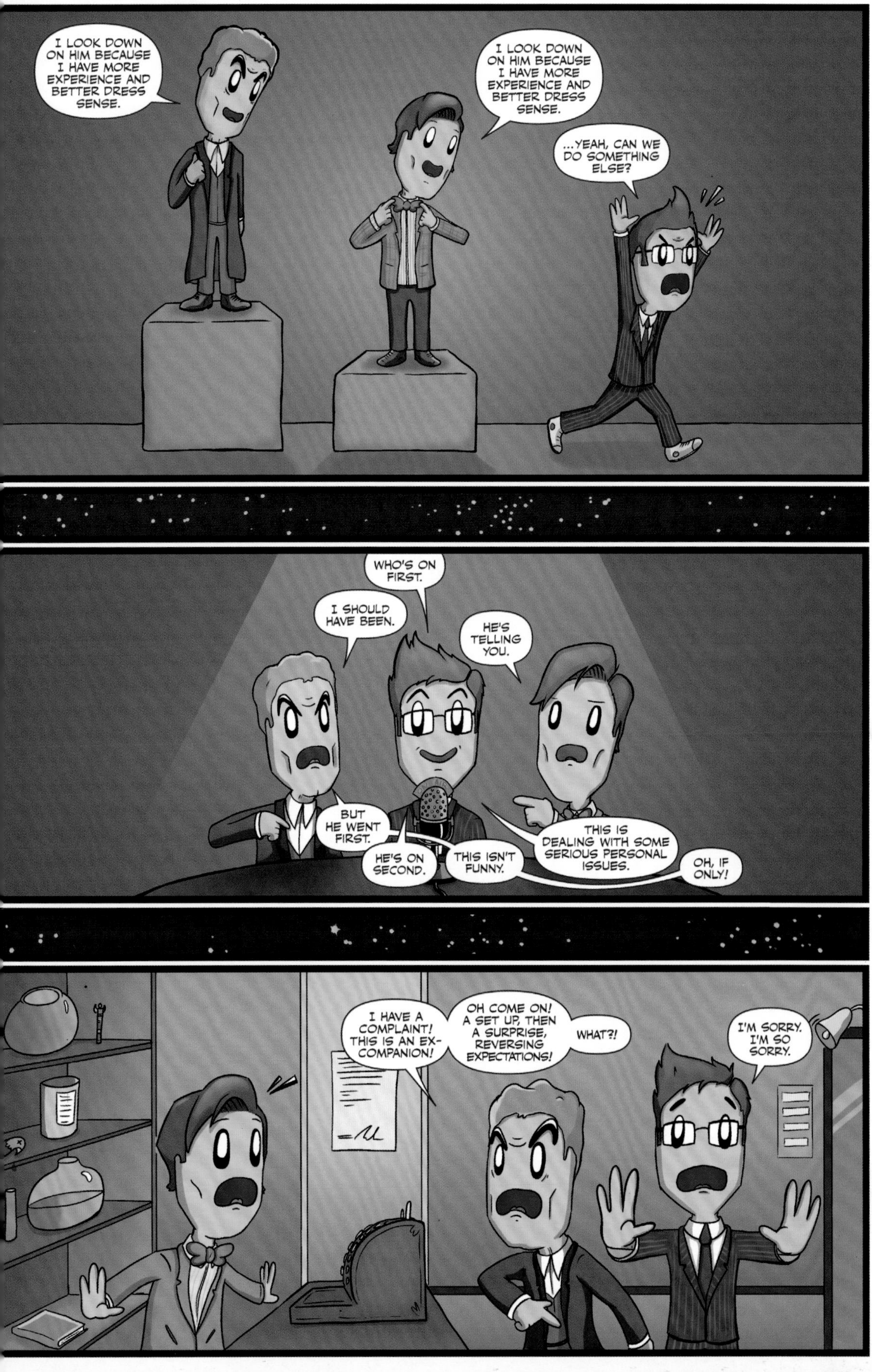

I LOOK DOWN ON HIM BECAUSE I HAVE MORE EXPERIENCE AND BETTER DRESS SENSE.
I LOOK DOWN ON HIM BECAUSE I HAVE MORE EXPERIENCE AND BETTER DRESS SENSE.
...YEAH, CAN WE DO SOMETHING ELSE?
WHO'S ON FIRST.
I SHOULD HAVE BEEN.
HE'S TELLING YOU.
BUT HE WENT FIRST.
HE'S ON SECOND.
THIS ISN'T FUNNY.
THIS IS DEALING WITH SOME SERIOUS PERSONAL ISSUES.
OH, IF ONLY!
I HAVE A COMPLAINT! THIS IS AN EX-COMPANION!
OH COME ON! A SET UP, THEN A SURPRISE, REVERSING EXPECTATIONS!
WHAT?!
I'M SORRY. I'M SO SORRY.

COVER 5

REGULAR Cover by Neil Edwards & Ivan Nunes

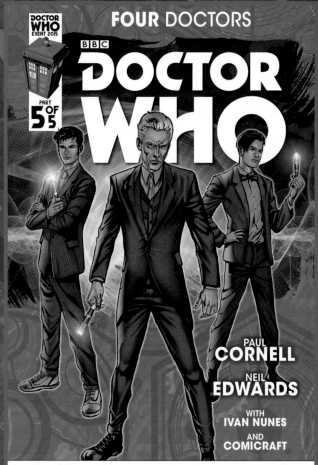

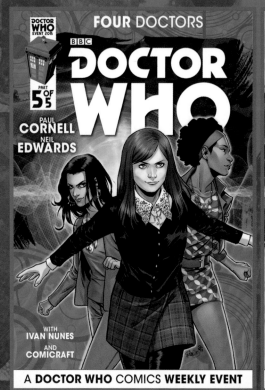

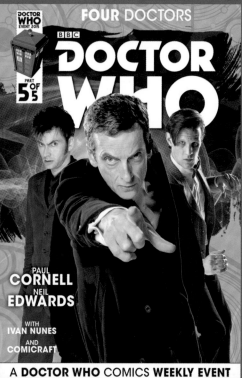

FOUR DOCTORS
DOCTOR WHO EVENT 2015
PART 5 OF 5
BBC
DOCTOR WHO
PAUL CORNELL
NEIL EDWARDS
WITH IVAN NUNES
AND COMICRAFT
A DOCTOR WHO COMICS WEEKLY EVENT

DOCTOR WHO EVENT 2015
FOUR DOCTORS
BBC
DOCTOR WHO
PART 5 OF 5
PAUL CORNELL
NEIL EDWARDS
WITH IVAN NUNES
AND COMICRAFT
A DOCTOR WHO COMICS WEEKLY EVENT

COMPANION Cover by Elena Casagrande, Eleonora Carlini & Claudia SG Iannicello

DOCTOR WHO EVENT 2015
FOUR DOCTORS
BBC
DOCTOR WHO
PART 5 OF 5
PAUL CORNELL
NEIL EDWARDS
WITH IVAN NUNES
AND COMICRAFT
A DOCTOR WHO COMICS WEEKLY EVENT

SUBSCRIPTION Cover by AJ & Rob Farmer

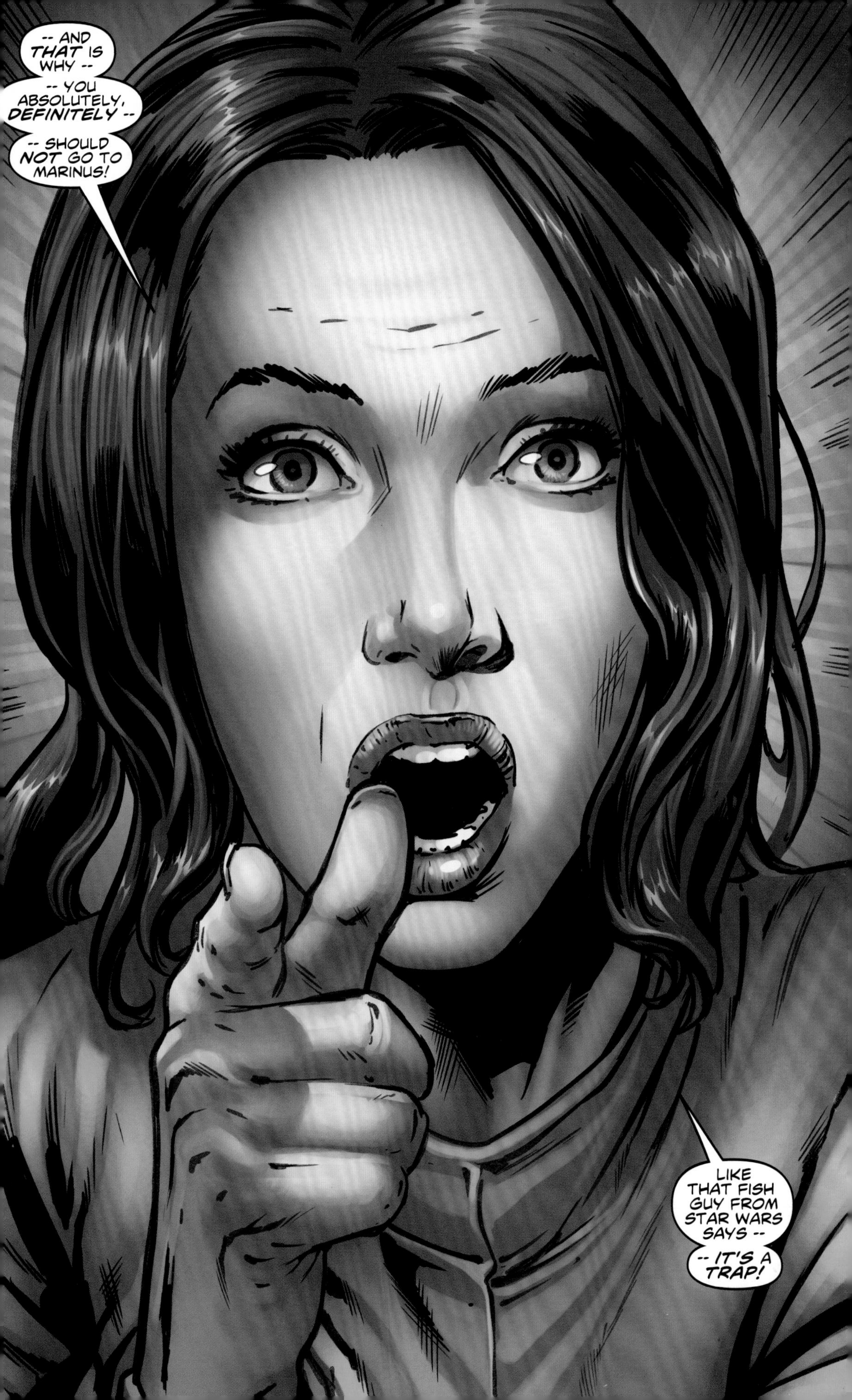
-- AND THAT IS WHY --
-- YOU ABSOLUTELY, DEFINITELY --
-- SHOULD NOT GO TO MARINUS!
LIKE THAT FISH GUY FROM STAR WARS SAYS --
-- IT'S A TRAP!

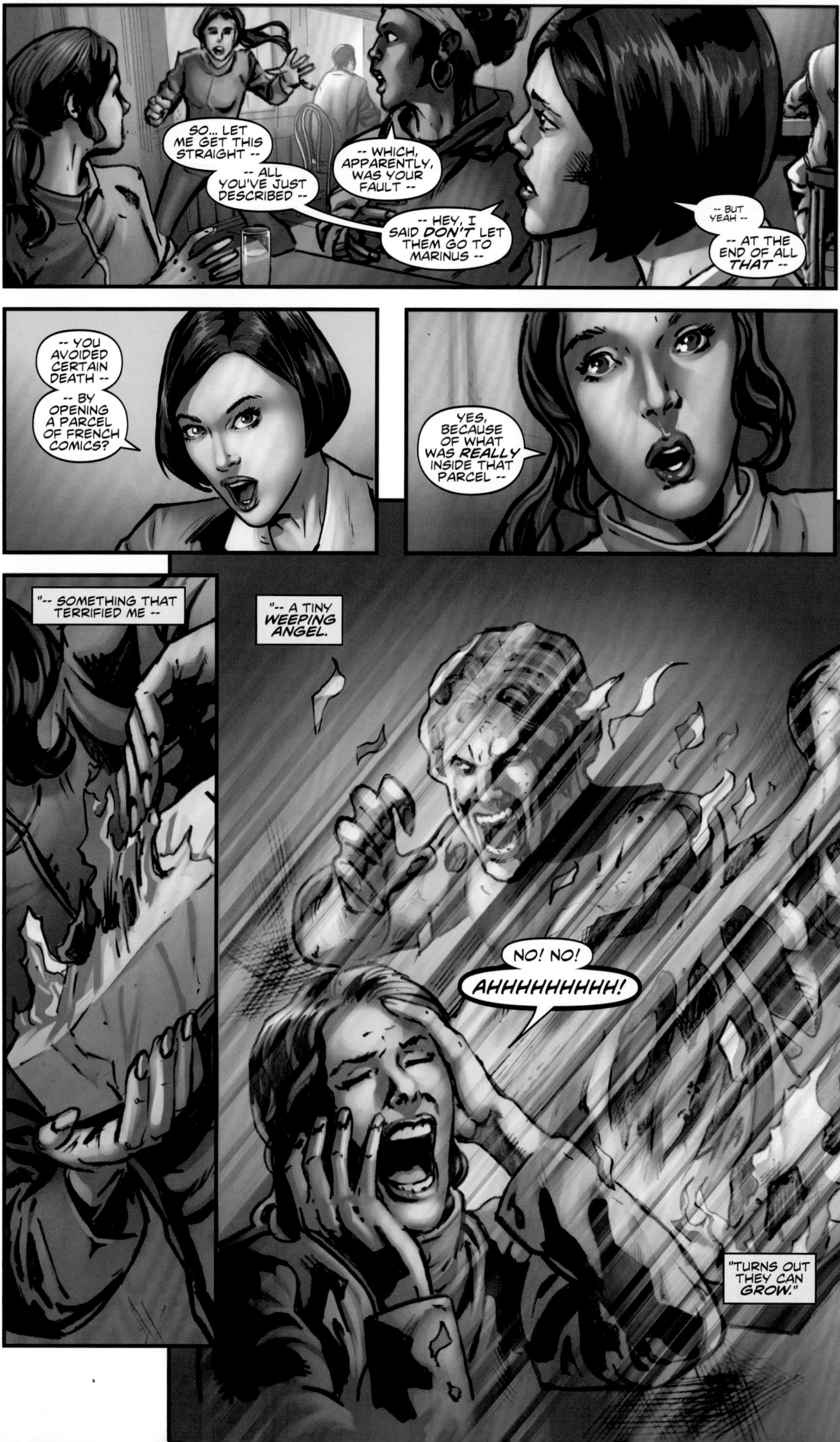
SO... LET ME GET THIS STRAIGHT --
-- ALL YOU'VE JUST DESCRIBED --
-- WHICH, APPARENTLY, WAS YOUR FAULT --
-- HEY, I SAID DON'T LET THEM GO TO MARINUS --
-- BUT YEAH --
-- AT THE END OF ALL THAT --
-- YOU AVOIDED CERTAIN DEATH --
-- BY OPENING A PARCEL OF FRENCH COMICS?
YES, BECAUSE OF WHAT WAS REALLY INSIDE THAT PARCEL --
"-- SOMETHING THAT TERRIFIED ME --
"-- A TINY WEEPING ANGEL.
NO! NO!
AHHHHHHHHH!
"TURNS OUT THEY CAN GROW."

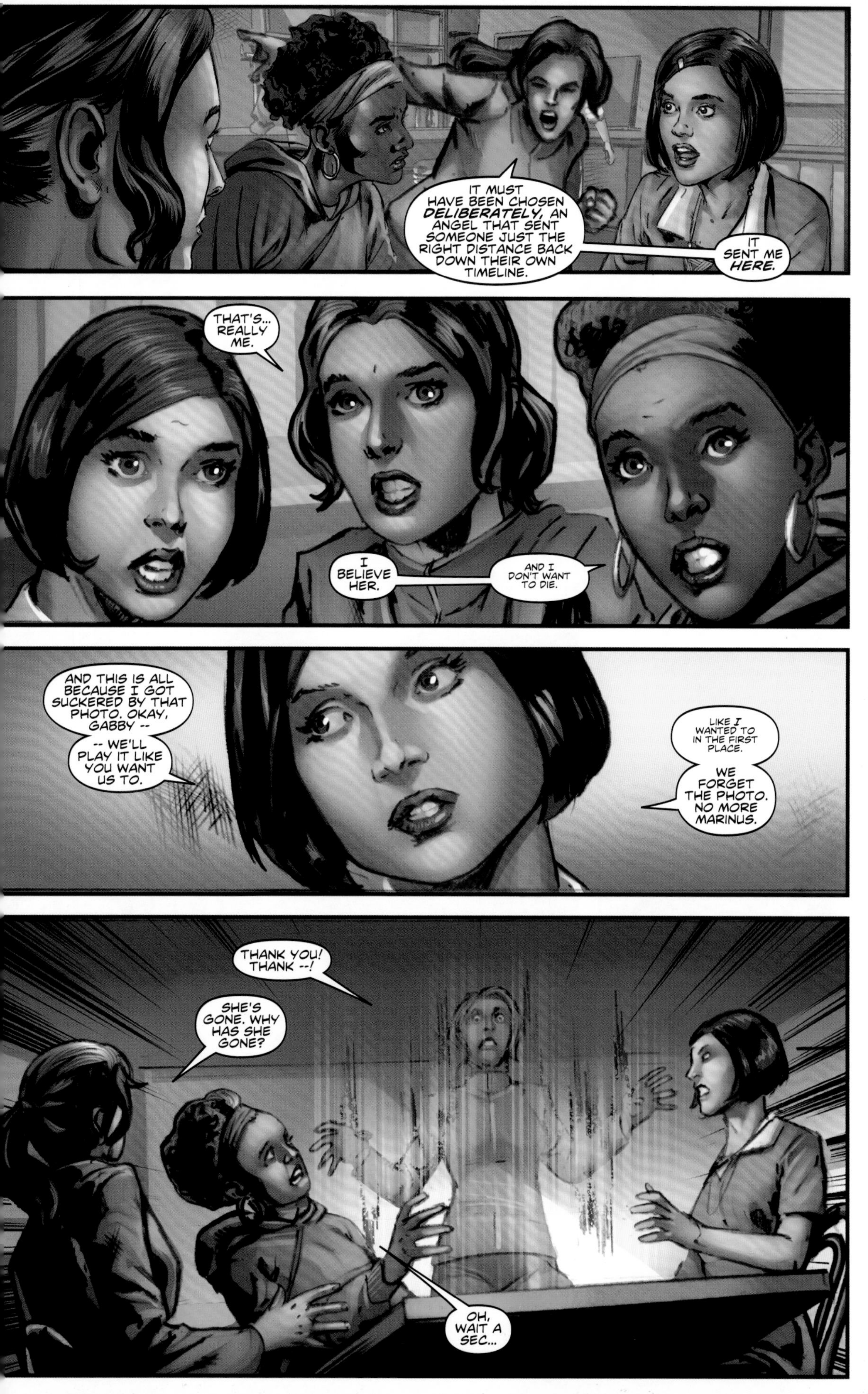
IT MUST HAVE BEEN CHOSEN DELIBERATELY, AN ANGEL THAT SENT SOMEONE JUST THE RIGHT DISTANCE BACK DOWN THEIR OWN TIMELINE.
IT SENT ME HERE.
THAT'S... REALLY ME.
I BELIEVE HER.
AND I DON'T WANT TO DIE.
AND THIS IS ALL BECAUSE I GOT SUCKERED BY THAT PHOTO. OKAY, GABBY --
-- WE'LL PLAY IT LIKE YOU WANT US TO.
LIKE I WANTED TO IN THE FIRST PLACE.
WE FORGET THE PHOTO. NO MORE MARINUS.
THANK YOU! THANK --!
SHE'S GONE. WHY HAS SHE GONE?
OH, WAIT A SEC...

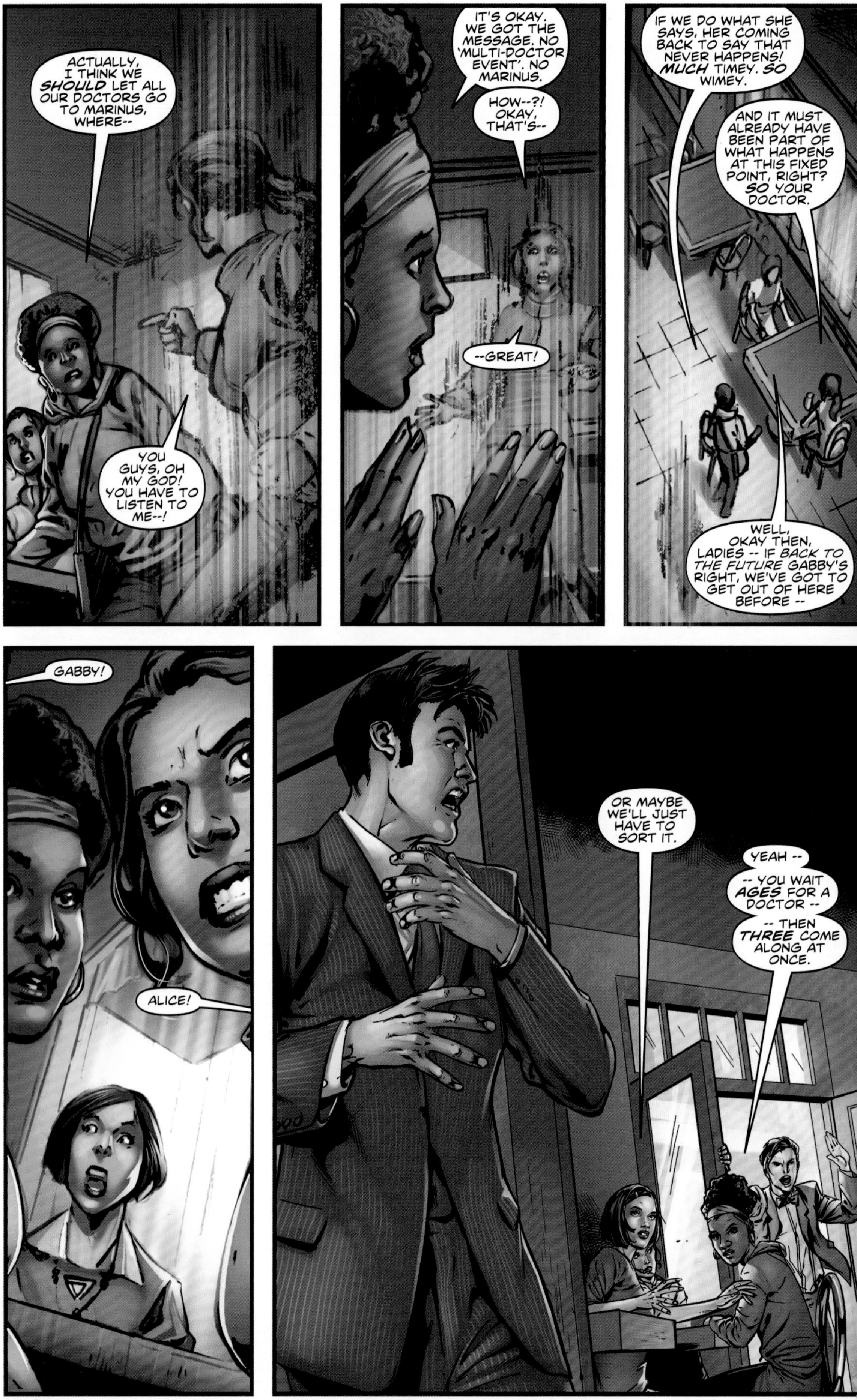
ACTUALLY, I THINK WE SHOULD LET ALL OUR DOCTORS GO TO MARINUS, WHERE--
YOU GUYS, OH MY GOD! YOU HAVE TO LISTEN TO ME--!
IT'S OKAY. WE GOT THE MESSAGE. NO 'MULTI-DOCTOR EVENT'. NO MARINUS.
HOW--?! OKAY, THAT'S--
--GREAT!
IF WE DO WHAT SHE SAYS, HER COMING BACK TO SAY THAT NEVER HAPPENS! MUCH TIMEY. SO WIMEY.
AND IT MUST ALREADY HAVE BEEN PART OF WHAT HAPPENS AT THIS FIXED POINT, RIGHT? SO YOUR DOCTOR.
WELL, OKAY THEN, LADIES -- IF BACK TO THE FUTURE GABBY'S RIGHT, WE'VE GOT TO GET OUT OF HERE BEFORE --
GABBY!
ALICE!
OR MAYBE WE'LL JUST HAVE TO SORT IT.
YEAH --
-- YOU WAIT AGES FOR A DOCTOR --
-- THEN THREE COME ALONG AT ONCE.

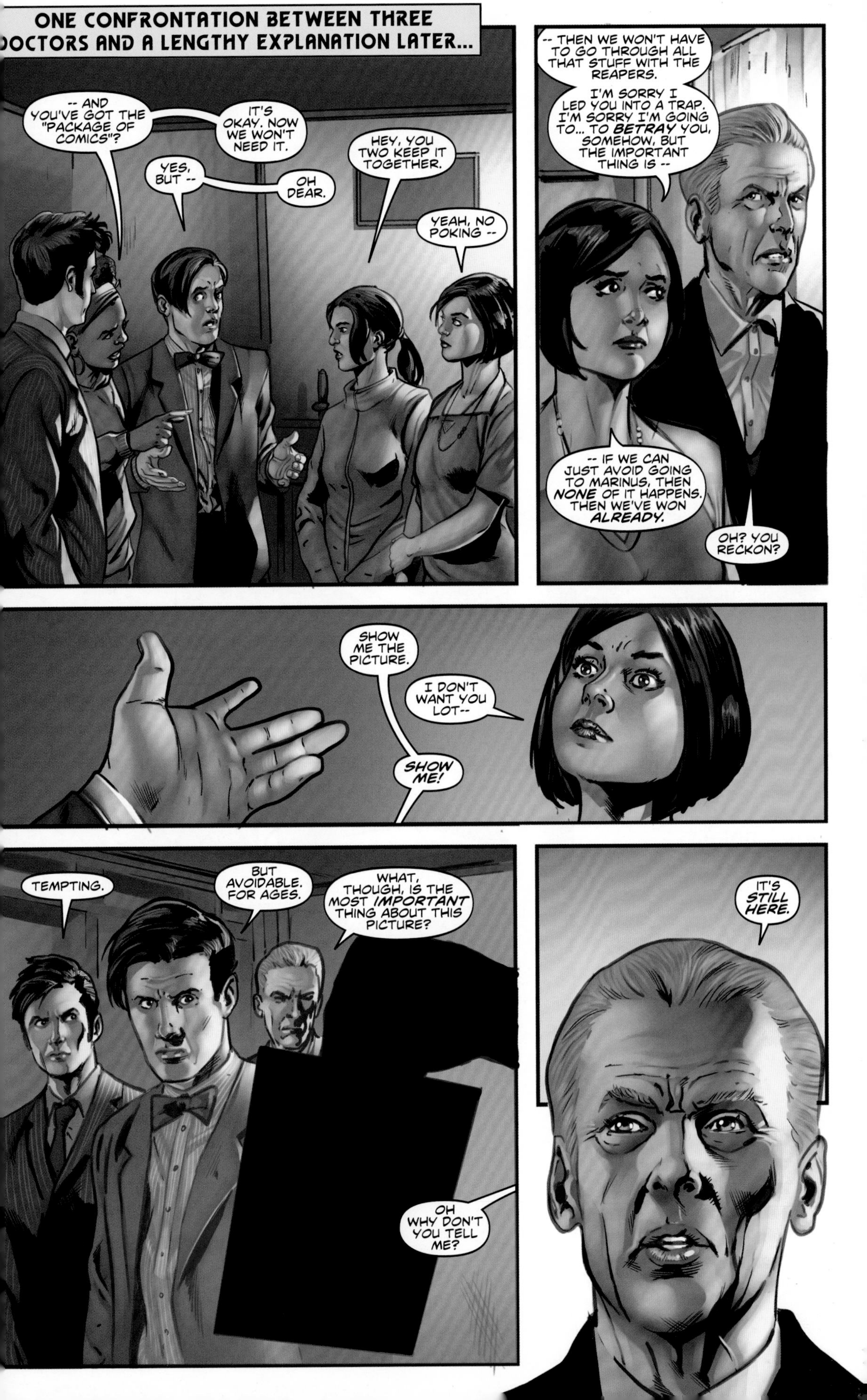
ONE CONFRONTATION BETWEEN THREE DOCTORS AND A LENGTHY EXPLANATION LATER...
-- AND YOU'VE GOT THE "PACKAGE OF COMICS"?
IT'S OKAY. NOW WE WON'T NEED IT.
YES, BUT --
OH DEAR.
HEY, YOU TWO KEEP IT TOGETHER.
YEAH, NO POKING --
-- THEN WE WON'T HAVE TO GO THROUGH ALL THAT STUFF WITH THE REAPERS.
I'M SORRY I LED YOU INTO A TRAP. I'M SORRY I'M GOING TO... TO BETRAY YOU, SOMEHOW, BUT THE IMPORTANT THING IS --
-- IF WE CAN JUST AVOID GOING TO MARINUS, THEN NONE OF IT HAPPENS. THEN WE'VE WON ALREADY.
OH? YOU RECKON?
SHOW ME THE PICTURE.
I DON'T WANT YOU LOT--
SHOW ME!
TEMPTING.
BUT AVOIDABLE. FOR AGES.
WHAT, THOUGH, IS THE MOST IMPORTANT THING ABOUT THIS PICTURE?
OH WHY DON'T YOU TELL ME?
IT'S STILL HERE.

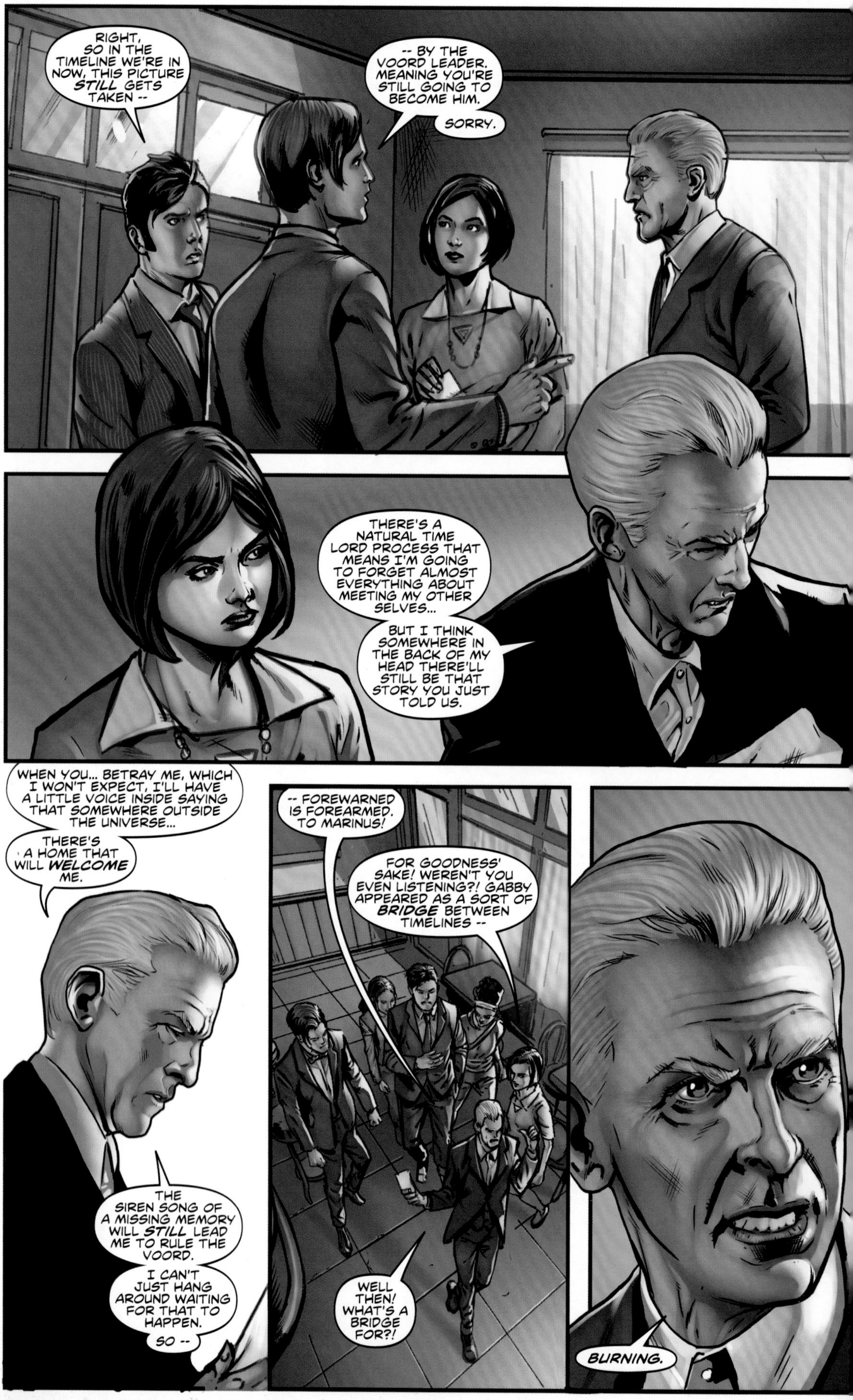

RIGHT, SO IN THE TIMELINE WE'RE IN NOW, THIS PICTURE STILL GETS TAKEN --
-- BY THE VOORD LEADER. MEANING YOU'RE STILL GOING TO BECOME HIM.
SORRY.
THERE'S A NATURAL TIME LORD PROCESS THAT MEANS I'M GOING TO FORGET ALMOST EVERYTHING ABOUT MEETING MY OTHER SELVES...
BUT I THINK SOMEWHERE IN THE BACK OF MY HEAD THERE'LL STILL BE THAT STORY YOU JUST TOLD US.
WHEN YOU... BETRAY ME, WHICH I WON'T EXPECT, I'LL HAVE A LITTLE VOICE INSIDE SAYING THAT SOMEWHERE OUTSIDE THE UNIVERSE...
THERE'S A HOME THAT WILL WELCOME ME.
THE SIREN SONG OF A MISSING MEMORY WILL STILL LEAD ME TO RULE THE VOORD.
I CAN'T JUST HANG AROUND WAITING FOR THAT TO HAPPEN.
SO --
-- FOREWARNED IS FOREARMED. TO MARINUS!
FOR GOODNESS' SAKE! WEREN'T YOU EVEN LISTENING?! GABBY APPEARED AS A SORT OF BRIDGE BETWEEN TIMELINES --
WELL THEN! WHAT'S A BRIDGE FOR?!
BURNING.

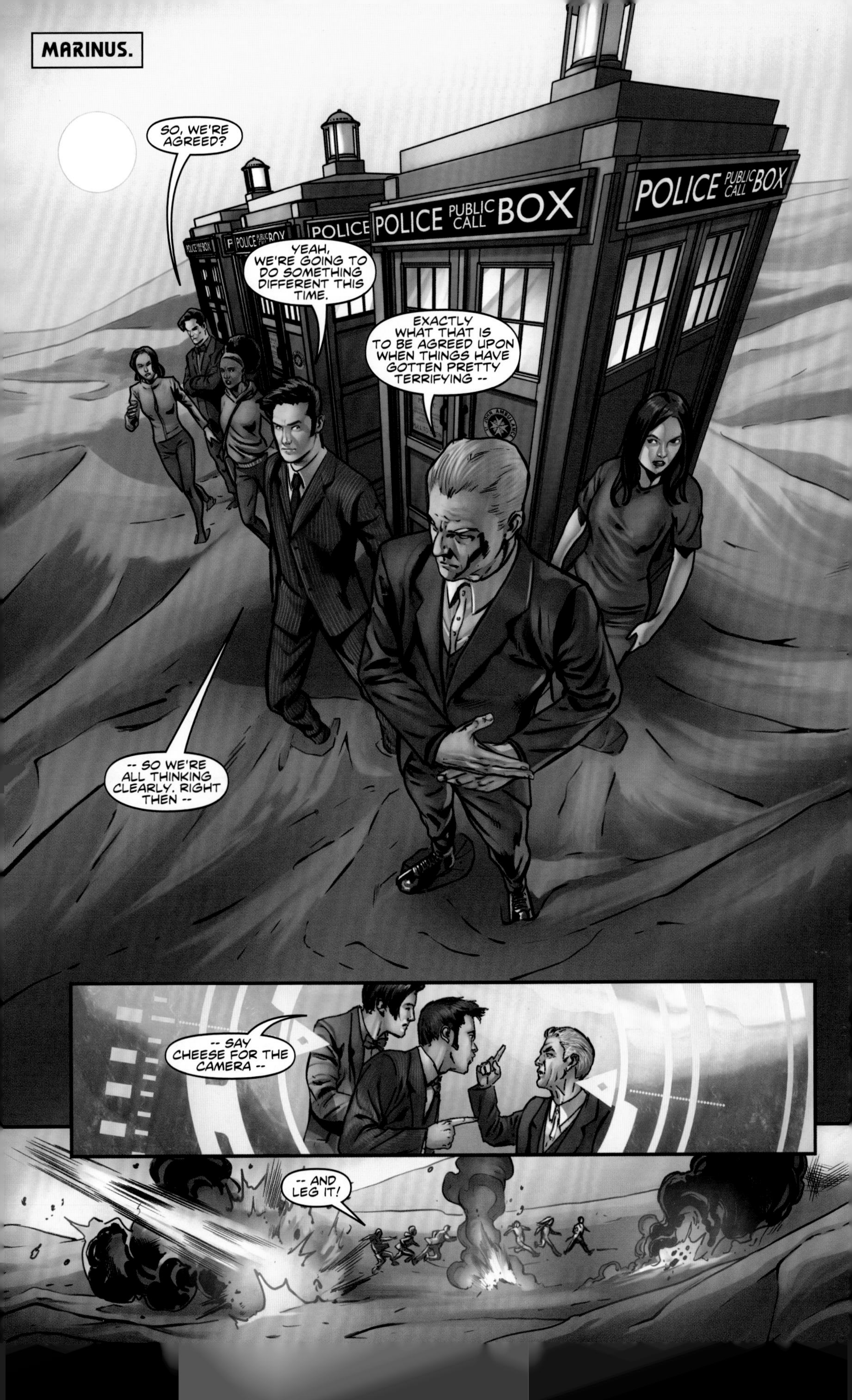
MARINUS.
POLICE PUBLIC CALL BOX
SO, WE'RE AGREED?
YEAH, WE'RE GOING TO DO SOMETHING DIFFERENT THIS TIME.
EXACTLY WHAT THAT IS TO BE AGREED UPON WHEN THINGS HAVE GOTTEN PRETTY TERRIFYING --
-- SO WE'RE ALL THINKING CLEARLY. RIGHT THEN --
-- SAY CHEESE FOR THE CAMERA --
-- AND LEG IT!

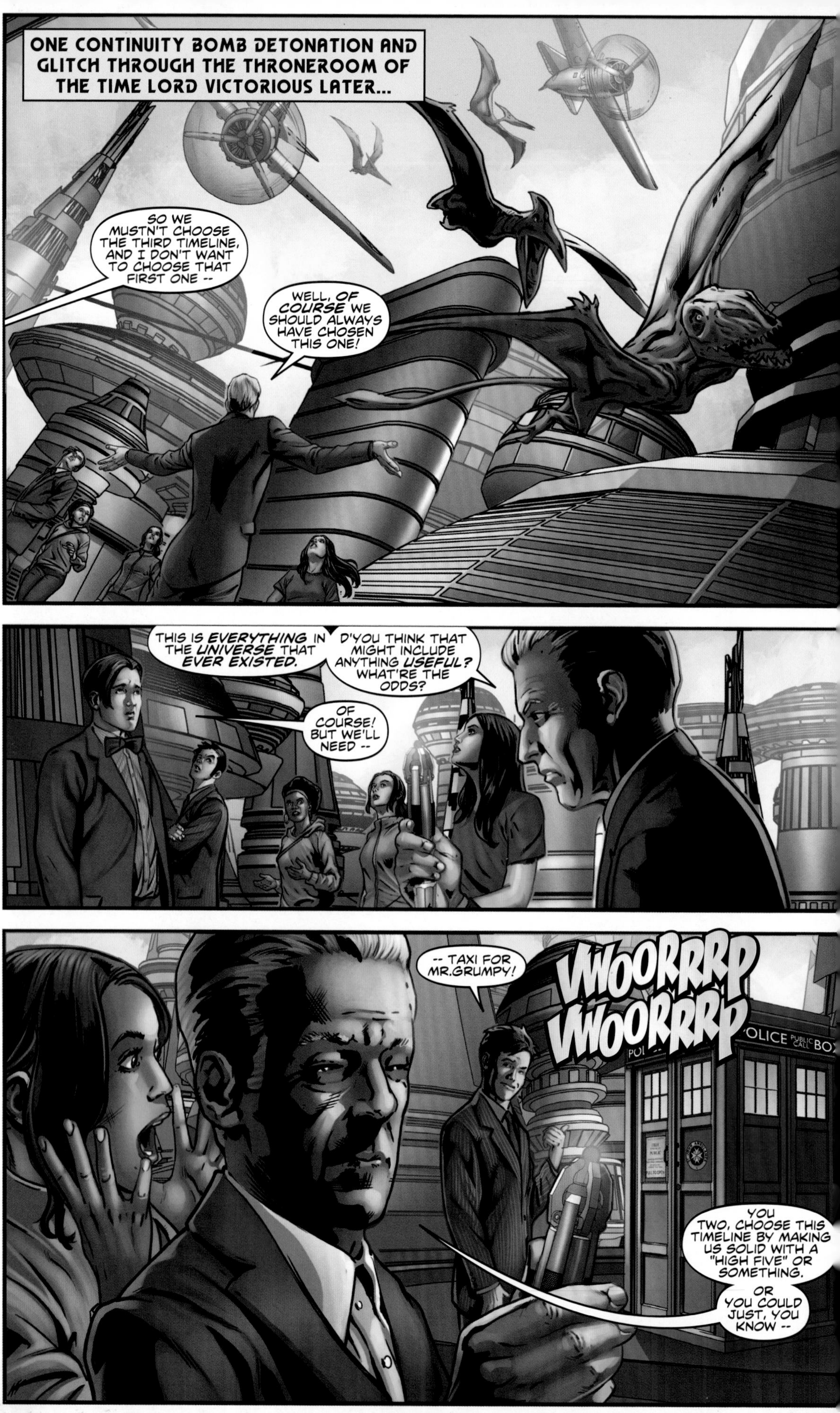
ONE CONTINUITY BOMB DETONATION AND GLITCH THROUGH THE THRONEROOM OF THE TIME LORD VICTORIOUS LATER...
SO WE MUSTN'T CHOOSE THE THIRD TIMELINE, AND I DON'T WANT TO CHOOSE THAT FIRST ONE --
WELL, OF COURSE WE SHOULD ALWAYS HAVE CHOSEN THIS ONE!
THIS IS EVERYTHING IN THE UNIVERSE THAT EVER EXISTED.
D'YOU THINK THAT MIGHT INCLUDE ANYTHING USEFUL? WHAT'RE THE ODDS?
OF COURSE! BUT WE'LL NEED --
-- TAXI FOR MR.GRUMPY!
VWOORRRP VWOORRRP
POLICE PUBLIC CALL BOX
YOU TWO, CHOOSE THIS TIMELINE BY MAKING US SOLID WITH A "HIGH FIVE" OR SOMETHING.
OR YOU COULD JUST, YOU KNOW --

"-- PUNCH EACH OTHER."

WE DON'T HAVE 'LONG' BEFORE THIS UNIVERSE COLLAPSES. FROM THIS GIANT TOOLBOX OF EVERYTHING, WE NEED TO FIND...

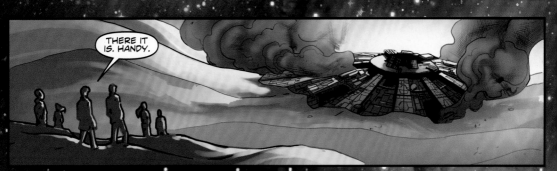

THERE IT IS. HANDY.

THIS IS IT, ANOTHER DALEK MONSTROSITY --

-- THE WEAPON THE VOORD ALTERED TO TAKE THEMSELVES OUT OF TIME AND SPACE.

AND WHAT *THEY* CAN DO--

-- AS LONG AS *YOU* STAY OVER THERE --

-- IF WE ALL JUST CONCENTRATE ON OUR OWN BIT --

AND WE ARE ON OUR WAY, OUT OF THIS UNIVERSE, HEADING BACK TO VOORD CITY--!

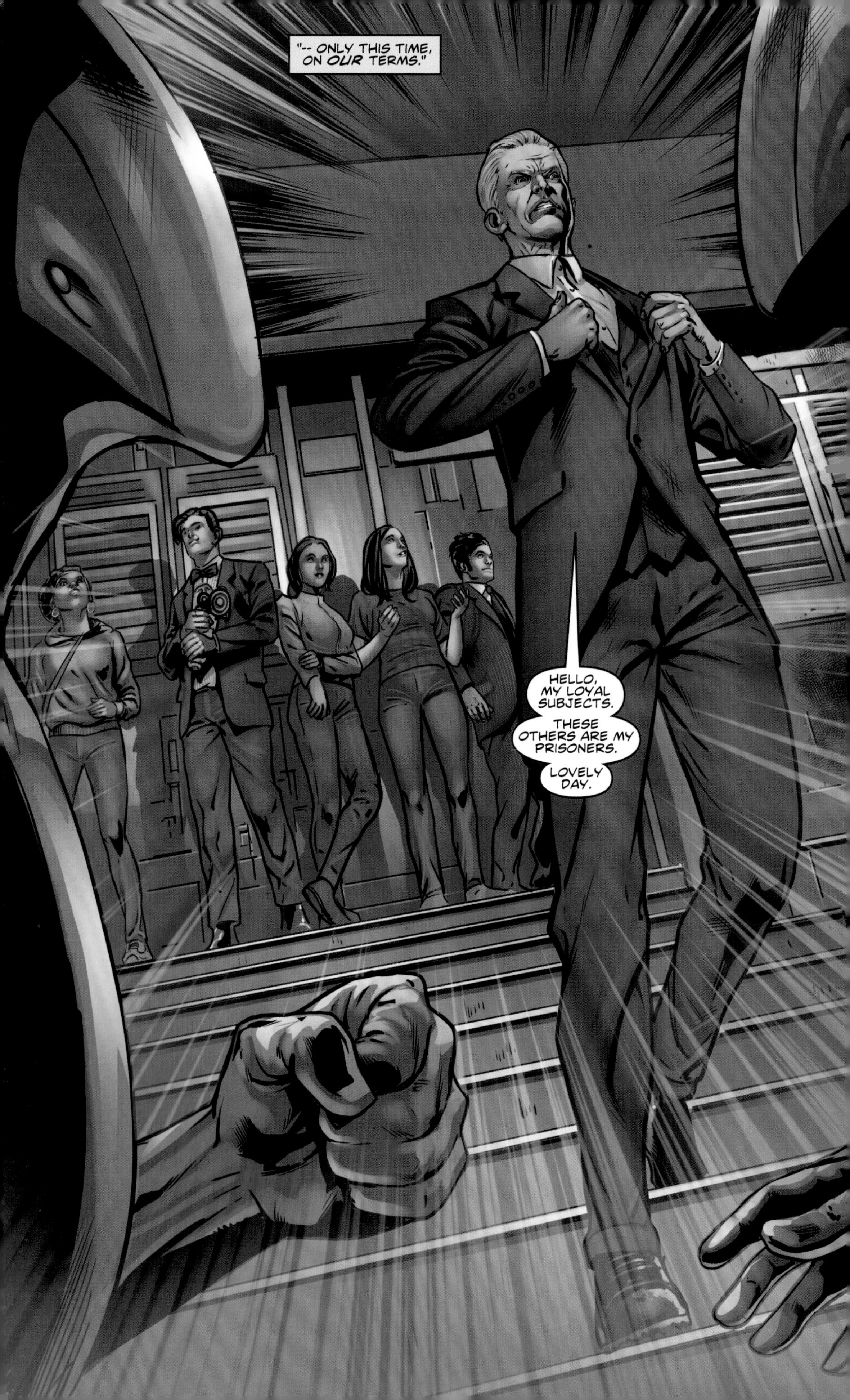
"-- ONLY THIS TIME, ON OUR TERMS."
HELLO, MY LOYAL SUBJECTS.
THESE OTHERS ARE MY PRISONERS.
LOVELY DAY.

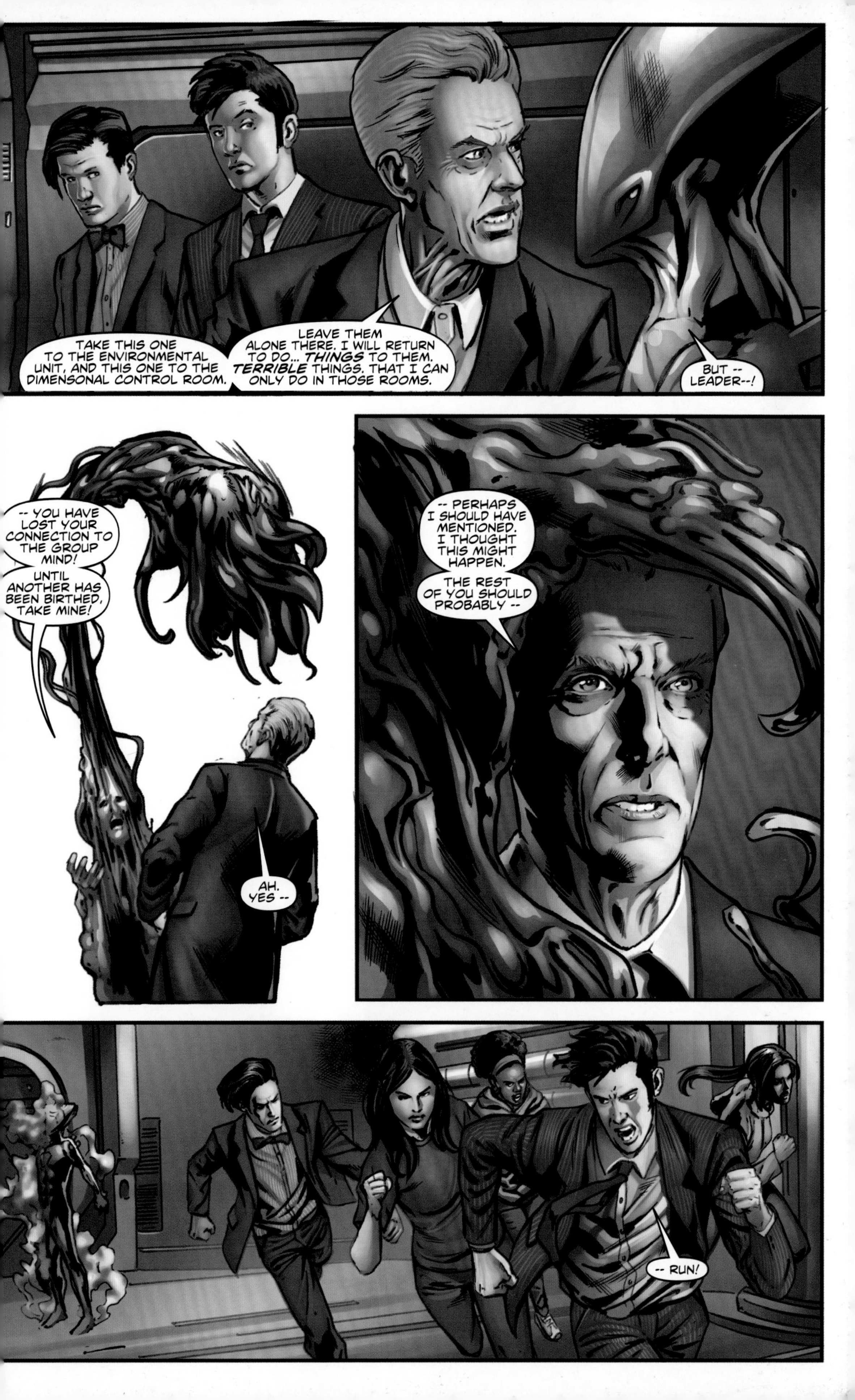
TAKE THIS ONE TO THE ENVIRONMENTAL UNIT, AND THIS ONE TO THE DIMENSONAL CONTROL ROOM.
LEAVE THEM ALONE THERE. I WILL RETURN TO DO... *THINGS* TO THEM. *TERRIBLE* THINGS. THAT I CAN ONLY DO IN THOSE ROOMS.
BUT -- LEADER--!
-- YOU HAVE LOST YOUR CONNECTION TO THE GROUP MIND!
UNTIL ANOTHER HAS BEEN BIRTHED, TAKE MINE!
AH. YES --
-- PERHAPS I SHOULD HAVE MENTIONED. I THOUGHT THIS MIGHT HAPPEN.
THE REST OF YOU SHOULD PROBABLY --
-- RUN!

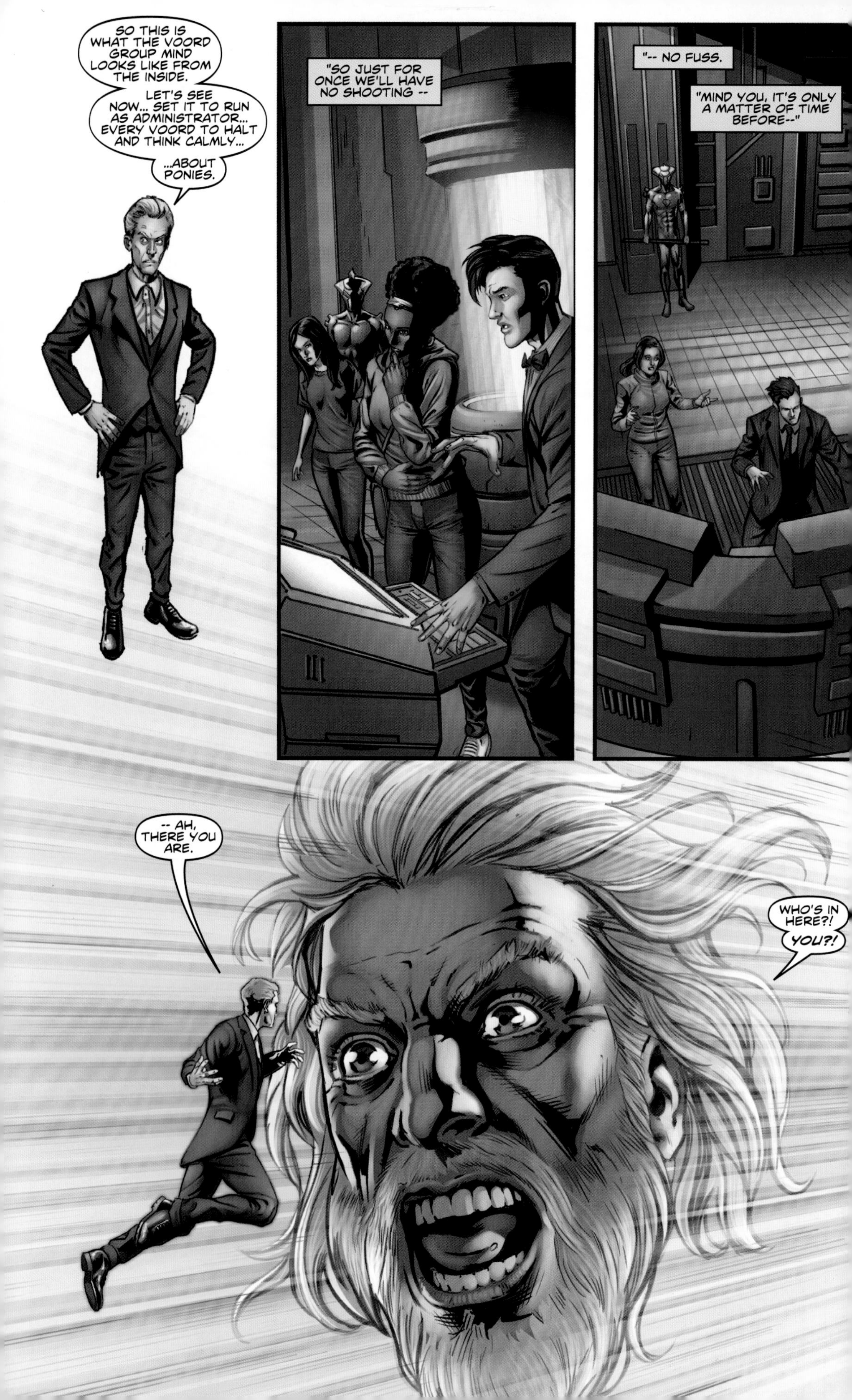
SO THIS IS WHAT THE VOORD GROUP MIND LOOKS LIKE FROM THE INSIDE.
LET'S SEE NOW... SET IT TO RUN AS ADMINISTRATOR... EVERY VOORD TO HALT AND THINK CALMLY...
...ABOUT PONIES.
"SO JUST FOR ONCE WE'LL HAVE NO SHOOTING --
"-- NO FUSS.
"MIND YOU, IT'S ONLY A MATTER OF TIME BEFORE--"
-- AH, THERE YOU ARE.
WHO'S IN HERE?!
YOU?!

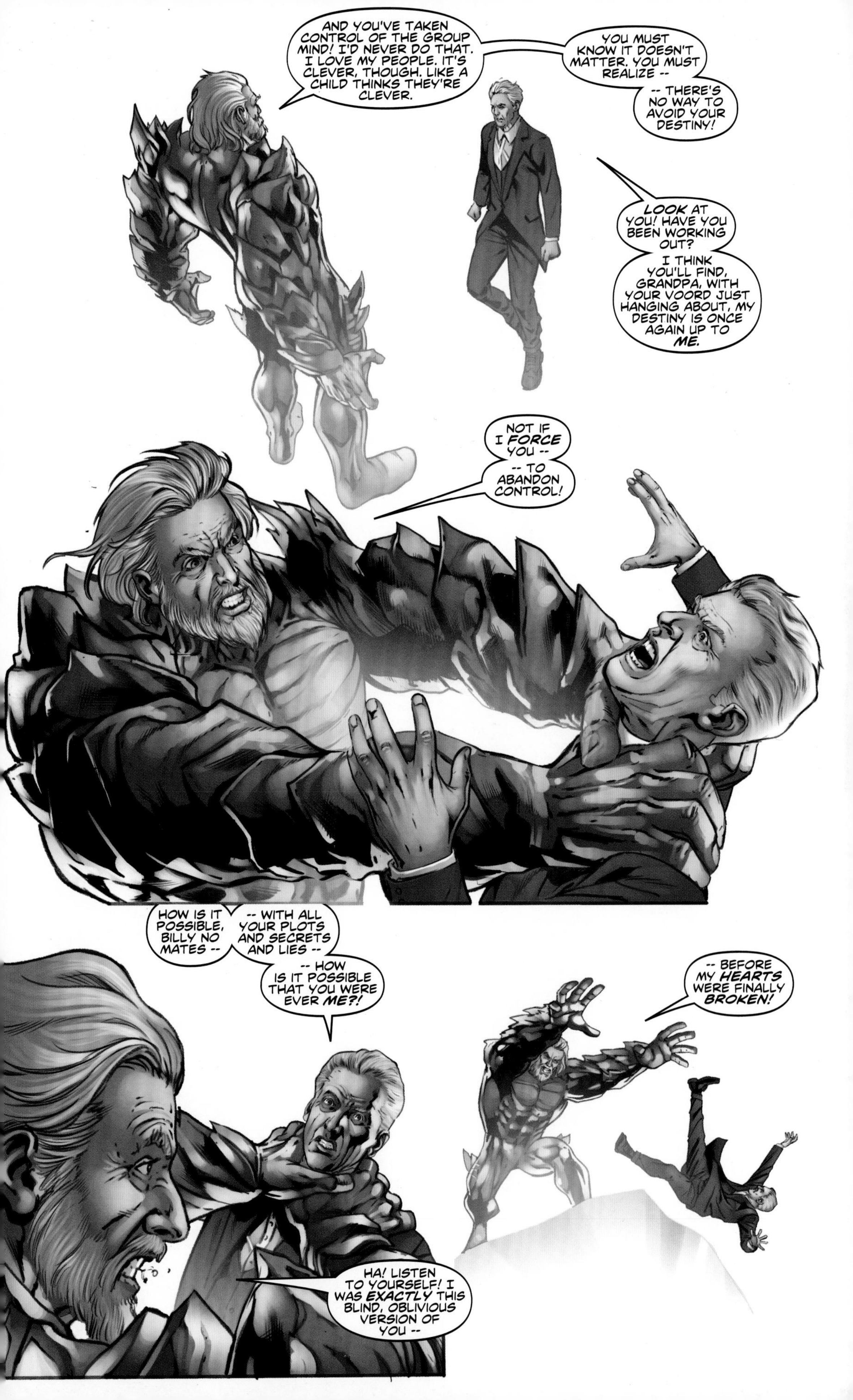
AND YOU'VE TAKEN CONTROL OF THE GROUP MIND! I'D NEVER DO THAT. I LOVE MY PEOPLE. IT'S CLEVER, THOUGH. LIKE A CHILD THINKS THEY'RE CLEVER.
YOU MUST KNOW IT DOESN'T MATTER. YOU MUST REALIZE --
-- THERE'S NO WAY TO AVOID YOUR DESTINY!
LOOK AT YOU! HAVE YOU BEEN WORKING OUT?
I THINK YOU'LL FIND, GRANDPA, WITH YOUR VOORD JUST HANGING ABOUT, MY DESTINY IS ONCE AGAIN UP TO ME.
NOT IF I FORCE YOU --
-- TO ABANDON CONTROL!
HOW IS IT POSSIBLE, BILLY NO MATES --
-- WITH ALL YOUR PLOTS AND SECRETS AND LIES --
-- HOW IS IT POSSIBLE THAT YOU WERE EVER ME?!
HA! LISTEN TO YOURSELF! I WAS EXACTLY THIS BLIND, OBLIVIOUS VERSION OF YOU --
-- BEFORE MY HEARTS WERE FINALLY BROKEN!

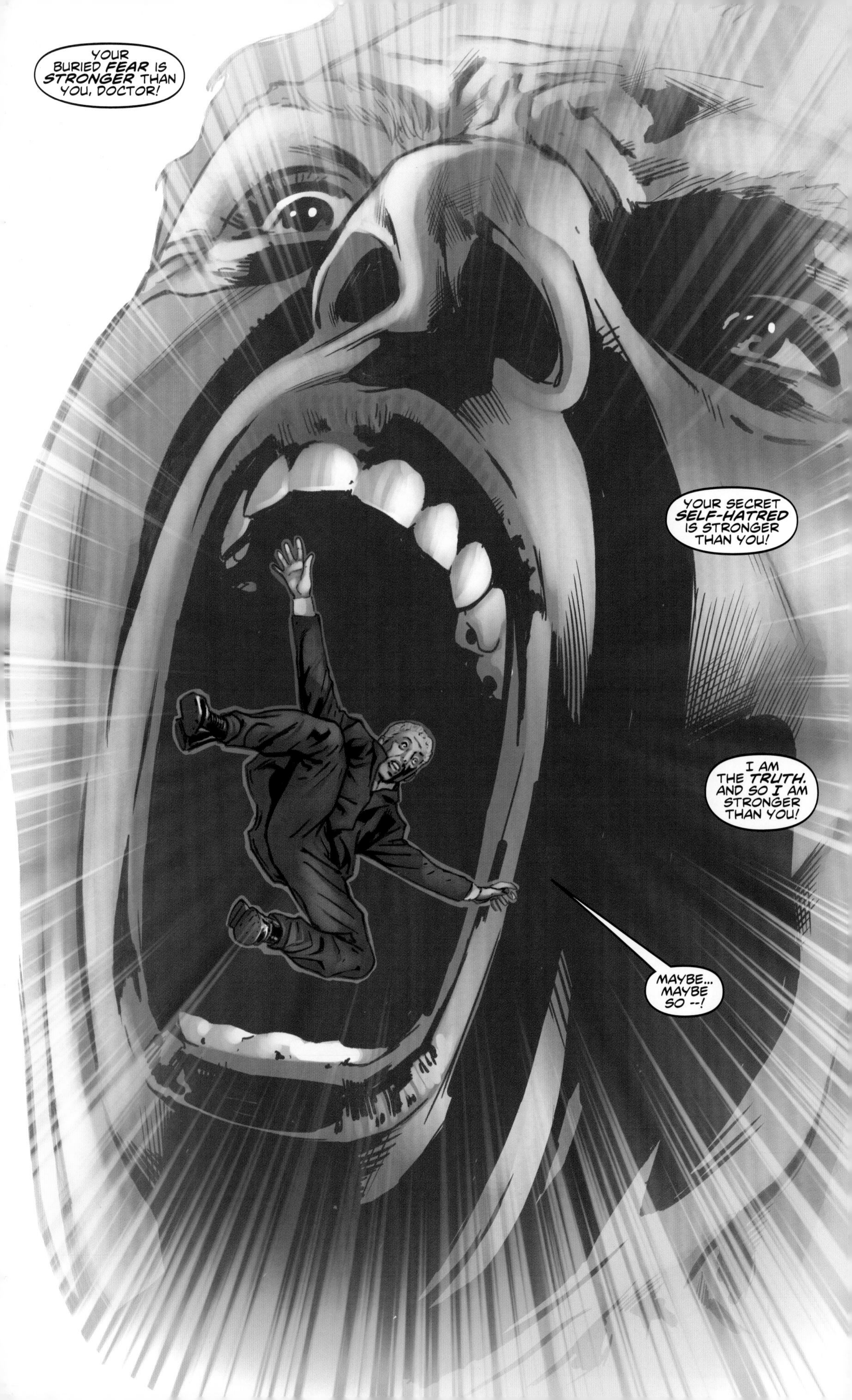
YOUR BURIED **FEAR** IS **STRONGER** THAN YOU, DOCTOR!
YOUR SECRET **SELF-HATRED** IS STRONGER THAN YOU!
I AM THE **TRUTH**. AND SO **I** AM STRONGER THAN YOU!
MAYBE... MAYBE SO --!

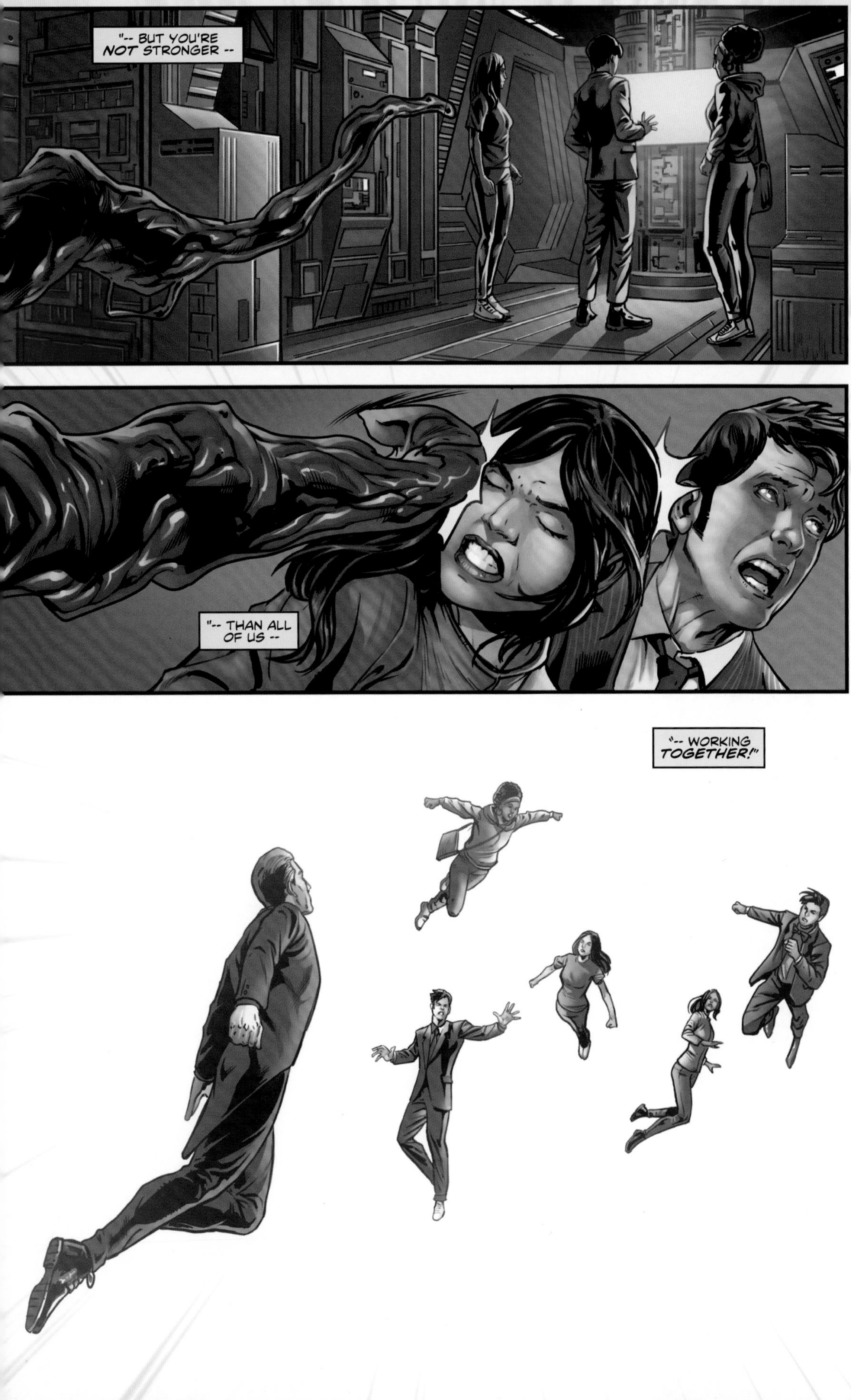
"-- BUT YOU'RE NOT STRONGER --
"-- THAN ALL OF US --
"-- WORKING TOGETHER!"

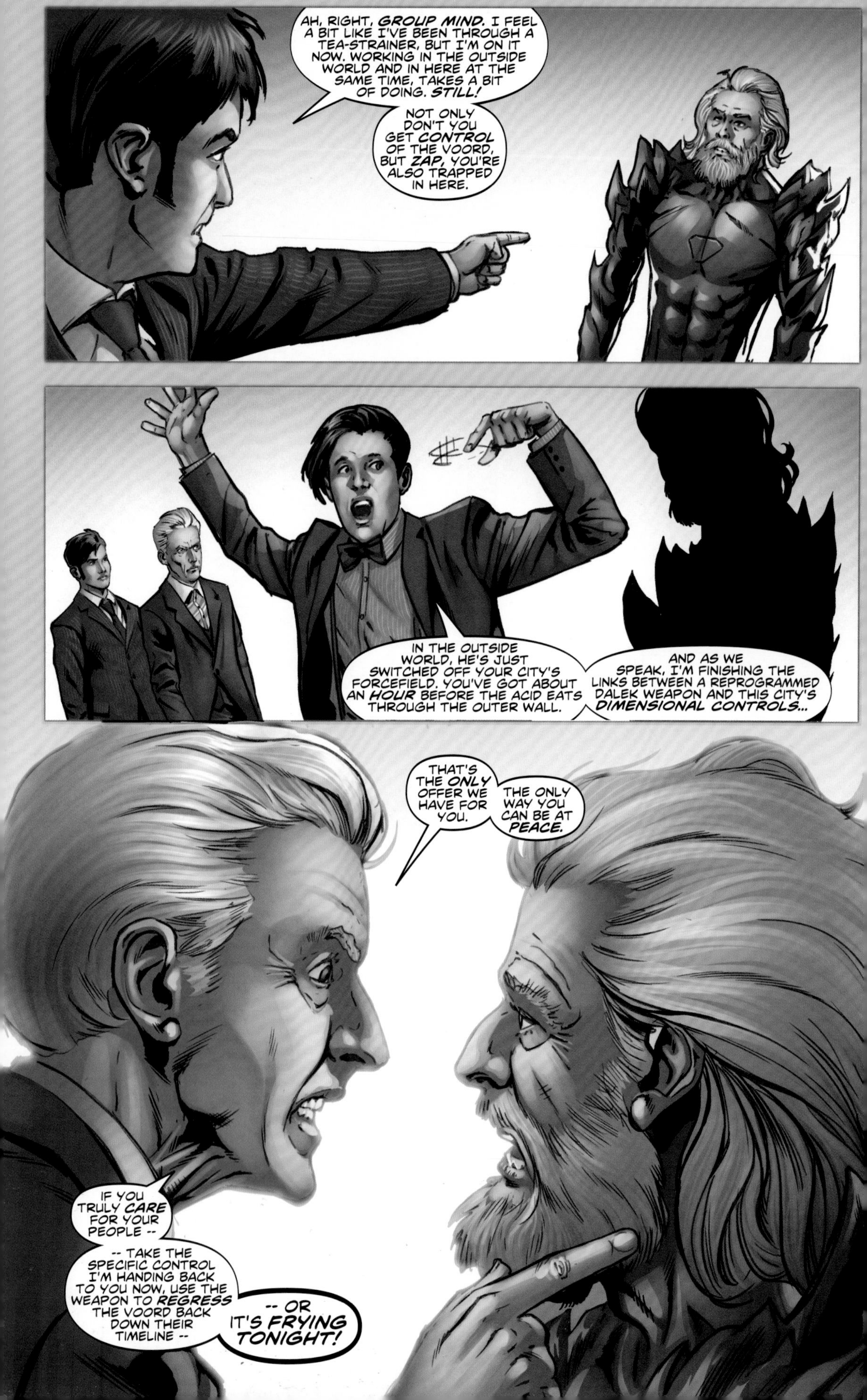
AH, RIGHT, GROUP MIND. I FEEL A BIT LIKE I'VE BEEN THROUGH A TEA-STRAINER, BUT I'M ON IT NOW. WORKING IN THE OUTSIDE WORLD AND IN HERE AT THE SAME TIME, TAKES A BIT OF DOING. STILL!
NOT ONLY DON'T YOU GET CONTROL OF THE VOORD, BUT ZAP, YOU'RE ALSO TRAPPED IN HERE.
IN THE OUTSIDE WORLD, HE'S JUST SWITCHED OFF YOUR CITY'S FORCEFIELD. YOU'VE GOT ABOUT AN HOUR BEFORE THE ACID EATS THROUGH THE OUTER WALL.
AND AS WE SPEAK, I'M FINISHING THE LINKS BETWEEN A REPROGRAMMED DALEK WEAPON AND THIS CITY'S DIMENSIONAL CONTROLS...
THAT'S THE ONLY OFFER WE HAVE FOR YOU.
THE ONLY WAY YOU CAN BE AT PEACE.
IF YOU TRULY CARE FOR YOUR PEOPLE --
-- TAKE THE SPECIFIC CONTROL I'M HANDING BACK TO YOU NOW, USE THE WEAPON TO REGRESS THE VOORD BACK DOWN THEIR TIMELINE --
-- OR IT'S FRYING TONIGHT!

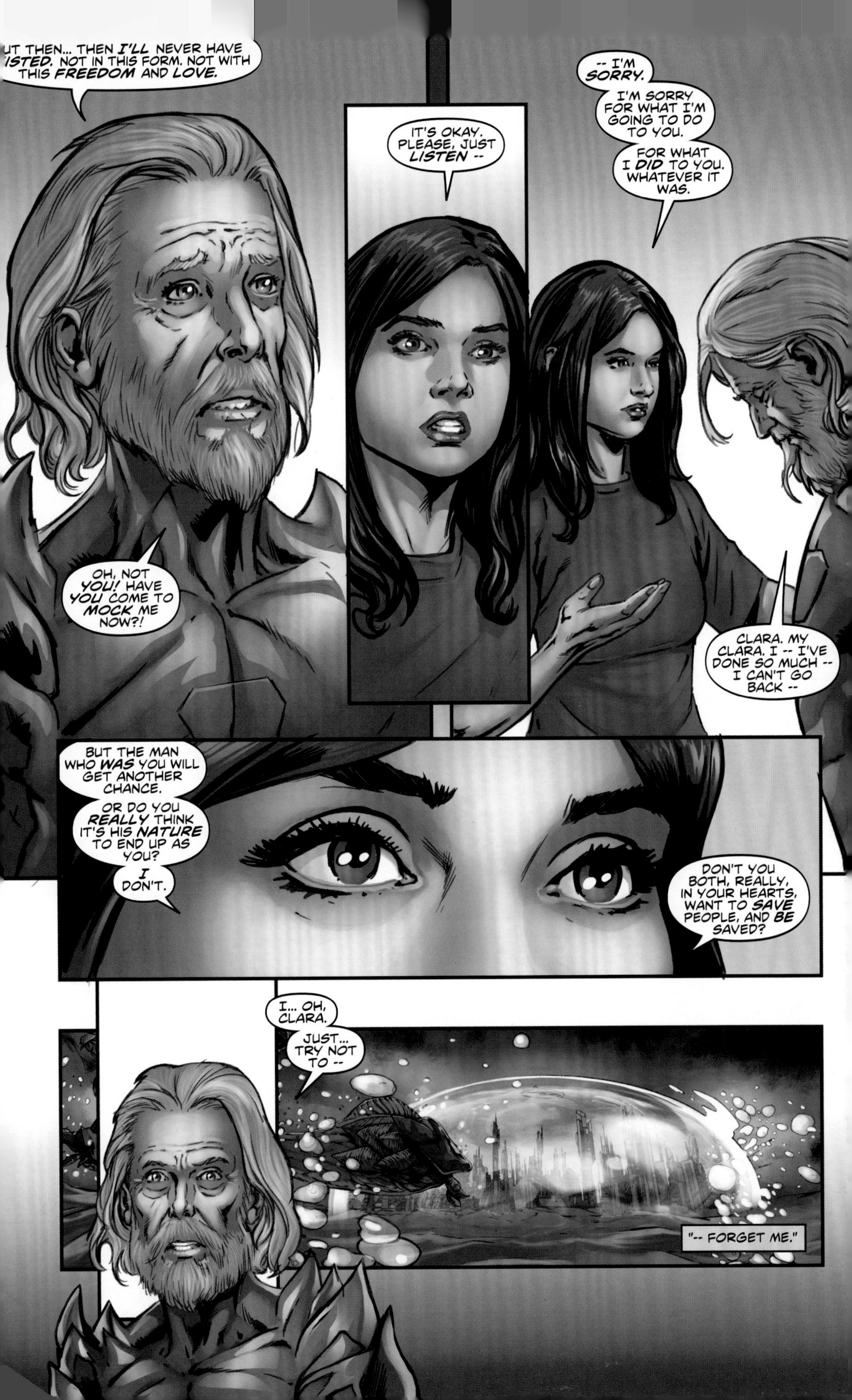
UT THEN... THEN I'LL NEVER HAVE ISTED. NOT IN THIS FORM. NOT WITH THIS FREEDOM AND LOVE.
OH, NOT YOU! HAVE YOU COME TO MOCK ME NOW?!
IT'S OKAY. PLEASE, JUST LISTEN --
-- I'M SORRY.
I'M SORRY FOR WHAT I'M GOING TO DO TO YOU.
FOR WHAT I DID TO YOU. WHATEVER IT WAS.
CLARA. MY CLARA. I -- I'VE DONE SO MUCH -- I CAN'T GO BACK --
BUT THE MAN WHO WAS YOU WILL GET ANOTHER CHANCE.
OR DO YOU REALLY THINK IT'S HIS NATURE TO END UP AS YOU?
I DON'T.
DON'T YOU BOTH, REALLY, IN YOUR HEARTS, WANT TO SAVE PEOPLE, AND BE SAVED?
I... OH, CLARA.
JUST... TRY NOT TO --
"-- FORGET ME."

MARINUS. AS IT WAS.
POLICE PUBLIC CALL BOX
I DON'T LIKE IT.
I DON'T LIKE WHAT WE'VE TAKEN FROM THE VOORD.
YES, WELL --
-- YOU NEVER DID LIKE IT WHEN YOUR ACTIONS HAD CONSEQUENCES.
LOOK WHO'S TALKING!
I THINK THE VOORD COULD DO WITH SUPPORT AND ADVICE AS MEMBERS OF THE WIDER COMMUNITY OF SPECIES, SOMETHING I INTEND TO ARRANGE --
-- AS SOON AS I'VE GOT BACK FROM FINDING JUST THE RIGHT WEEPING ANGEL TO HIDE IN A PACKAGE OF COMICS... ALL OF WHICH I'LL ASK ALICE TO REMEMBER FOR ME!
THE MOST IMPORTANT THING IS, THOUGH --
-- THE PICTURE HAS GONE.

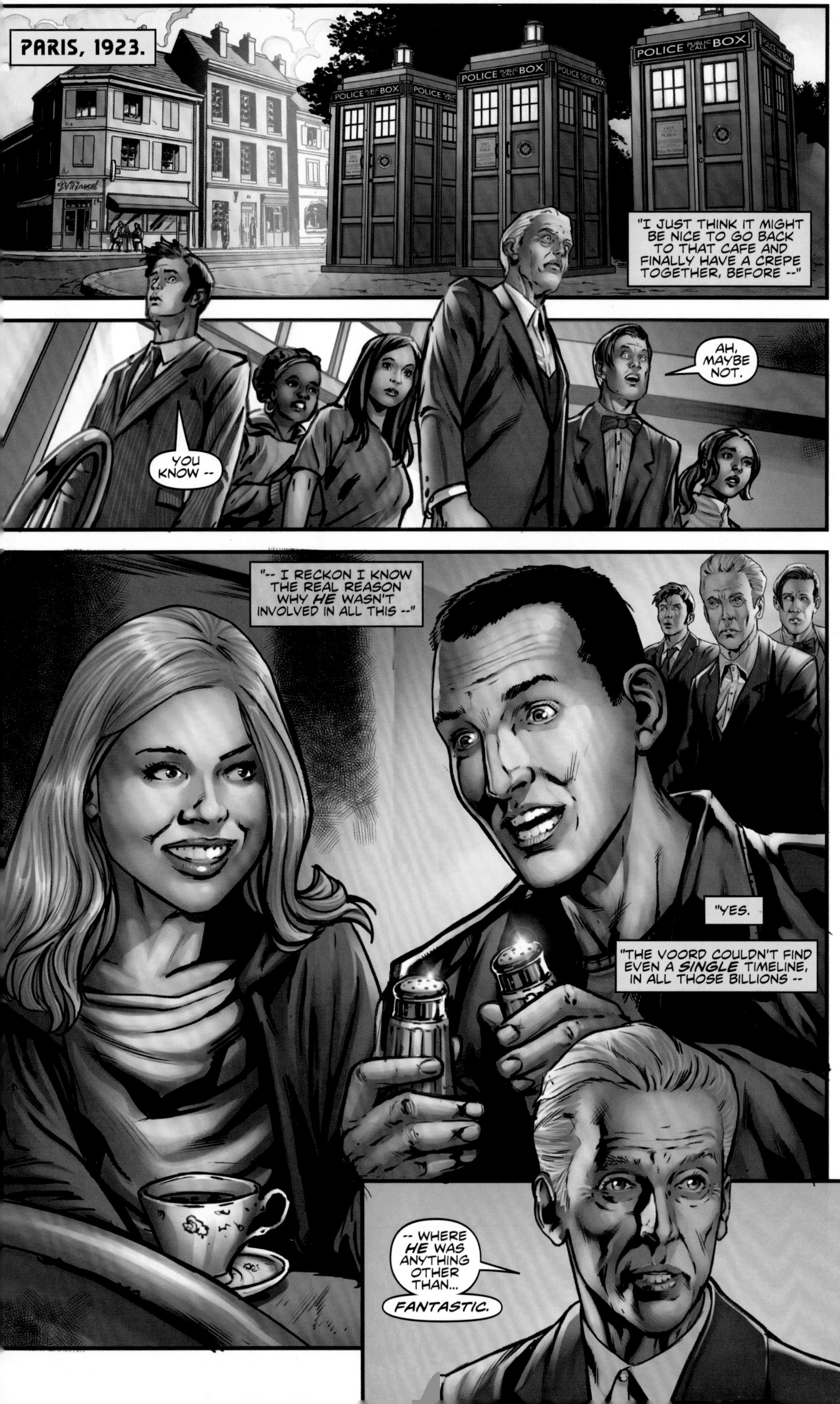
PARIS, 1923.
POLICE PUBLIC CALL BOX
"I JUST THINK IT MIGHT BE NICE TO GO BACK TO THAT CAFE AND FINALLY HAVE A CREPE TOGETHER, BEFORE --"
YOU KNOW --
AH, MAYBE NOT.
"-- I RECKON I KNOW THE REAL REASON WHY HE WASN'T INVOLVED IN ALL THIS --"
"YES.
"THE VOORD COULDN'T FIND EVEN A SINGLE TIMELINE, IN ALL THOSE BILLIONS --
-- WHERE HE WAS ANYTHING OTHER THAN...
FANTASTIC.

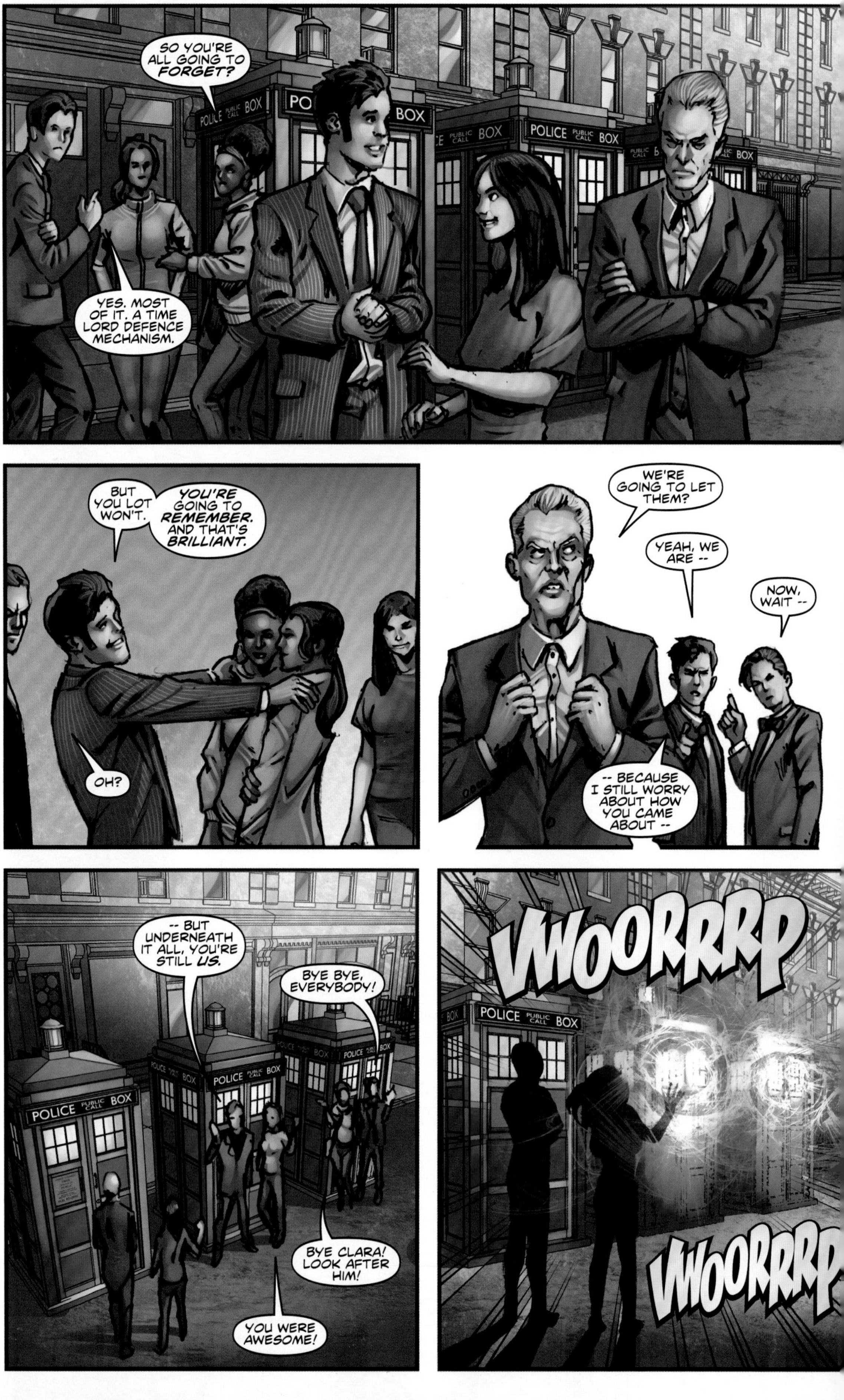
SO YOU'RE ALL GOING TO FORGET?
YES. MOST OF IT. A TIME LORD DEFENCE MECHANISM.
BUT YOU LOT WON'T.
YOU'RE GOING TO REMEMBER. AND THAT'S BRILLIANT.
OH?
WE'RE GOING TO LET THEM?
YEAH, WE ARE --
NOW, WAIT --
-- BECAUSE I STILL WORRY ABOUT HOW YOU CAME ABOUT --
-- BUT UNDERNEATH IT ALL, YOU'RE STILL US.
BYE BYE, EVERYBODY!
BYE CLARA! LOOK AFTER HIM!
YOU WERE AWESOME!
VWOORRRP
VWOORRRP
POLICE PUBLIC CALL BOX

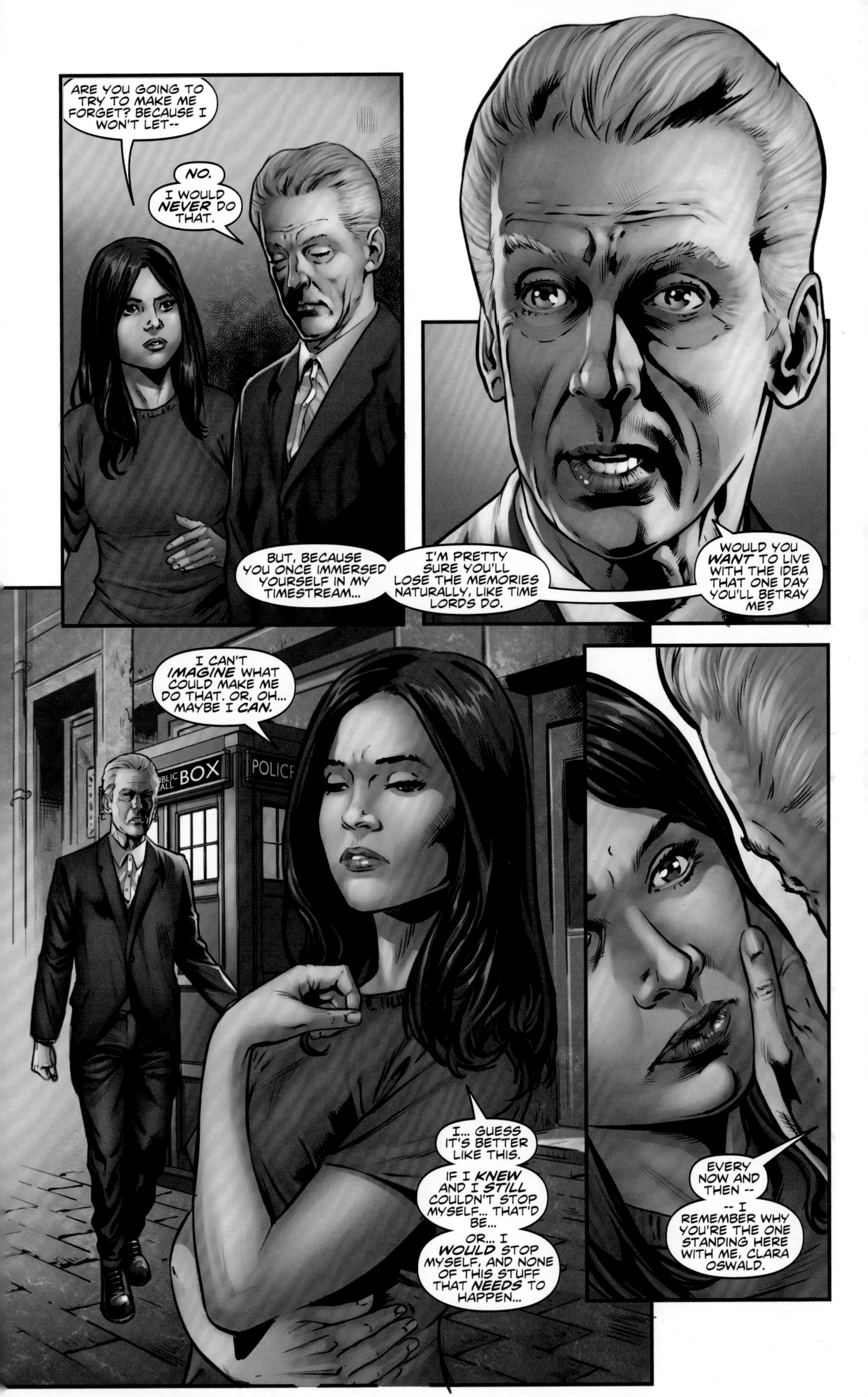
ARE YOU GOING TO TRY TO MAKE ME FORGET? BECAUSE I WON'T LET--
NO.
I WOULD NEVER DO THAT.
BUT, BECAUSE YOU ONCE IMMERSED YOURSELF IN MY TIMESTREAM...
I'M PRETTY SURE YOU'LL LOSE THE MEMORIES NATURALLY, LIKE TIME LORDS DO.
WOULD YOU WANT TO LIVE WITH THE IDEA THAT ONE DAY YOU'LL BETRAY ME?
I CAN'T IMAGINE WHAT COULD MAKE ME DO THAT. OR, OH... MAYBE I CAN.
BOX
POLICE
I... GUESS IT'S BETTER LIKE THIS.
IF I KNEW AND I STILL COULDN'T STOP MYSELF... THAT'D BE...
OR... I WOULD STOP MYSELF, AND NONE OF THIS STUFF THAT NEEDS TO HAPPEN...
EVERY NOW AND THEN --
-- I REMEMBER WHY YOU'RE THE ONE STANDING HERE WITH ME, CLARA OSWALD.

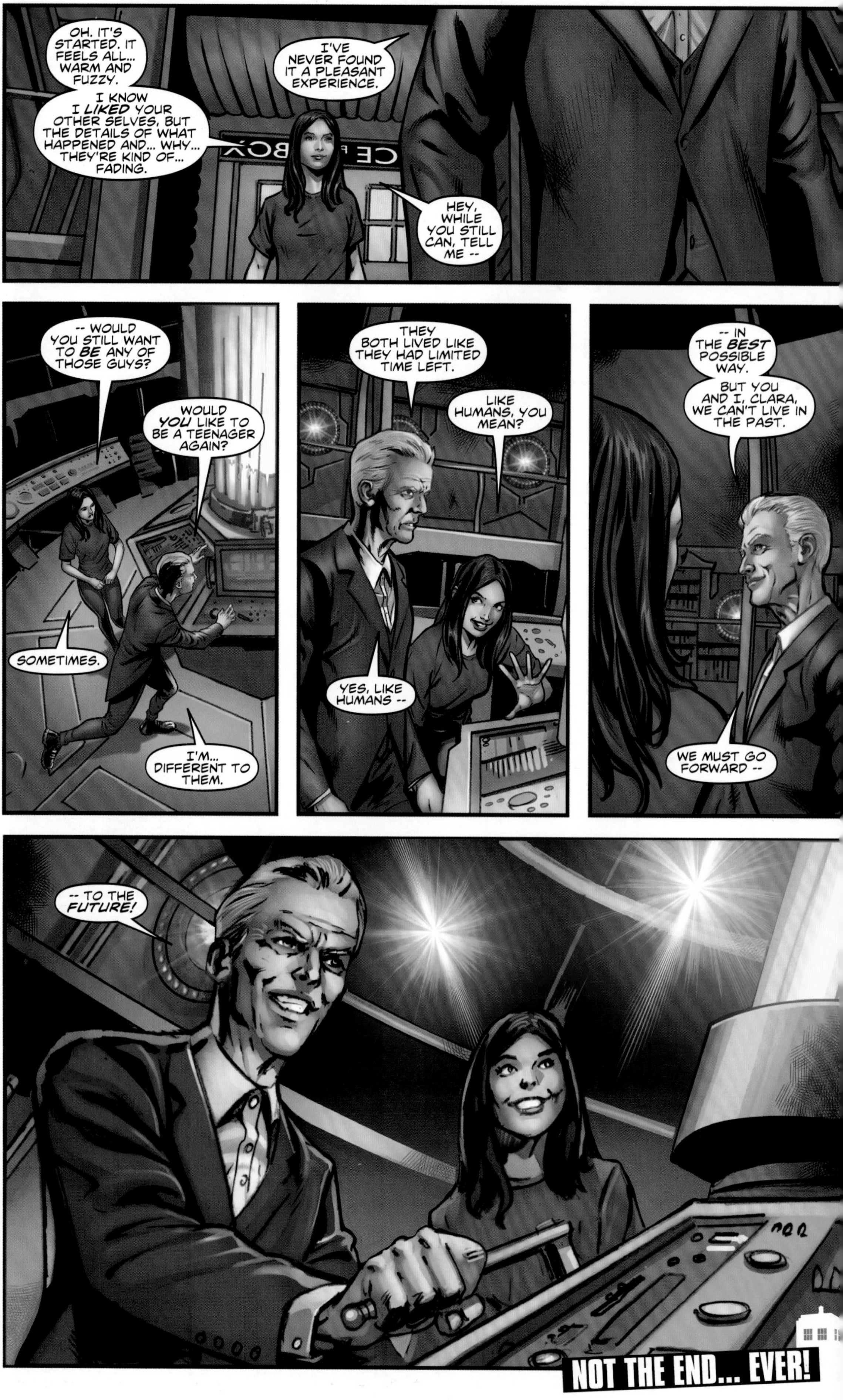
OH. IT'S STARTED. IT FEELS ALL... WARM AND FUZZY.
I KNOW I *LIKED* YOUR OTHER SELVES, BUT THE DETAILS OF WHAT HAPPENED AND... WHY... THEY'RE KIND OF... FADING.
I'VE NEVER FOUND IT A PLEASANT EXPERIENCE.
HEY, WHILE YOU STILL CAN, TELL ME --
-- WOULD YOU STILL WANT TO *BE* ANY OF THOSE GUYS?
WOULD *YOU* LIKE TO BE A TEENAGER AGAIN?
SOMETIMES.
I'M... DIFFERENT TO THEM.
THEY BOTH LIVED LIKE THEY HAD LIMITED TIME LEFT.
LIKE HUMANS, YOU MEAN?
YES, LIKE HUMANS --
-- IN THE *BEST* POSSIBLE WAY.
BUT YOU AND I, CLARA, WE CAN'T LIVE IN THE PAST.
WE MUST GO FORWARD --
-- TO THE *FUTURE!*
NOT THE END... EVER!

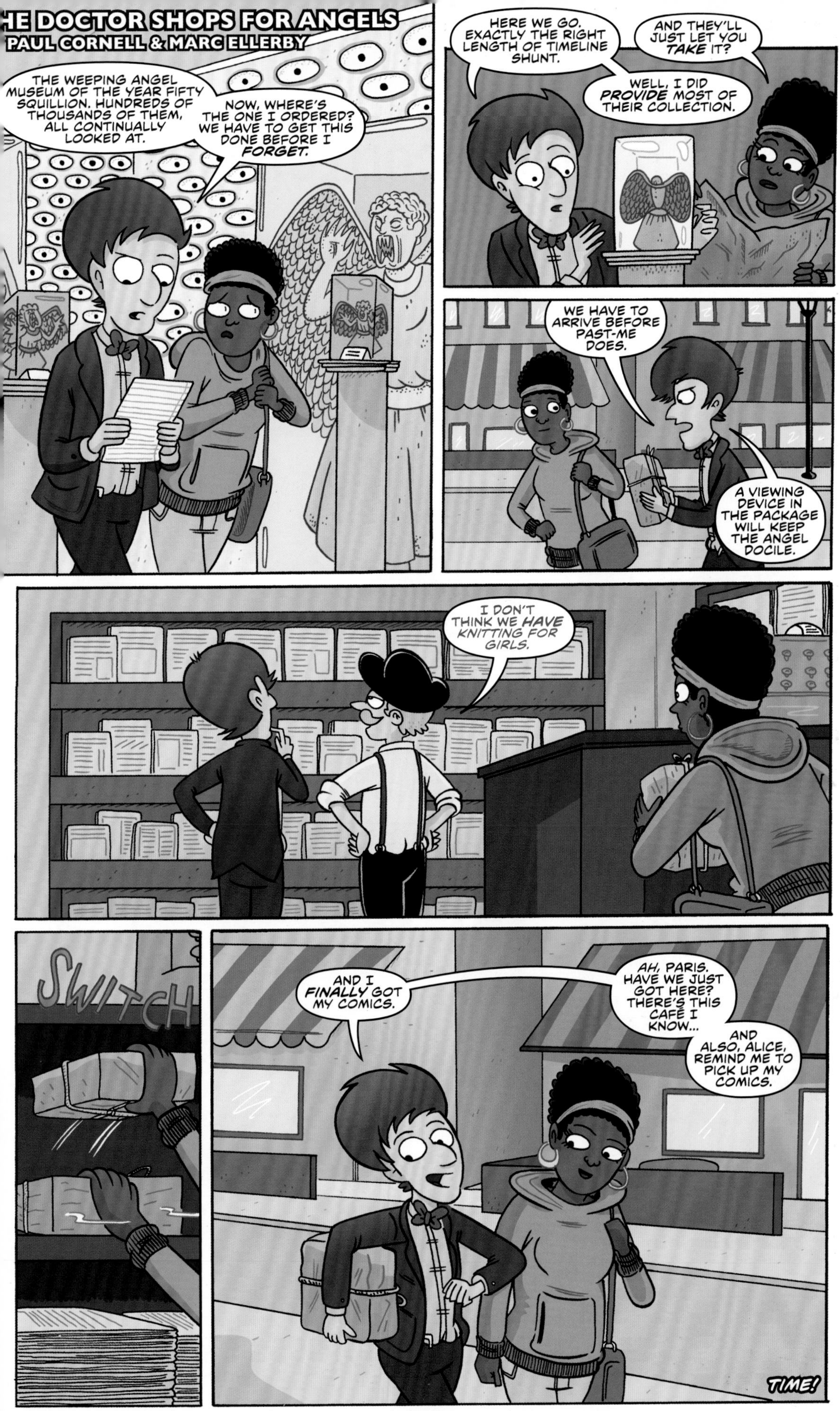
HE DOCTOR SHOPS FOR ANGELS
PAUL CORNELL & MARC ELLERBY
THE WEEPING ANGEL MUSEUM OF THE YEAR FIFTY SQUILLION. HUNDREDS OF THOUSANDS OF THEM, ALL CONTINUALLY LOOKED AT.
NOW, WHERE'S THE ONE I ORDERED? WE HAVE TO GET THIS DONE BEFORE I FORGET.
HERE WE GO. EXACTLY THE RIGHT LENGTH OF TIMELINE SHUNT.
AND THEY'LL JUST LET YOU TAKE IT?
WELL, I DID PROVIDE MOST OF THEIR COLLECTION.
WE HAVE TO ARRIVE BEFORE PAST-ME DOES.
A VIEWING DEVICE IN THE PACKAGE WILL KEEP THE ANGEL DOCILE.
I DON'T THINK WE HAVE KNITTING FOR GIRLS.
SWITCH
AND I FINALLY GOT MY COMICS.
AH, PARIS. HAVE WE JUST GOT HERE? THERE'S THIS CAFÉ I KNOW...
AND ALSO, ALICE, REMIND ME TO PICK UP MY COMICS.
TIME!

FOLLOW YOUR FAVORITE INCARNATIONS ACROSS THESE FANTASTIC COLLECTIONS!

DOCTOR WHO: THE TWELFTH DOCTOR VOL. 1: TERRORFORMER

ISBN: 9781782761778
ON SALE NOW - $19.99 / $22.95 CAN / £10.99
(UK EDITION ISBN: 9781782763864)

DOCTOR WHO: THE TWELFTH DOCTOR VOL. 2: FRACTURES

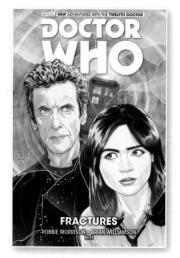

ISBN: 9781782763017
ON SALE NOW - $19.99 / $25.99 CAN / £10.99
(UK EDITION ISBN: 9781782766599)

DOCTOR WHO: THE TWELFTH DOCTOR VOL. 3: HYPERION

ISBN: 9781782767473
COMING SOON - $19.99 / $25.99 CAN / £10.99
(UK EDITION ISBN: 9781782767444)

DOCTOR WHO: THE ELEVENTH DOCTOR VOL. 1: AFTER LIFE

ISBN: 9781782761730
ON SALE NOW - $19.99 / $22.95 CAN / £10.99
(UK EDITION ISBN: 9781782763857)

DOCTOR WHO: THE ELEVENTH DOCTOR VOL. 2: SERVE YOU

ISBN: 9781782761754
ON SALE NOW - $19.99 / $22.95 CAN / £10.99
(UK EDITION ISBN: 9781782766582)

DOCTOR WHO: THE ELEVENTH DOCTOR VOL. 3: CONVERSION

ISBN: 9781782763024
COMING SOON - $19.99 / $25.99 CAN / £10.99
(UK EDITION ISBN: 9781782767435)

Titan COMICS

For information on how to subscribe to our great Doctor Who titles, or to purchase them digitally, visit:
WWW.TITAN-COMICS.COM

COMPLETE YOUR COLLECTION!

**DOCTOR WHO: THE TENTH DOCTOR
VOL. 1: REVOLUTIONS OF TERROR**

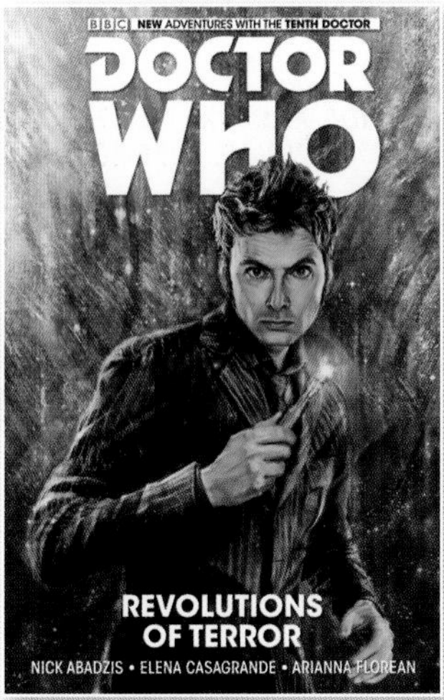
BBC NEW ADVENTURES WITH THE TENTH DOCTOR
DOCTOR WHO
REVOLUTIONS OF TERROR
NICK ABADZIS • ELENA CASAGRANDE • ARIANNA FLOREAN

ISBN: 9781782761747
ON SALE NOW - $19.99 / $22.95 CAN / £10.99
(UK EDITION ISBN: 9781782763840)

**DOCTOR WHO: THE TENTH DOCTOR
VOL. 2: THE WEEPING ANGELS
OF MONS**

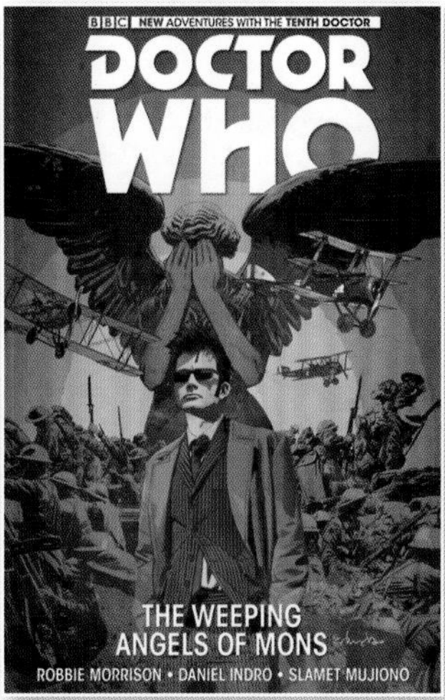
BBC NEW ADVENTURES WITH THE TENTH DOCTOR
DOCTOR WHO
THE WEEPING ANGELS OF MONS
ROBBIE MORRISON • DANIEL INDRO • SLAMET MUJIONO

ISBN: 9781782761754
ON SALE NOW - $19.99 / $25.99 CAN / £10.99
(UK EDITION ISBN: 9781782766575)

**DOCTOR WHO: THE TENTH DOCTOR
VOL. 3: THE FOUNTAINS
OF FOREVER**

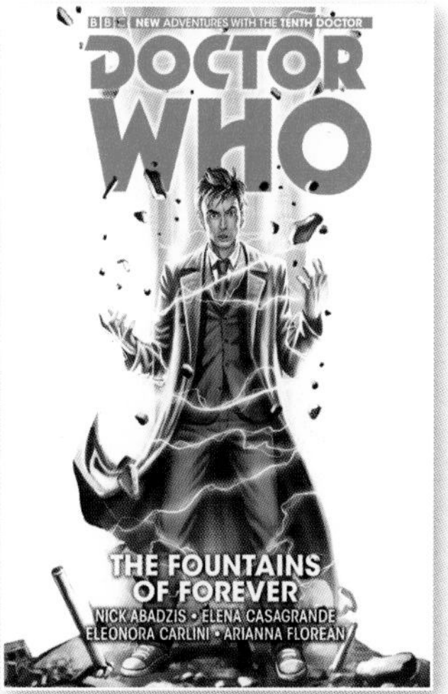
BBC NEW ADVENTURES WITH THE TENTH DOCTOR
DOCTOR WHO
THE FOUNTAINS OF FOREVER
NICK ABADZIS • ELENA CASAGRANDE
ELEONORA CARLINI • ARIANNA FLOREAN

ISBN: 9781782763024
ON SALE NOW - $19.99 / $25.99 CAN / £10.99
(UK EDITION ISBN: 9781782767404)

COMING SOON!

**DOCTOR WHO: THE NINTH DOCTOR
VOL. 1: WEAPONS OF PAST DESTRUCTION**

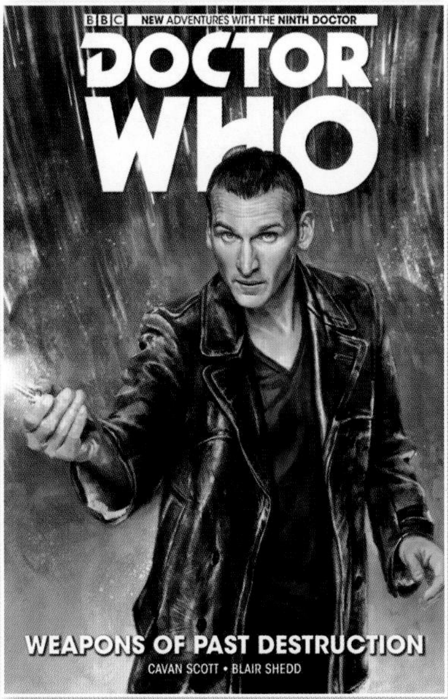
BBC NEW ADVENTURES WITH THE NINTH DOCTOR
DOCTOR WHO
WEAPONS OF PAST DESTRUCTION
CAVAN SCOTT • BLAIR SHEDD

ISBN: 9781782763369
COMING SOON - $19.99 / $25.99 CAN / £10.99
(UK EDITION ISBN: 9781782761056)

**DOCTOR WHO: THE EIGHTH DOCTOR
VOL. 1: A MATTER OF LIFE AND DEATH**

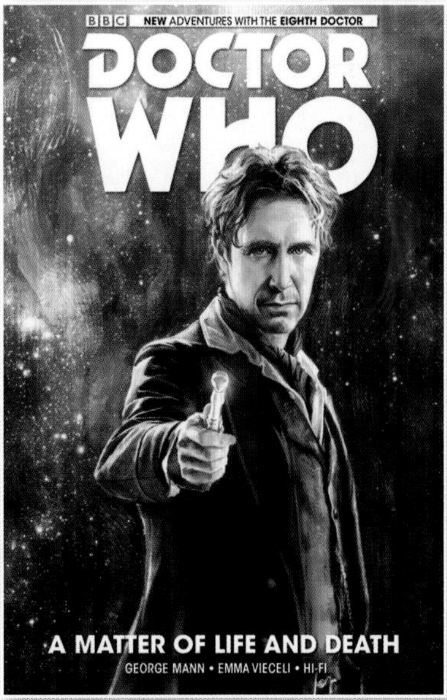
BBC NEW ADVENTURES WITH THE EIGHTH DOCTOR
DOCTOR WHO
A MATTER OF LIFE AND DEATH
GEORGE MANN • EMMA VIECELI • HI-FI

ISBN: 9781782767534
COMING SOON - $19.99 / $25.99 CAN / £10.99
(UK EDITION ISBN: 9781785851063)

AVAILABLE FROM ALL GOOD COMIC STORES, BOOK STORES, AND DIGITAL PROVIDERS!

BBC

BBC

DOCTOR WHO

FOUR DOCTORS

BIOGRAPHIES

Paul Cornell is a writer of science fiction and fantasy in prose, comics and TV, one of only two people to be Hugo Award-nominated for all three media. He has written *Doctor Who* for the BBC ('Father's Day', 'Human Nature', 'Family of Blood'), *Action Comics* for DC, and *Wolverine* and *Captain Britain* for Marvel. He has won the BSFA Award for his short fiction, an Eagle Award for his comics, and shares in a Writer's Guild Award for his television writing. His urban fantasy novel series, from Tor, begins with *The Severed Streets*. He lives in Buckinghamshire with his wife and son.

Neil Edwards is a British comics artist whose skillful pencils have enlivened *Fantastic Four, Spider-Man, Justice League United, Legion of Superheroes, Dark Avengers, Iron Man,* and many more, including the forthcoming *Assassin's Creed: Trial by Fire*, also from Titan Comics.

Ivan Nunes is a Brazilian colorist whose past works have included Marvel's *New Avengers* and *Thor, Game of Thrones* and *The Bionic Man*.

Marc Ellerby is a British freelance illustrator and comics artist. As well as *Doctor Who*, he currently contributes comic strips to *Rick and Morty* and *Regular Show*.

Rachael Smith's first graphic novel, *House Party*, debuted to critical acclaim in 2014. Her second, *The Rabbit,* has just been released by Avery Hill Publishing. Rachael is also the creator of *Flimsy the Kitten* and *One Good Thing*. She is currently working on her new webcomic, *Bess*, at besscomic.tumblr.com.

Neil Slorance is an illustrator, painter and comics artist, and one half of the team behind the award-winning *Dungeon Fun* comic, now available in its first collection.

Colin Bell is a writer, letterer and publisher, who writes the regular *Twelfth Doctor* back-ups. As well as being the other half of the *Dungeon Fun* team, he also publishes comics under the DoGooder Comics label.

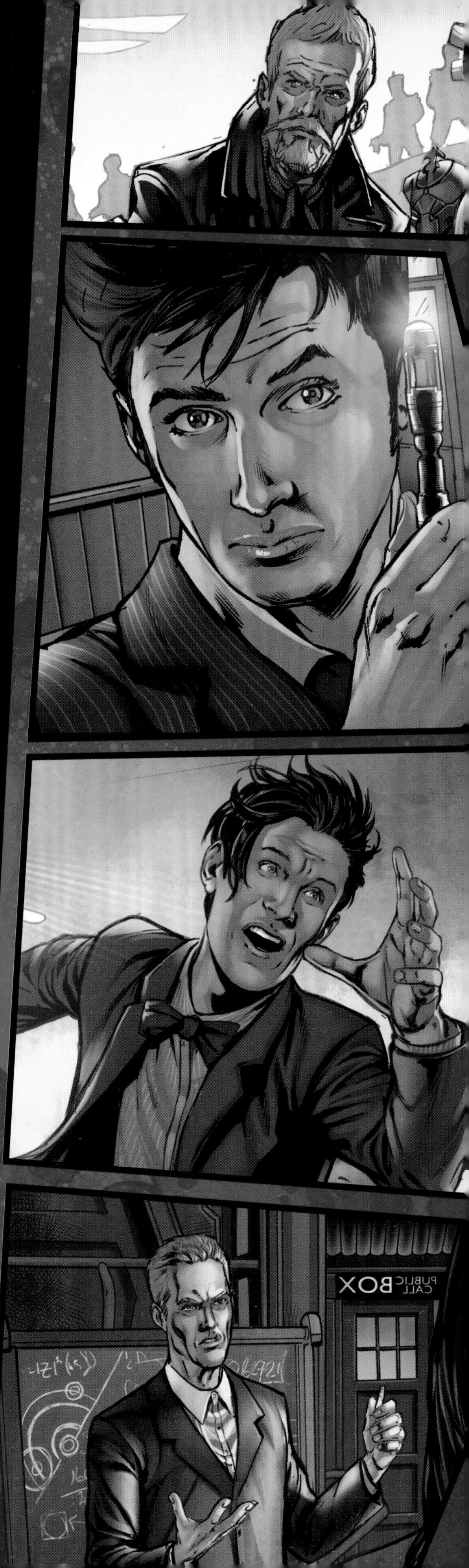